Action Research and New Media

Concepts, Methods and Cases

NEW MEDIA: POLICY AND SOCIAL RESEARCH ISSUES
Ronald E. Rice, *Series Editor*

Double Click: Romance and Commitment Among Couples Online
  Andrea Baker

Action Reseach and New Media: Concepts, Methods and Cases
  Greg Hearn, Jo Tacchi, Marcus Foth, and June Lennie

The Role of Culture and Political Institutions in Media Policy:
  The Case of TV Privatization in Greece
  Theomary Karamanis

Media Policy for the 21st Century in the United States and
  Western Europe
  Yaron Katz

Telecommunications and Development in China
  Paul S.N. Lee (ed.)

Impact and Issues in New Media: Toward Intelligent Societies
  Paul S.N. Lee, Louis Leung and Clement Y.K. So (eds.)

Global Trends in Communication Research and Education
  Kenneth W.Y. Leung, James Kenny, and Paul S.N. Lee (eds.)

Communication Technology and Society: Audience Adoption and Uses
  Carolyn A. Lin and David J. Atkin (eds.)

Foundations of Communication Policy: Principles and Process in the
  Regulation of Electronic Media
  Philip M. Napoli

Media Ownership: Research and Regulation
  Ronald E. Rice (ed.)

Language and New Media: Linguistic, Cultural and Technical Evolutions
  Charley Rowe and Eva L. Wyss (eds.)

Virtual Politicking: Playing Politics in Electronically Linked
  Organizations
  Celia T. Romm

Automating Interaction: Economic Reason and Social Capital in
  Addressable Networks
  Myles A. Ruggles

The Playful Audience: From Talk Show Viewers to Internet Users
  Tony Wilson

Action Research and New Media

Concepts, Methods and Cases

Greg Hearn
Queensland University of Technology

Jo Tacchi
Queensland University of Technology

Marcus Foth
Queensland University of Technology

June Lennie
June Lennie Research and Evaluation

HAMPTON PRESS, INC.
CRESSKILL, NJ 07626

Printed in the United States of America

Library of Congress Cataloging-in-Publication Data

Action research and new media : concepts, methods, and cases / Greg Hearn ... [et al.].
    p. cm. — (New media)
  Includes bibliographical references and index.
    ISBN 978-1-57273-866-9 (hardbound) — ISBN 978-1-57273-867-6 (paperbound)
    1. Action research.   2. Mass media—Technological innovations.   3. Action research—Case studies.   I. Hearn, Greg, 1957–
    H62.A513 2009
    302.23072—dc22   2008047691

Hampton Press, Inc.
23 Broadway
Cresskill, NJ 07626

Contents

Foreword

Douglas Schuler
The Evergreen State College
The Public Sphere Project

For over 20 years I've been working at the junction of activism, research, and community work in the field of new media and communication networks, a region that although rich in research issues and urgent social needs, is to a large degree, still *terra incognita*. Unfortunately working where these three realms meet is to work on the margins of each. The book you're holding should help mitigate that problem. It's the book that I needed at the beginning of those 20 years.

Action research is simultaneously a set of methodologies, a philosophical orientation, and a research culture. Action research is, of course, *timeless* in itself; research that is *engaged* was needed yesterday and will be needed tomorrow. Nevertheless, as the authors of this book make clear, new media and the advent of the internet, and increasingly ubiquitous digital networking adds a degree of urgency to this endeavour.

This urgency shows up in a "perfect storm" of opportunities and challenges:

- new possibilities for connecting people across boundaries, with more information at their disposal, for use in new venues;

- an increase in collaborative, transnational research/action projects that provide real meaning and connect to the lives of real people;

- evolving technologies, institutions, and policies of new information and communication systems; and

- a backdrop of globalisation, surveillance, poverty, militarism, and ecocide

Research that is totally "objective" or "disengaged" is a myth, yet, like all myths, it has a reality in the sense that it guides and orients our thinking and, hence, our actions, in ways that are often implicit. The fact that action research and other participatory approaches still meet resistance is a testament to institutional inertia, the enduring force that polices intellectual enquiry and thereby constrains both thought and action. This book is part of a gathering force to describe and define participatory and collaborative approaches to new media research that are both rigorous and meaningful in a *real* way; that is to say in a way that moves research forward (thus satisfying the critical objectives of the academy) while providing ideas and actions of significance beyond the academy, to the world where people live.

Action research should not be championed solely because of the good effects that it could have on the world, although if that were all it accomplished, it would be enough to warrant a lot more of it. Action research is also key to high-quality scholarship. The insistence on *social engagement* (that action research is built upon) is indispensable for any intellectual enquiry. For one thing, it helps keep the research *honest*. Statistics and other quantitative data don't (of course!) tell the whole story. (This helps explain the tragedy of economics.) For another thing, this type of research helps keep the *researcher* honest—not just in the narrow sense of "not lying" but in the broader sense of being true to the realities (and possibilities!) of conditions and systems of influence and interrelationships.

As this book makes clear, a pragmatic approach to action research that is underpinned by principles such as methodological pluralism, and takes a critical yet inclusive approach to social problems, is absolutely critical for both the validity of the social sciences and the future of the planet. It's also critical that the work that it describes becomes vastly more prominent within the social sciences (perhaps renamed social *enquiries?*).

In the past few years I've been working on new theoretical models and structures that would more actively bridge the worlds of research, activism, and community work. These include a participatory project to develop a complex theory of social change—the "Liberating Voices" pattern language (Schuler, 2008)—and a boundary-blurring concept of civic intelligence (Schuler, 2001), which focuses on the idea of collective intelligence for addressing major problems that are shared around the world.

So although I didn't have a copy of this book 20 years ago, it's presumably not too late for me to take advantage of it now. In fact, I'm anticipating the involvement of the nascent community of action researchers in the evaluation of Liberating Voices pattern language and in the definition, development, cultivation, and evaluation of civic intelligence in society. The most important thing now, however, is that the next generation of researchers/activists will be able to consult this book and use it to simultaneously improve their work—*and the world.*

References

Schuler, D. (2001). Cultivating society's civic intelligence: Patterns for a new "world brain." *Information, Communication & Society*, 4(2), 157–181.
Schuler, D. (2008). *Liberating voices: A pattern language for communication revolution*. Cambridge, MA: MIT Press.

About the Author

Although **Douglas Schuler**'s educational background focused on computer science, he has spent much of the past two decades looking at the opportunities and risks of information and communication systems. Doug has given presentations around the world on democratic, equitable, and sustainable uses of technology. Locally, Doug co-founded the Seattle Community Network, an all-volunteer, free public access computer network. In 2008 Doug was awarded a Safeco Community Hero award for his work. Doug is a faculty member (Evening and Weekend Studies) at The Evergreen State College where he teaches interdisciplinary programs such as Community Information Systems and Global Citizenship. Over the last eight years Doug coordinated an online, participatory "patterns language" for social change project. Doug and 85 co-authors developed 136 patterns for *Liberating Voices: A Pattern Language for Communication Revolution* which is being published by MIT Press. Doug is also the author of *New Community Networks*, co-editor of six books, and author of numerous articles and book chapters. Doug is former chair of Computer Professionals for Social Responsibility, a public-interest organisation concerned about the impact of computers on society, and organised 11 CPSR conferences. He is the director of the Public Sphere Project where he is working on projects such as e-Liberate, a web-based application that supports distributed meetings using Roberts Rules of Order. Doug will be exploring the idea of "civic intelligence," the collective capability of society to address its problems, during his upcoming sabbatical.

Abbreviations

AAL	anticipatory action learning
AAR	anticipatory action research
CD	compact disc
CLA	causal layered analysis
CLC	community learning centre
CMC	computer-mediated communication
CSCW	computer supported cooperative work
DFID	Department for International Development (Britain)
DVD	digital versatile disc
EAR	ethnographic action research
EU	European Union
ICT	information and communication technology
ictPR	ICT for Poverty Reduction
IT	information technology
KCRIP	Kothmale Community Radio and Internet Project
LEARNERS	Learning, Evaluation, Action & Reflection for New technologies, Empowerment and Rural Sustainability
MMS	multimedia messaging service
NGO	nongovernment organisation
OECD	Organisation for Economic Cooperation and Development
PAR	participatory action research

PM&E	participatory monitoring and evaluation
QUT	Queensland University of Technology (Brisbane, Australia)
SHG	self-help group
SLQ	State Library of Queensland (Brisbane, Australia)
SMS	short message service
UN	United Nations
UNDP	United Nations Development Program
UNESCO	United Nations Educational, Scientific and Cultural Organisation
YIRN	Youth Internet Radio Network

Acknowledgements

We would like to acknowledge a number of people who assisted in the production of this book. First, in addition to writing parts of the book, June Lennie had a significant role in pulling the book together. She compiled and edited several chapters from early drafts, sourced and organised references, ensured the overall flow of the book made sense, and wrote the overview. Natalie Collie acted as editor of the final draft and assisted with permissions and coordination. Jaz Hee-jeong Choi did a great job on illustrations, and Lucy Hearn proofread from beginning to end. Julie Blakey and Camille Short conducted literature searches early in the book's life. We would also like to thank Doug Schuler for his review of the book and writing a great foreword as well as Ron Rice for his very thorough review of the manuscript and his thoughtful suggestions.

This book represents the culmination of many years of work applying action research to new media by all of the authors. Although the book was a team effort and all chapters benefit from input from the team as a whole, each chapter has its own pedigree. Formal acknowledgements for each chapter follow.

Chapters 1 and 2: Some parts of these chapters are used with permission from: Hearn G., & Foth M. (2005). Action research in the design of new media and ICT systems. In K. Kwansah-Aidoo (Ed.), *Current Issues in Communications and Media Research* (pp. 79–94). New York: Nova Science.

Chapters 3 and 5: Some sections in these chapters were adapted from the *Ethnographic Action Research Handbook* by Tacchi, Slater, and Hearn (2003). Ethnographic action research was developed initially through funding from the UK Department for International Development in 2002, applied and refined through the UNESCO funded ictPR project (Slater & Tacchi, 2004), and is being developed further through the Australian Research Council (ARC), UNESCO, and UNDP funded Finding a Voice research project (see below for project details). Jo Tacchi and colleagues in the Finding a Voice project are currently preparing an updated CD ROM version of the handbook (Tacchi et al., 2007).

Chapter 4: The section on tools and systems in this chapter was adapted with the permission of Sage Publications from: Foth M. (2006). Network action research. *Action Research*, 4(2), 205–226.

Chapter 6: This chapter is a revised version (with the permission of Sage Publications) of: Foth M. (2006). Network action research. *Action Research*, 4(2), 205–226. The tools and systems section of the original article was revised and integrated into Chapter 4. The work was supported by the Australasian CRC for Interaction Design (ACID), established and supported under the Cooperative Research Centres Programme through the Australian Government's Department of Education, Science and Training.

Chapter 7: The key idea for this chapter "anticipatory action research" began its life in *Anticipating Social and Policy Implications of Intelligent Networks: Complexity, Choice and Participation* (Hearn et al., 1995).

Chapter 8: This chapter draws on the ictPR research project which was funded by UNESCO and led by Jo Tacchi (whilst she was employed as a Visiting Fellow at the Oxford Internet Institute, University of Oxford), in collaboration with Don Slater of the London School of Economics (see Slater & Tacchi, 2004). The research depended on a network of nine local EAR researchers together with Ian Pringle and Savithri Subramanian who were based, at the time, in UNESCO's Delhi office. It also draws on Finding a Voice: Making Technological Change Socially Effective and Culturally Empowering, an ARC Linkage Project (project number LP0561848, 2006–2009). This is a collaboration between the Queensland University of Technology (QUT), the University of Adelaide, UNESCO (South Asia), and UNDP (Indonesia). In addition there are numerous local partner organisations involved through 15 ICT initiatives. This research project depends on the contribution of three Australian researchers—Emma Baulch, Joann Fildes, and Kirsty Martin—who support and coordinate the contributions of a network of 12 local EAR researchers. Support is also provided by M. S. Kiran in Delhi and Karma Tshering in Nepal. Seema Nair provides project support from UNESCO's Delhi office. Chief Investigators are Jo Tacchi, Stuart Cunningham, and Hitendra Pillay from QUT, and Andrew Skuse from the University of Adelaide. Full details of the partner organisations and personnel can be found at www.findingavoice.org.

Chapter 9: This chapter draws on content creation activities in the Finding a Voice project. A series of workshops has been conducted in Nepal, Indonesia, and India by Jerry Watkins of QUT. Jerry's contribution to thinking about the potential for participatory content creation in this and other research projects has been invaluable. An early workshop in digital storytelling was conducted in India by Tanya Notley and Ben Grubb, also of QUT. Kelly McWilliams of QUT kindly helped us to position our work in relation to the Californian and British models of digital storytelling.

This chapter also draws upon the ARC Linkage Project *Youth Internet Radio Network: Ethnographic Action Research of an Emerging Media Technology* (project number LP0349078, 2004–2006). Collaborating organisations were the Queensland Government's Office of Youth Affairs and Arts Queensland, the Brisbane City Council, and QMusic. Chief Investigators were John Hartley and Greg Hearn. The Project Leader was Jo Tacchi. Researchers were Tanya Notley, Justin Brow and Mark Fallu. A range of local organisations partnered with us in the delivery of the content creation workshops.

Chapter 10: The research reported in this chapter was supported under the ARC's Discovery funding scheme (project number DP0663854). The project also received support from the Queensland Government's Department of Housing. Figure 10.1 is courtesy of the Kelvin Grove Urban Village project. Figure 10.2 is reproduced with permission from: Foth M. & Hearn G. (2007). Networked individualism of urban residents: Discovering the communicative ecology in inner-city apartment complexes. *Information, Communication & Society*, 10(5) (available at http://informaworld.com).

Chapter 11: Material in this chapter draws on the final report on the LEARNERS project by Lennie, Hearn, and Simpson et al. (2005) and a paper by Lennie, Hearn, Simpson, and Kimber (2005) published in the *International Journal of Education and Development Using ICT*. The case study of the use of the EvaluateIT kit was previously published in Lennie, Hearn, and Hanrahan (2005). The following organisations provided funding and support for the LEARNERS project.

• The ARC, which funded Dr. Lennie's Postdoctoral Fellowship through a Strategic Partnerships with Industry—Research and Training (SPIRT) grant.

• The Department of Family and Community Services (Australian Government).

• Learning Network Queensland.

• The Office for Women, Queensland Government, which provided funding through an Assisting Rural Women Leadership grant.

• QUT, which funded Marcus Foth's website design for the EvaluateIT resource kit through a QUT Community Service grant.

The development of the EvaluateIT resource kit was supported by a project funded by the State Library of Queensland and QUT through a QUT Strategic Links with Industry grant.

Chapter 12: Some of the text in this chapter on digital inclusion was drawn from a draft UNESCO paper by Jo Tacchi entitled "Poverty reduction and the role of communication and information."

About the Authors

Greg Hearn is Research Professor in the Creative Industries Faculty at QUT. His work focuses on the application, development, and evaluation of new technologies and services in the creative industries. He has been involved in high level consulting and applied research examining new media and industry/organisational forms for more than two decades, with organisations including British Airways, Hewlett Packard, and many Australian national and state government agencies. He was a consultant to the Broadband Services Expert Group, the national policy group that formulated Australia's foundational framework for the internet in 1994. In 2005 he was an invited member of a working party examining the role of creativity in the innovation economy for the Australian Prime Minister's Science Engineering and Innovation Council. He has authored or co-authored over 20 major research reports and a number of books including *The Communication Superhighway: Social and Economic Change in the Digital Age* (1998: Allen and Unwin) and *The Knowledge Economy Handbook* (2005: Edward Elgar).

Jo Tacchi holds a PhD in Social Anthropology from University College London. She is an Associate Professor in the Centre of Excellence for Creative Industries and Innovation, Queensland University of Technology. She has specialized in research on radio and new media and currently works on a range of media research and development projects in Australia and the Asia and Pacific region. She has worked closely with UNESCO's Regional Bureau for Communication and Information for the Asia and Pacific region to develop and test the Ethnographic Action Research methodology. In collaboration with local, national, and international partners she is First Chief Investigator on three Australian Research Council funded projects which have in common the application of ethnographic methods to creative old and new media practices.

Marcus Foth is a Senior Research Fellow at the Institute for Creative Industries and Innovation, Queensland University of Technology (QUT), Brisbane, Australia. He received a BCompSc(Hon) from Furtwangen University, Germany, a BMultimedia from Griffith University, Australia and an MA and PhD in digital media and urban sociology from QUT. Dr. Foth is the recipient of an Australian Postdoctoral Fellowship supported under the Australian Research Council's Discovery funding scheme. He was a 2007 Visiting Fellow at the Oxford Internet Institute, University of Oxford, UK. Employing participatory design and action research, he is working on cross-disciplinary research and development at the intersection of people, place and technology with a focus on urban informatics, locative media and mobile applications. Dr. Foth has published over fifty articles in journals, edited books, and conference proceedings in the last four years. He is the conference chair of OZCHI 2009, a member of the Australian Computer Society and the Executive Committee of the Association of Internet Researchers. More information at www.urbaninformatics.net

June Lennie is an independent research and evaluation consultant based in Brisbane, Australia. She has significant expertise in managing and conducting participatory action research and evaluation projects in collaboration with government, nongovernment and business organisations. Her research interests include critical feminist analysis of gender, rurality, and empowerment related to communication technologies and community participation processes, and the use of participatory research and evaluation methodologies for improving community development and health. From 1990–2005 she worked on several research, evaluation, and consulting projects in various fields at Queensland University of Technology. They included a Postdoctoral Fellowship project which successfully built community capacities in evaluating rural IT initiatives. In early 2007 she took up a part-time position as Senior Research Associate in the Creative Industries Faculty at QUT. Dr. Lennie has authored 50 publications, including 20 refereed papers in journals and conference proceedings; invited book chapters; and research and evaluation reports.

Introduction

The first chapter of Part I: Key Concepts, Methods and Tools introduces the two key concepts of the book: namely, new media and action research. We point out that 'new' media is not really a new term; but it does have validity as a descriptor that points to emerging innovations. We also suggest that its current use in the information and communication technology (ICT) field is distinctive because of the growing importance of the audiovisual content layer of these technologies (principally, internet and cell phones). Thus, we emphasise three layers in new media applications: the content, the technology, and the social layers. As a democratic and participatory approach that focuses on practical problem solving, we propose that action research is a particularly appropriate methodology for new media projects. Action research is seen as a methodology, an overarching process for managing enquiry, and a research culture that can engage all stakeholders in ongoing cycles of planning, acting, observing, and reflecting. We argue that action research is a valid method to apply to new media because it requires an approach that is thoroughly sensitive to the social and creative context of new media. We suggest that a method that is participatory and cyclical, and amenable to feedback, can best address such a context. We trace the history and intellectual origins of action research as well as the history of sociotechnical and interpretive approaches to technology studies as a foundation for the idea of applying action research to emerging new media contexts.

Chapter 2 considers the relationship between the technology and social domains from the perspectives of technological determinism and the social construction of technology. To overcome these bipolar positions, we propose an alternative co-evolutionary perspective, which assumes a reciprocal relationship between the social and the technical. We argue that new media action research is most usefully guided by this position. The theoretical and conceptual framework that underpins our approach to new media action research is set out, including a detailed explanation of the key concept 'communicative ecology.' We also present a number of methodological principles that guide our approach.

Chapter 3 introduces the basic processes and methods involved in using action research in new media projects. We describe the action research process as evolving through ongoing, flexible cycles of planning, taking action, observation, and reflection. Commonly used methods for new media action research are outlined. We provide more detailed descriptions of less familiar methods such as cultural probes. We suggest that the ideal is to build a research culture in which action research becomes an everyday, integrated component of new media projects and highlight the need for effective skills in communication, listening, and facilitation. Key practices for ethical action research and strategies for increasing the rigour of this approach are suggested.

Chapter 4 discusses new media tools that can enable and support collaborative research. We illustrate these via the fields of knowledge management and computer-supported cooperative work. We discuss how findings from the literature can be transferred from a business context to an academic context, highlighting the specific needs of action researchers. We argue that these tools offer vast potential to create more inclusive and democratic environments. We present a number of case studies that illustrate the use of these tools for action research and collaboration, and we consider issues of access, technology literacy, maintenance continuity, and intellectual property.

Part II, Advanced Approaches to Action Research and New Media, begins with an introduction to ethnographic action research (EAR) in Chapter 5. We outline the background to the development of EAR, how it emerged, what perceived needs it was responding to, and what it consists of. We suggest that through using this methodology, media for development initiatives can develop in ways that recognise and respond to local social, political, cultural, and economic contexts, and each media technology can be seen as part of a wider communicative ecology that predates their intervention and is at the same time altered by it. We outline current applications of EAR in south and southeast Asia and the various theories of ICTs, inclusion, and development that underpin this approach. The basic principles of EAR are outlined and the role of the EAR researcher in developing a research culture and working as a sociocultural animator is discussed. We describe the mix of methods that are typically used in EAR projects and new media tools that can support these projects. The limitations and issues in using this methodology are highlighted, such as those related to inclusion, power, and ethics.

Chapter 6 introduces network action research as a methodological variation which considers the network qualities of community and the implications on action research. We begin by discussing research that is situated in the nexus of people, place, and technology, the shifting quality of community as networks, and the challenges for action researchers emerging from this shift. Network action research is proposed as a means of addressing some of those challenges and as a way to recognise the significance of human networks within communities and society. To provide empirical support, we draw on an example from an investigation of social networks in inner-city apartment buildings. Some of the broader ethical imperatives associated with this approach, including anonymity, confidentiality, and inclusion are considered.

Chapter 7 discusses the theory and practices associated with anticipatory action research (AAR). This approach proposes that by anticipating the ways in which new media innovations could impact on existing social structures we can plan, prepare, make choices, and take responsibility for these future impacts. We consider various methodologies for generating new and alternative futures of new media, including appreciative enquiry and causal layered analysis. The value of anticipatory studies of new media in identifying the intentional and unintentional effects of the introduction of ICTs such as cell phones is demonstrated. We present a case study that shows how AAR could be used to assist a telecommunications provider and other groups understand, co-learn and co-develop applications and services for cell phones. The various steps involved in conducting workshops for this purpose are described. Finally, we suggest some uses of AAR in identifying emerging social innovations in cell phone use.

Part III, Case Studies and Applications, presents four case studies or examples of the use of new media action research in different contexts. Chapter 8 describes the use of EAR in various ICT projects that aim to alleviate poverty in developing countries. We argue that the gap between technology and development is a more appropriate focus than the digital divide between developed and developing countries. The potential role of the concept 'voice' in understanding ICTs and poverty in terms of the following is considered: local content creation and voice poverty; research methods, monitoring, evaluation, and impact assessment; and access and use, mixing old and new media and advocacy. The successful development and testing of EAR in various ICT projects conducted in south and southeast Asia over the past four years is described. These examples illustrate the value of EAR as a model of embedded and ongoing participatory research and evaluation in ICTs for poverty alleviation initiatives.

Chapter 9 describes two research projects that used action research to develop creative content: the *Youth Internet Radio Network* (*YIRN*); and Finding a Voice. The *YIRN* project was based in Australia and focused on young people, whereas the Finding a Voice project (described in Chapter 8), was based in south and southeast Asia and involved community-based ICT centres. We explain how the content creation activities undertaken in

YIRN influenced the content creation activities of the subsequent Finding a Voice project. The digital storytelling format that was used for local content creation is outlined and we explain how and why this was applied across both projects. We explain how Finding a Voice highlighted the importance of context and the value of embedded action research in the process of encouraging participatory content creation and creative engagement. We conclude this chapter by discussing our learnings about the local conditions and technological, cultural, social, economic, and political contexts that facilitate (or restrict) creative engagement with digital technologies in low infrastructure areas or among marginalised groups.

Chapter 10 outlines a work in progress that provides an effective case study to examine if and how residents of an inner-city residential development connect with each other to create and maintain social networks, and how new media and ICT systems can better support the interaction in those networks. The sociotechnical challenges of master planning ICT and new media systems for a community that does not exist yet are discussed, along with other issues. Based on this analysis, we critique conventional approaches to community-building and propose a way forward. We conceptualise a theoretical framework for studying place-based communication technology and new media applications used by urban residents in the context of their other ICT and media usages, which is based on the concept of a communicative ecology. From this model, we present a methodological variation that combines network action research and participatory design. This is seen as overcoming some of the negative side effects of the top–down approach of master planning.

Chapter 11 draws on the outcomes of two inter-related projects that aimed to build the capacities of people in rural Australia to plan and evaluate their local new media projects. The capacity-building process that was trialed in two communities was considered innovative in that it took a whole of community systems approach, used participatory action research (PAR) and participatory evaluation methods, encouraged analysis of differences such as gender and levels of information literacy, and aimed to develop learning communities. A critical perspective was taken that recognised the significant role of rural women in the uptake of new media and community development. Our research identified many issues related to the sustainability of new media initiatives in rural areas. A key outcome of the PAR projects was the development of an online evaluation toolkit. We present a case study of the use of this toolkit by a community group to evaluate a rural library website. This highlights the value of this toolkit in structuring and focusing the evaluation process. Both the empowering and disempowering impacts of the LEARNERS project on the participants and communities involved are discussed.

The concluding Chapter 12 summarises the key elements of the theoretical and conceptual framework for new media action research that was set out in the book and outlines our broad methodological framework for new media action research. We suggest that these frameworks offer a valuable guide to action research in this field. Finally, we consider some future directions for action research and new media based on the themes and issues we have identified in this book and elsewhere, and recent work in this field.

Part I

Key Concepts, Methods, and Tools

Chapter 1

Action Research and New Media Overview

Action research is a particularly valuable methodology for developing, researching, evaluating, and managing new media projects. As a democratic and participatory approach that focuses on practical problem solving, action research is especially appropriate to new media initiatives that involve constant innovation and change; have unpredictable outcomes; and require flexibility, creativity, and an inclusive, user-centred approach.

In this chapter, we begin by defining the two key terms used in this book: 'new media' and 'action research.' We then provide an overview of the complex history of action research, the diverse approaches to action research that have developed over the past 60 years, and the various contexts in which action research has been conducted. They include business, education, community development, and social services. Next, we provide a rationale for using action research in new media projects, and consider the various ways in which this methodology is closely connected to the technology design or evaluation process. We then discuss the various approaches to the complex process of undertaking the user-centred design of new media initiatives and systems. We demonstrate how action research can overcome many of the problems experienced in using traditional methodologies for media and communication research. To illustrate our arguments, we use practical examples throughout this chapter.

What Are New Media?

When researchers use the term *new media* they most often refer to communication technologies that contrast with the 'old' media: namely, the mass broadcasting media, radio, television, and newspaper. New media are networked and digital. The internet (and within that, innovations such as blogging, streaming, tagging, etc.) and cell phones are the most obvious and defining technologies of the term *new media*. There is of course a se-

9

mantic problem with the term *new media* that some have suggested renders the term meaningless: many of these new media are no longer exactly 'new.' Indeed, the field was defined and mapped by Rice (1984). More recently, what's new about new media has been the subject of two special issues of the *New Media & Society* journal (Jankowski, Jones, Lievrouw, & Hampton, 2004; Jankowski, Jones, Samarajiva, & Silverstone, 1999). Flew (2005) also provided a useful overview that underlines the semantic benefit of the term for this book's purpose in that it directs our attention to the cutting edge of technological evolution. It is on this cutting edge, this frontier of change, that action research—which began as a change management and community development methodology—is of particular relevance. So although acknowledging that *new* is always a relative term, we think the term is appropriate to the field of research and development to which we apply action research.

There is another reason we prefer the term to others like information and communication technology (ICT). We think of new media as a communicative ecology having three layers: the technology, the social, and the content layers. The technology layer includes the material artifact (the gadget) and any other technical knowledges required in its operation. The social layer simply pertains to the people, their relationships, and the social and cultural contexts of use. The first two layers also apply to ICTs. It is the third layer that makes these technologies media: the content layer, which self-evidently comprises 'what' is communicated, consumed, or exchanged. This is the realm of human creativity and expression—and it is a layer that is amenable to action research as much as the technology and social domains. This layer has become more and more important in the evolution of ICT, as the capacity and portability of devices has increased.

What Is Action Research?

The imperative of an action research project is not only to *understand* a problem, but also to provoke *change* (Dick, 2002; Reason & Bradbury, 2001; Smith, Willms, & Johnson, 1997). As discussed further in the next section, *action research* is a generic term that covers a wide range of methodologies and approaches. However, at its core, action research is an approach that 'focuses on simultaneous action and research in a participative manner' (Coghlan & Brannick, 2001, p. 7). Reason and Bradbury (2001) provided a comprehensive definition of action research, which they see as:

> a participatory, democratic process concerned with developing practical knowing in the pursuit of worthwhile human purposes. . . . It seeks to bring together action and reflection, theory and practice, in participation

with others, in the pursuit of practical solutions of pressing concern to people, and more generally the flourishing of individual persons and their communities. (p. 1)

Action research is operationalised by constant cycles of planning, acting, observing, and reflecting. Findings and theory-building, which the researcher drives, are balanced by the phase of planned action, which benefits the participants by giving them a solution to their problem or at least by making a step toward a solution. This approach is especially suitable in new media studies where innovation and change are continual, and where processes and outcomes are usually not predictable and often involve fuzzy and emotional human parameters (Hirschheim, 1985). Additionally, the field of new media is highly technical and the process of designing software and media systems naturally embodies many action research principles, such as participatory design, feedback on trials, cycles of innovation, and so on.

Moreover, action research can also be thought of as an overarching process for managing other forms of new media research. Thus, although action research frequently incorporates qualitative methods, it may in fact incorporate any primary method at all. Action research can also be thought of as a research *culture* (Tacchi, Slater, & Hearn, 2003), which engages all project stakeholders in a constant process of oscillation between knowledge generation and critical-informed reflection. This oscillating process functions like a helix, directed at reaching a stage of improvement from which the process can start all over again—but this time toward an even higher level of understanding and achievement. In this regard there are many similarities to other traditions of research and intervention that incorporate participatory cyclical processes (e.g., total quality management [TQM] and communication audits, in their more participatory and organisational development incarnations).

Thus, the features of action research that recommend it as a vehicle for enquiry into new media include its grounding in actual processes of change; the primacy it gives to the lived experiences of participants; its flexible, open, and eclectic process of enquiry; and its cyclical experimental character.[1]

History and Forms of Action Research

Action research has a long and complex history and numerous forms of action research have been developed since it first emerged more than 60

---

[1]As shown in Chapter 2, these all grow to some extent out of a critique of more dominant modes of enquiry in media and communication research.

years ago. As Brydon-Miller, Greenwood, and Maguire (2003) pointed out: 'action research is a work in progress' (p. 11). Stringer (1999) commented that quite 'disparate' histories of action research have been written by authors such as Kemmis and McTaggart (1988) and Reason (1994). Although most authors consider the American social psychologist Kurt Lewin (1946) as the first advocate of action research in the English language, McTaggart (1992) argued that it originated in the much earlier work of J.L. Moreno. Historical research shows that Moreno was the first to employ the terms *interaction research* and *action research* and used group participation and the idea of *co-researchers* as far back as 1913 in community development initiatives conducted in Vienna (McTaggart, 1992).

The intellectual origins of action research are diverse. As well as the pioneering contributions of Moreno and Lewin, action research can be linked to the pragmatic philosophy of John Dewey, Paulo Freire's influential work in the field of emancipatory education (Freire, 1970, 1982), and to the critical theories of Jürgen Habermas (1979). Feminist activists such as Maria Mies (see Klein, 1983), Patricia Maguire (1987), Marion Martin (1994), and Patti Lather (1991) have also greatly influenced the theories and practice of participatory forms of action research.

Action research has much in common with fields such as action enquiry and community development (Stringer, 1999), as well as with participatory, empowerment, and feminist research (Small, 1995). As Coghlan and Brannick (2001) pointed out, it can also be likened to action learning (Revans, 1998), cooperative enquiry (Reason, 1988), and reflective practice (Schön, 1995). As discussed later in this chapter, action research is also closely connected to the technology design or evaluation process. Indeed, design methodologies such as participatory design, agile methods, interaction design, and design studio methodologies use reflective methods that are similar to those employed in action research (Foth & Axup, 2006; Greenbaum & Kyng, 1991; Schuler & Namioka, 1993).

Some of the distinctive, but overlapping, forms of action research include participatory action research (PAR) (Kemmis & McTaggart, 2000; McTaggart, 1991, 1992; Reason, 1994; Tandon, 1996), community-based action research (Stringer, 1999), and pragmatic action research (Greenwood & Levin, 2006). PAR is described in Box 1.1. Based on their critique of the marginalisation of women and gender in participatory research, feminists such as Maguire (1987) and Gatenby and Humphries (1996) developed and successfully applied feminist PAR.

Other approaches to action research aim to improve organisational, work, and technical systems, including internet-based systems (Mumford, 2001). 'Appreciative enquiry' (Cooperrider & Whitney, 2005) is a form of practice that is 'designed to create democratically based, visionary change'

Box 1.1: Overview of Participatory Action Research

Participatory action research (PAR) is the most widely practiced participatory research methodology. It was influenced by participatory research, an approach that is popular in developing countries, and emerged from the work of radical adult educator Paulo Freire, Orlando Fals-Borda, and others in Latin America. Lewin's notion of action research, which argued for 'acting' as the basis of learning and knowing, influenced the development of PAR (Tandon, 1996). The terms *participatory research* and *participatory action research* are often used interchangeably.

Like action research, there is no single, agreed definition of PAR. Indeed, Kemmis and McTaggart (2000) consider it a 'contested concept' (p. 567). Drawing on de Koning and Martin (1996), Kemmis and McTaggart (2000), McTaggart (1991), Reason (1994), and Tandon (1996), the following key features of PAR can be identified.

The key principles of PAR include participation, action and reflection; the empowerment and emancipation of individuals and groups, and the improvement of their situations; changing the culture of groups and organisations; the production of various forms of knowledge; and engaging in 'the politics of research action' (McTaggart, 1991, p. 177).

PAR seeks to involve all stakeholders in the whole research process. However, it is useful to conceive of PAR as taking place along a continuum of participation, which can range from 'co-option' to 'collective action,' and involves varying degrees of control by researchers (Martin, 1997).

PAR is critical and begins with a concern for power and powerlessness. It aims to produce knowledge from the perspective of those who are marginalised or disadvantaged. The experiences and knowledge of local community members and workers are legitimised. Contemporary approaches to PAR draw on Foucault's model of power, which sees power as existing in action, intimately connected to knowledge, ever present in social interactions, and analysed as coming from the bottom–up, rather than from the top–down (Humphries, 1994).

Identifying the needs and priorities of people in a local community or organisation is a key aim of PAR. The issues identified are placed in the context of local people's lives so as to develop socially and culturally appropriate solutions.

Authentic commitment to 'genuine collaboration' in the research project and to 'democratic values' is a further feature of PAR (Reason, 1994). This emphasises the importance of communication and dialogue in the PAR process, which can occur both face to face and mediated by technology. Through dialogue, the academic knowledge of researchers works 'in a dialectical tension' with community knowledge 'to produce a more profound understanding of the situation' (Reason, 1994, p. 328).

PAR aims to transform theory and practice. In PAR projects theory is not given more emphasis than practice. The aim is to transform both the theories and practices of researchers and the theories and practices of people working at the local level Through this process, PAR aims to connect the local and the global (Kemmis & McTaggart, 2000).

in organisations (Gergen, 2003, p. 53). Another variety of action research that has focused on change in organisational systems is 'action science' (Argyris, 1982). We draw on Argyris later in this chapter when we discuss new media design processes.

Rationale of Action Research for New Media

New media systems or applications not only have a relatively young history, but also may be very transitory and have a very short life span. The executive protagonists of this new era are programmers and designers. Their products—software applications, internet websites, multimedia presentations, and animations—are digital, weightless, and intangible, which makes them ever more pervasive and ubiquitous. Although new media products only come to life when both the code and the design aspects work together seamlessly to create a functional and useful unit, the programmers and designers themselves come from quite different backgrounds and do not understand each other by default when they think, communicate, and act in their respective professional spheres. For example, although there are of course interdisciplinary influences, programmers are strongly influenced by mathematical and computer science traditions, whereas designers come from an arts and aesthetics background.

It is still quite rare that the position of a programmer and a designer is filled by one employee who has the educational and practical background of both disciplines, and understands the interface, and thus the transcendence, of working comfortably in both disciplines. This is especially the case when each discipline itself is still progressing and evolving rapidly to reach out to new frontiers while unifying the understanding and knowledge of the existing territory (e.g., Hirschheim, 1985; Markus, 1984; Shedroff, 1999).

Furthermore, new media professionals have to deal with another important variable when developing products and applications: the client or user. New media applications require a high level of expertise in order to be developed, customised, deployed, and maintained. The conventional relationship between a client facing a problem and a developer willing to provide an appropriate solution is usually constrained by a lack of understanding on both sides, because both parties plan, act, and reflect within a different knowledge space: the client within a problem-specific knowledge space of their business or community, and the developer within a solution-specific knowledge space of their particular area of expertise. Additional limitations on time and budget frequently result in two key issues. First, the developer's solution does not meet all needs the client is aware of, and second, the developer's portfolio of solutions could have addressed other needs the client is not currently aware of. Thus, the two apparent communication conflicts occur internally between different professional groups of developers, and externally between the developer and the client. Only if an awareness of these conflicts is raised and the conflicts are successfully addressed by strategic methodological decisions, will it be possible to develop and deploy a solution to the client's problem. Yet, this is anything but trivial.

For example, a particular business interested in advancing and streamlining their sales operations and acquiring more customers through online channels might be offered an inexpensive 'brochure ware' website from a contractor not familiar with database programming, whereas another supplier might offer a dynamic website that fully integrates with the business's existing information technology infrastructure.[2] The question is, how can we expect to find a solution to a problem if we do not know what we are looking for? Polanyi (1983) offered a simple but far-reaching way out of this classic contradiction by stating that 'we can know things, and important things, that we cannot tell' (p. 22), something he termed *tacit knowledge*.

So, for an ICT or new media developer it is essential to tap into a client's tacit knowledge, because it will help to surface the inner processes of the client's business operations—information that is significant for the successful development of any potential solution. The discovery of this meta problem, which has to be looked at before any exploration of the client's actual problem can begin, enables the search for, and endeavours to span, connections between the problem-specific knowledge space of the client and the solution-specific knowledge space of the developer—between explicit and tacit strata on each side.

The distinction between tacit and codified knowledge is important in action research. Most research methods only acknowledge codified knowledge, privileging the development of theory, via formal definitions, arguments, or other publicly verifiable knowledge forms. Action research, however, trades in both codified and tacit knowledge. Tacit knowledge is embedded in the actions and phenomenology of participants. This is an important source for the construction of knowledge about the local life

---

[2]This is an example of a common problem in ICT and new media development—and even in media and communication research—that goes back to the issue Plato (1956) illustrated in Meno. Plato presents a dialogue between Socrates and a slave boy who gives right answers to a geometrical problem although he knows no geometry. In our example, Socrates is the new media developer trying to discover which applications would be best suited to meet the business's needs, although the business itself is not familiar with the inner workings of new media applications (and the reverse as well: The developer is not familiar with the business).

space as well as the implementation of changes in that life space. Additionally, action research produces codified knowledge that can be related to the theory produced by both action research and other research methods.[3]

The interplay of codified and tacit knowledge toward an actionable solution is fostered by setting up a culture of action research. With its focus on participative development, soft or agile methods, qualitative analysis, adaptive procedures, reflective practice, and informed action, many new media professionals and businesses start to adopt de facto principles of action research in their strategy and operations, in order to translate these ideas and concepts into a design and development process that yields a sustainable and user-friendly new media product.

This has been accompanied by a shift in the traditional social research disciplines as outlined previously, but also in technical and practice-oriented disciplines such as software engineering and systems design (see Arnold, 2002). In fact, the well-established product life-cycle models (e.g., ISO 12207) do already resemble the act–reflect cycle of action research in that they both propose alternating phases of planning (initiation, specifications, design), action (production, delivery and implementation), and reflection (review and evaluation). The development of updates and service releases to software products and websites corresponds with the stage of informed reflection and change at the end of each action research cycle. Nevertheless, the fast spreading shift toward action research is more groundbreaking than the mere adoption of a life-cycle process that limits itself in most cases to a top-down view of the technology itself and the correction of its flaws and faults, rather than adding a holistic and user-inclusive bottom-up perspective.

There is a long history of research in technology studies that has acknowledged the importance of the issues just raised and developed research methods to address them. This extends back to the sociotechnical systems school (Emery, 1969; Emery & Trist, 1973) and the range of participatory methods it prefigured—for example, TQM (Oakland, 2003) and organisational development interventions (Waddell, Cummings, & Worley, 2004)—as well as those researchers who have advocated ethnographic and interpretive approaches to technology design and implementation (e.g., Bloomfield, 1980; Harvey & Myers, 1995; Hirschheim, 1985; Markus; 1984; Orlikowski, 1992; Urquhart, 2007; Walsham, 1993). These foundations laid the groundwork for the current upshot in action-oriented methods applied to design and implementation of new media. The most recent work includes reflective practitioners advocating action research

---

[3]Action research exists in a meta-theoretical space that has seen, for example, Marxist (Kemmis & McTaggart, 1988), feminist (Gatenby & Humphries, 1996), and liberal (Argyris, 1982) forms emerge.

through participative development and soft systems methodology (Checkland & Holwell, 1998; Checkland & Scholes, 1999), scenarios and use cases (Rosson & Carroll, 2002), agile methods (Cockburn, 2002; Fowler, 2003; Highsmith, 2002), interaction design (Cooper, 1999; Cooper & Reimann, 2003; Preece, Rogers, & Sharp, 2002), participatory design (Greenbaum & Kyng, 1991; Schuler & Namioka, 1993) and the sociotechnical approach to action research (Mumford, 2001).

Additionally, the authors, and others, have conducted a limited number of new media studies that are explicitly informed by action research. Research involving the authors includes anticipatory studies of the incorporation of 'intelligence' into the telephone network (Hearn et al., 1993; Lennie, Hearn, Stevenson, Inayatullah, & Mandeville, 1996); design and evaluation of internet services for Australians in rural and regional locations (Lennie & Hearn, 2003; Lennie et al., 2004; Lennie, Hearn, Simpson, & Kimber, 2005); evaluation of community websites in rural Australia (Lennie, Hearn, & Hanrahan, 2005); design and evaluation of community media projects in south Asia (Tacchi, Slater, & Hearn, 2003); research and design of residential community networks (Foth, 2006a, 2006b; Foth & Hearn, 2007); and research to animate youth through music, creativity, and ICT (Hartley, Hearn, Tacchi, & Foth, 2003); and a project that facilitated isolated rural women's access to online conversation groups and other ICTs (The Rural Women and ICTs Research Team, 1999). We present case studies of a number of these projects in Part III.

Research in this field by others includes the evaluation of an African telecentres project (Hudson, 2001); the application of ethnographic action research (EAR) in a collaboration project conducted in a distributed university research centre (MacColl, Cooper, Rittenbruch, & Viller, 2005); and a study that explored the actual and potential uses of ICTs in rural, regional, and outback Queensland for personal, organisational, and community development purposes (Simpson, Wood, Daws, & Seinen, 2001). A further example from the commercial world is a major action research project that involved using information technology to build a 'new' retail bank (Reynolds, Thorogood, & Yetton, 2005).

In these examples, the action research process is typically engaged either to design or to evaluate some aspect of a new technology, or to better understand the context of its use. The approach focuses on actual practices of use and interaction with new media technology in the wider context of people's lives—what has been termed *communicative ecologies* (see Box 2.1 in Ch. 2). Placing users and producers at the centre of the research process is important if useful analytical and action frameworks are to be developed. This necessitates the complete range of social relationships and processes within which a project is doing its work. It includes the immediate circle of participants, how they are organised, and how the project fits into their everyday lives. It also involves the wider social context of the project—for example, social divisions within the community, language issues, community economic, social and cultural resources, power, and institutions in the community—and social structures and processes beyond the locality—for example, infrastructure, government policies, and economic developments.

Action research means that the research process is tightly connected to the technology design or evaluation in three main ways:

1. *Active participation.* The people who should benefit from the research participate in defining the aims and direction of the research and in interpreting and drawing conclusions from it.

2. *Action-based methods.* The activities and experiences of participants generate knowledge alongside, or in combination with, more formal methods.

3. *Generating action.* Research is directly aimed at generating things like medium and long-term plans, including business plans; ideas for new initiatives; solving problems; targeting sectors of the user constituency; finding new resources or partners. Action-generating research can be a combination of general, wide-ranging, background research and very specific focused research.

Knowledge produced via these processes ranges from tacit, tactical knowledge of most relevance to local participants, through to more general codified knowledge relevant for transfer to other communities.

Issues and Challenges

As shown in this volume, action research and related participatory research and evaluation methodologies raise complex theoretical, methodological, and ethical issues and challenges that have implications for the quality of new media projects and the trustworthiness of the findings and outcomes. Lennie (2006) identified the following issues that need to be taken into account:

1. *Ensuring stakeholder representativeness.* Several studies have highlighted the complex barriers and issues, which need to be addressed, that arise when action researchers attempt to involve a broad diversity of participants and stakeholders in projects (Lennie, 2002; Mathie & Greene, 1997).

2. *Conflicting agendas and perspectives.* There is a potential that the conflicting agendas and perspectives of various stakeholder groups will

hinder the effectiveness of an action research project. However, although power is a central issue in participatory research and evaluation, it is often ignored (Gregory, 2000; LeCompte, 1995). Critical assessments of both the empowering and potentially disempowering impacts of action research projects are therefore required.

3. *Critique of key action research concepts.* There is a need to critique key concepts such as 'collaboration,' 'empowerment,' and 'participation' when assessing the outcomes of PAR. Idealistic or naive assumptions are sometimes made, for instance that participation will automatically lead to empowerment. However, the concept of empowerment is often used in contradictory ways, while the forms of participation range from co-option to collective action (Hirschheim, 1985; Martin, 2000).

4. *Time, energy, and resources required.* Compared with other research methods, action research requires significant amounts of time, energy, and resources to build research capacity, plan and conduct projects, and develop relationships based on mutual trust and open communication. To be effective, action research projects require sufficient time and resources, particularly in the early stages when some participants may be unfamiliar with participatory methods or prefer more traditional research methodologies. Kelly (1985) pointed out that action research in schools 'makes more demands than traditional research on the teachers' time and energy. This can lead to reluctance to become over-involved.'

Other issues and challenges that need to be considered in conducting new media action research include the following:

1. *Hearing the voices of the marginalised or less confident.* Our research indicates that it is often those who are more advantaged, empowered, and willing to participate in processes such as workshops and meetings who are typically heard in action research projects.

2. *Effective capacity building.* New media action research requires a wide range of skills and abilities, including skills in planning, organising, facilitation, communication, research, evaluation, and in the design and use of various technologies. However, there are many challenges involved in effectively building capacities in these areas, as Lennie, Hearn, Simpson, and Kimber (2005) suggested.

3. *Widely disseminating results.* For the outcomes of the learning and enquiry to be put to best use, they need to be widely spread within organisations and communities, including to those who have not actively participated in the project.

4. *Making effective use of new media.* When working with participants who are geographically distant from the research team, a key question is whether action research projects can be effectively conducted at a distance. This raises issues such as equal community access to new media and ensuring that the technologies used are relevant to the needs, interests, and goals of participants.

Several of these issues are discussed further in Chapter 6, when we consider the contributions of network action research in responding to these challenges.

Conclusion

We began this chapter by arguing for the appropriateness of using the term *new media* in this book, rather than terms such as *information and communication technology*. New media are networked and digital and have technology, social, and content layers. We suggested that the content layer—the realm of creativity and expression—is what makes technology media. This layer is just as amenable to action research as the technology and social domains.

Action research was seen as particularly appropriate to new media initiatives because they involve constant innovation and change, have unpredictable outcomes, and require flexibility, creativity, and an inclusive, user-centred approach. The importance of the distinction between tacit and codified knowledge, the interplay between these forms of knowledge, and the need to focus on the wider context of people's lives in action research were highlighted. We also noted the various ways in which this methodology is closely connected to the technology design or evaluation process.

The strengths of action research in relation to new media enquiry should not blind us to its various challenges and issues, which we have outlined in this chapter. These and other issues continue to be discussed by researchers and practitioners in the field (e.g., Avison, Baskerville, & Myers, 2001; Lennie, 2005; McKay & Marshall, 2001; Mumford, 2001). First and foremost is the difficulty of finding participants willing to engage in protracted and intense enquiry, but also the difficulty of building mutually inclusive frames of reference between researchers and participants in the research process. There are clearly many methodological challenges and opportunities that recent technological advances and social changes pose for new media action research. In the next chapter we suggest a number of methodological principles for new media action research that seek to address these issues and challenges.

Chapter 2

Guiding Concepts and Principles

There are three levels of knowledge used in the application of an action research approach to new media:

1. The underlying philosophy adopted; for example, assumptions about the social problems or processes being investigated, and, in particular, assumptions about the operation of media technologies in the social contexts in question. A related issue is the guiding assumptions about how knowledge can be produced and the status of this knowledge (i.e., the underlying epistemological questions).

2. Principles and concepts that guide the use of action research methodology. This layer is more operational than the first, although of course informed by it.

3. The methods and tools that can be most effectively used in new media action research projects.

In this chapter, we deal with Levels 1 and 2 and the discussion is necessarily more abstract than operational. Level 3 is discussed in detail in Chapters 3 and 4.

We begin by considering a number of philosophical positions related to the relationship between the technology and social domains. Positions at either end of the spectrum, namely technological determinism and the social construction of technology perspectives are detailed. As a means of overcoming these polar positions, we present an alternative co-evolutionary perspective on technology and society. We then outline the theoretical and conceptual framework that underpins our approach to new media action research. This includes an explanation of the key concept *communicative ecology* and the notion that everything is connected. Finally, we identify a number of methodological principles that guide our approach. They include adopting methodological pluralism, taking an open enquiry approach, and facilitating participation that respects diversity and difference. Definitions of the social research key concepts used in this volume are provided in Box 2.1.

Box 2.1: Definitions of Key Social Research Concepts

Although Greenwood and Levin (2006) abandoned the concepts *method* and *methodology* in their recent introduction to action research, we find it useful to continue using these terms. To clarify what we mean by the various social research concepts used in this volume, we provide definitions of the terms *methods*, *tools*, *methodology*, *theoretical perspective*, and *epistemology*. The following definitions (other than for *tools*) are based on those given by Crotty (1988).

Methods: The techniques or procedures used to gather and analyse data related to a research question or problem (e.g., participant observation, focus groups, interviews).

Tools: New media technology and software used to maintain communication and foster collaboration between researchers, co-researchers, participants, and stakeholders involved in social or action research projects (e.g., e-mail, discussion boards, community networks, blogs). These tools are also useful to gather, store, and discuss research data.

Methodology: The strategy, plan of action, process, or design lying behind the choice and use of particular methods for data collection and analysis and linking the choice and use of methods to the desired outcomes (e.g., ethnography, action research).

Theoretical perspective: The philosophical stance informing the methodology, which provides a context for the process used and a way of grounding its principles and criteria (e.g., pragmatism, interpretivism, feminism).

Epistemology: The theory of knowledge embedded in the theoretical perspective and therefore in the methodology used in a research project (e.g., constructionism, subjectivism).

The Philosophical Underpinnings of New Media Action Research

Action research is a method of enquiry that produces practical outcomes. It can equally be seen as a practical problem-solving process that also produces enquiry outcomes. Indeed, the production of practical outcomes is part of the enquiry process. Put simply, figuring out what does and does not work requires defining and collecting information about all parts of the practical puzzle at hand. In effect, this is a loose kind of experimentation. But can we justify these claims? How good is action research at producing knowledge? And how good is it at producing practical outcomes? It is not the only process that purports to do each of these. More particularly for this book, is action research useful in producing knowledge and practical outcomes in the field of new media?

To reiterate, by *new media* we simply mean the ever-expanding range of networked and digital technologies that are used by people to communicate, and send and receive content. They include the internet, e-mail, cell phones, personal digital assistants (PDAs), and digital television, among others. As discussed in Chapter 1, new media has three layers: the content, the technology, and the social layers, which are of course inter-related. An important first step in explaining the rationale for using action research is to examine the way these relationships have been explained in social theory.

An important starting point is the long-standing distinction between objective and subjective enquiry approaches to, and explanations of, the social sphere. Although objective approaches were once dominant, increasingly, the subjectively oriented constructivist (and constructionist) positions have gained acceptance. Although there are many variants and traditions,[1] pre- and poststructuralist, they share an emphasis on language (and there-fore culture) as a determining factor in the constitution and (therefore) change of society. We accept and acknowledge that this strand of theorising is an important corrective to purely objective views of social theory. In attacking the taken-for-grantedness of social realities, especially those held unreflectively, social constructivists open the way for critique and remaking of social life. They rightly make it more possible that the many socially constructed realities, which sometimes function to legitimate inequality and serve various sets of interests, can be challenged. They remind us that the natural order of things is not natural at all. These considerations are important to an enquiry approach that examines and seeks change in systems, content, or relationships around new media.

However, we also question any moves by the constructivists toward cultural determinism, particularly when considering any social behaviours related to technologies. As such, we suggest that technology systems of any kind share much with other systems that are not primarily mediated by language (e.g., rainforests, animal species, human biology). In not talking about the systemic effects of *the material* as opposed to the merely linguistic or cultural, we can be distracted from the important task of understand-ing how technology and culture interact. Understanding the conjunction

---

[1]An important distinction is between constructivist and constructionist traditions which reflect micro, sense making perspectives and social institutional determinist perspectives respectively. Both are at issue here. Whereas constructivism asserts that each individual's way of making sense of the world is 'as valid and worthy of respect as any other,' social constructionism 'emphasises the hold our culture has on us: it shapes the way in which we see things . . . and gives us a quite definite view of the world' (Crotty, 1998, p. 58).

of material systems and cultural systems is, in our view, a most pressing theoretical imperative facing social theory in general and the study and practice of new media technologies in particular.

Deriving from this basic philosophical starting point are a number of conceptual positions about the relationship between the technology layer and the social layer of new media. As Hearn, Mandeville, and Anthony (1998) and Volti (2006) showed, there is extensive literature discussing the relationship between technology and society and many philosophical positions that could be taken. At one end of the spectrum is the viewpoint labeled *technological determinism* (implied in the work of Bell, 1982; Innis, 1950, 1951; McLuhan, 1967a; Pool, 1983; and more recently Castells, 1996, 1997, 2000a, 2000b, 2001, 2003).[2] This is the label given to those who advocate or at least argue that the technology layer drives change in the social layer and indeed, more broadly, is a fundamental driver of social change. Technology is seen as a powerful and inevitable factor in human affairs. Its inevitability makes consideration of the social and political interests it serves beside the point. That is, in this perspective the social and political interests associated with technological choices are not problematised and those who produce them are viewed as 'independent of their social location and above sectional interests' (Wajcman, 1991, p. 20). This influential viewpoint is common among some media sociologists, governments and business organisations, and the community in general. Technological determinists can usually point to a succession of innovations in technology and broadly identify their impacts on society. Traditional descriptions of various technology revolutions depend on this basic argument (see e.g., Diamond, 1999).

For example, when questions such as 'How is the internet changing society?' are asked they betray an underlying technological determinist frame of reference. Technological determinists usually suggest that technologies evolve independently of society and social forces. To put it crudely, they emerge and exert their impacts regardless of what people do with them. As such, technology operates essentially as a material force that changes the material substratum of society—the logistics of information flows. Marshall McLuhan (1967b) famously asserted that 'the medium is the message.' He argued that it is not the content but the rearrangement of the modes of communication which affects society and culture. For example, the extent to which a medium is visual- or text-based, the speed of information flow,

---

[2]Two other positions are often identified, namely technological optimism (or utopianism) and technological pessimism (or dystopianism). Logically speaking, both fall under the technological determinist position because implicit in them is the view that technological change leads to social outcomes. However in much of the literature, technological determinism is assumed to infer mindless technological optimism.

and its distributive characteristic all affect the outcomes of communication. According to this argument, it is the technology itself, not the way it is appropriated or adopted, that is the essential cause of change.

As a viewpoint, technological determinism manifests itself in different ways and within different situations. In research, it can be seen in questions that are framed in terms of the effects of a technology on society or social practices: 'Is the internet making us less sociable?' 'Is the internet destroying social capital?' and so on (see Bargh & McKenna, 2004, for a review of studies that frame the internet and social life in some cases). This perspective also influences the policies of national governments by emphasising that investment in technology is a key spearhead for economic growth and development. An example of this is the belief that information and communication technologies (ICTs) will, by themselves, play a critical role in national and regional development. In companies, this viewpoint may be found in the drive to stay at the cutting edge of technology. Those who implement technology may focus on simply getting the technology working, without considering user preferences or aesthetic considerations.

Many technological determinists could be described as utopian in their view of the possibilities of technology. However, many of the most pessimistic views of the technologisation of the human condition rest on the same deterministic assumption: that technology is the prime mover in human affairs (see Diamond, 1999, for a compelling technological determinist perspective of history).

One alternative view to technological determinism has been termed the *social construction of technology* position (exemplified by Khong, 2003; Krug, 2005; Latour, 2005; Mackay & Gillespie, 1992; MacKenzie & Wajcman, 1985; Volti, 2006; Winner, 1993). From this viewpoint, in the analysis of social issues, technology is considered no different from other phenomena or institutions, in that it is ultimately and inescapably a product of society. In other words, technology arises and changes because of social processes according to the interests of different social groups. Furthermore, technologies are translated and apprehended culturally: they are named and integrated, and become taken for granted. Thus, technology is a social and cultural artifact. MacKenzie and Wajcman (1985) critiqued the notion that technologies follow a predetermined course of development. MacKay and Gillespie (1992) used the example of research and development decisions that are significant determinants of the sorts of technologies that are developed. And, although technologies clearly have impacts, their nature is not built into the technology, but depends on a complex range of social, political, and economic factors, including the values and ideologies of technology designers and developers (MacKay & Gillespie, 1992; Wajcman, 1991).

The social construction of technology perspective has gained increasing recognition over the past 20 years. In their view, *our understanding* of technology determines its impact, not the technology itself. Social constructivists as policymakers are critical of new technology hype. They recognise that vendors of technology often exaggerate its potential, and that users may exaggerate the negative consequences. Additionally, they usually raise questions about the social implications of new technology (e.g., issues of equity, access, or privacy). For technology managers, the socially constructed perspective is a reminder that it is the market that will ultimately determine the success or failure of a technology, rather than the technology itself. Technology implementers who are sensitive to the needs of users also reflect an implicit appreciation for the socially constructed view of technology.

An important contribution to the social construction of technology debate has been made by feminist researchers, who have drawn attention to the mutual shaping of gender and technology (Rakow, 1988; van Zoonen, 1992, 2001; Wajcman, 1991). As Williams and Edge (1996) pointed out, feminist research has raised questions about 'how the gendered nature of society influences technological development' and also the ways in which the use of technologies 'may reinforce particular gendered social relations' (p. 879). Given the continuing dominance of men in the technological sphere, the view that technology is socially constructed and gendered suggests a need for close attention to gender-related issues when conducting new media action research. For example, an action research project on Australian rural women's access to ICTs showed that these women were often early adopters of technologies such as the internet but also experienced many barriers in accessing this technology, including training programs that did not meet their particular needs and lack of effective ongoing technical support (The Rural Women and ICTs Research Team, 1999).

An Alternative Co-Evolutionary Perspective

In contrast to either the technological determinist or social constructivist views, we take the position in this volume that technologies and society are co-evolutionary. As many theorists have noted (e.g., Hirschheim, 1985; Orlikowski, 1992, 2000; Poole & Desanctis, 1990), people appropriate, understand, and use technologies in a social context. At the same time, we believe there are impacts of technology that are not that dependent on their cultural appropriation: for example, compression of time and space, changes in the location and logistics of information, physical access or lack of access (see Rice, McCreadie, & Chang, 2001), and whether a device actually works. Sociologist William Ogburn (cited in Volti, 2006) suggested the following:

> The whole interconnected mass (i.e., social institutions, customs, tech-
> nology, and science) is in motion. When each part is in motion and
> banging up against some other part, the question of origins seems
> artificial and unrealistic. If one pushes the question to the extreme,
> origins are lists in a maze of causative factors. (p. 272)

Furthermore, as Volti (2006) suggested: 'no reasonable person could deny that technology has been a major force in making the world we live in, but it is important to always keep in mind that technology has not operated as an agent independent of the society in which it is embedded' (p. 272). Similarly, Katz and Rice (2002) advocated a 'syntopia' position—rejecting both utopian and dystopian visions of the internet.

The policy and practical imperatives of a co-evolutionary view are to advance and resource both technical and social issues. Thus, the co-evolutionary view of technological change offers ways around the bipolar positions that bog us down. This leads us to our methodological position. We maintain that new media systems cannot completely be explained or understood solely by recourse to either constructivist or objectivist think-ing. There are phenomena that are evident in systems that do not have language (at least the human variant). However, there are phenomena that are also language based or cultural and this has reciprocal effects. We assert that rather than pitting constructivist views against materialist views, a more fruitful task is to understand the possible relation between the two (e.g., the relationship between ecological and cultural systems, or gender and biology, or ideology and productive capacity). In the case of new media, we believe that both enquiry and practice demand an understanding of the relationship between the cultural as well as the technical domains. That is, we assume a reciprocal relationship between the social and the technical (Orlikowski, 1992, 2000).

Of course it is possible, and for many purposes desirable, to stand apart from new media systems and to conduct research as if it was object-ive. However, in real terms it is impossible to achieve this perfectly. For a start, to address many research questions the researcher must interact with people to obtain answers to their questions, and this engagement poten-tially changes the answers to the questions asked. Even the most carefully constructed objective research enquiries are not neutral and 'inert.' Action research acknowledges this and does not purport to be inert, objective, or value-free. Because social fields are constructed communicatively, new media systems are interventions into the very fabric of a social field. New media—and the social systems in which they are embedded—are always evolving, and action research is part of that evolution.

But can such an enquiry produce valid knowledge about new media systems? As Hearn and Foth (2005) argued, communication and media studies have always been fragmented (Ellis, 1995; Gerbner, 1983), with functionalist, interpretivist, and critical traditions vying with each other (Hearn, 1999; Hearn & Stevenson, 1998). Ironically, it is a feature that these three traditions share that is the point of departure for new media action research—namely, the split between the theoriser and those theorised about, the observer and the observed (Guba & Lincoln, 1994).

For example, it is the functional/empirical school's pursuit of generalisable, predictive scientific formulae that requires disengagement between the observer and the observed, in particular the observer's disengagement from action. As such, it treats social phenomena as concrete, materialistic entities—types of social facts. As a result, this approach is beset by problems that help distance theory from action: the stripping of context from actions, dissociation of meaning from purpose, inapplicability of general data to individual cases, and exclusion of the discovery dimension in enquiry. The meaning of communication from the actor's point of view is obscured, as a new 'scientific discourse' is developed to more effectively explain what is happening.

Interpretivists, while acknowledging social context and stressing the importance of local meaning-making, are ultimately no less guilty than functionalists of putting words into the mouths of others. Indeed, perhaps their basis for doing so is even more suspect than that of the functionalists, because their right to 'tell the story' as they see it ultimately cannot be disputed. Moreover, the pursuit of grand theoretical schemes is also no less pronounced than among the functionalists (e.g., Schoening & Anderson, 1995). Interpretivists are motivated by theory-building as much as functionalists, and their claim to know the mind of the observed is equally spurious because it, too, is based on the attributions of the observer. It is the construction of a story from the point of view of an observer, living in a different phenomenal world to the observed.

The critical stance also embodies an inability to develop a full understanding from the point of view of the observed or theorised about, even from poststructuralist and postmodernist perspectives. Embedded within the critical approach is a claim to know what is better, more just, or more humane, and a belief that these claims must be defended rather than interrogated. In this sense, the critical approach is antireflective. In other words, the fixed macro positions that critical theorists take toward the social world interfere with their ability to embrace local problems in fresh and open-minded ways. Ironically, therefore, the critical position leads to the same kind of problem—disengagement from phenomena—that they find the functionalists guilty of in their objective stance (Burrell & Morgan, 1979).

Therefore, in a basic sense it can be argued that the three research traditions share the same epistemological stance, namely that of the observer—an objective observer, a sensemaking observer, and a critical observer, respectively. Although each of these may at times be a valid perspective in its own right, each misses an essential point, namely that communication and mediated communication inherently involves an interactive process. As a result, the observer stance leads to a disjunction between theory and action. A disjunction between theory and action renders each tradition more intent on theory-building and less open to seeing the ultimate poverty of its approach. Theories built are theories defended.

An engagement with action challenges prior theory, exposing its limited dimensionality and the necessity for further development. Therefore, the field of action inculcates perceptual openness rather than defense and thus increases the chances for dialogue across paradigms. Conducted effectively, such an approach also increases the validity of the research by including the whole range of perspectives, values, agendas, and interpretations (of researchers, stakeholders, participants) in the process of planning and conducting the research, gathering and interpreting the data, reflecting on the action, and reporting results.

In recent years, a number of researchers from different traditions have begun to move toward a position that accentuates local dialogical knowledge, rejects strictly objective characterisations of human communication activities, and shares a concern to enact their theory (see e.g., Dockery, 2000; Lather, 1991; Mumby, 1997; Sanger, 1996). As we suggested initially, this turn in research philosophy is particularly relevant to the field of new media.

Thus, action research deviates from many other research approaches in what it considers to be valid knowledge. Certainly, action research does not reject the importance of verification and reliability and so on. But, unlike many forms of empirical social research that set out to produce objectified knowledge, action research, as described in Chapter 1, seeks to produce learning toward insight and actionable knowledge. It questions both the philosophical validity of objectified knowledge as well as its practical utility. Nevertheless, issues of validity, 'trustworthiness' (Guba & Lincoln, 1989) and quality are still criteria that can be brought to bear in assessing outputs for such research methodology. We discuss ways of increasing the rigour of action research in Chapter 3, drawing on recent work in this area by Lennie (2006).

Deriving from the pragmatic philosophical tradition of John Dewey and William James is a concern with the 'primacy of the practical' (Heron, 1996). In Dewey's view, traditional epistemologies, whether rationalist or empiricist, had drawn too stark a distinction between thought, the domain of knowledge, and the world of fact to which thought purportedly referred. Thought was believed to exist apart from the world, epistemologically, as the object of immediate awareness, and ontologically as the unique aspect of the self. Dewey and James maintained that an idea agrees with reality, and is therefore true, if and only if it is successfully employed in human action in pursuit of human goals and interests, that is, if it leads to the resolution of a problematic situation in Dewey's terms. The pragmatic position suggests that 'when judging ideas, we should consider their empirical and practical consequences' (Johnson & Onwuegbuzie, 2004, p. 17). Philosophers such as Dewey and James were not only interested in using this approach to help understand the importance of their philosophical positions, they also wanted to use their findings to help decide which actions to take next 'as one attempts to better understand real-world phenomena' (Johnson & Onwuegbuzie, 2004, p. 17).

Given these philosophical considerations, we now outline a broad theoretical and conceptual framework that guides our approach to action research. Following this, we set out the methodological principles that underpin our work.

Theoretical and Conceptual Framework

Although we have used a variety of different concepts and theories in our work in this field—several of which are explained elsewhere in this volume—the key elements of our broad theoretical and conceptual framework are as follows:

- A **critical perspective** that questions assumptions about both action research and new media.

- Consideration of the **communicative ecology** (see Box 2.2) of project locations. This entails taking the wider social and cultural context and existing local communication networks into account.

- A **holistic perspective** that recognises **the connectedness of everything**.

- Recognition that any explanation of a phenomenon, such as the introduction of new technologies, involves **multiple causes and effects**. Our

Box 2.2: Communicative Ecology

In order to understand the potential and real impacts of individual media technologies in any given situation, you need to place this experience within a broader understanding of the whole structure of communication and information in people's everyday lives.

Each instance of communication or information takes place within an already existing 'communicative ecology,' and each place has its own unique communicative ecology that we need to understand.

Key questions to understand a local communicative ecology:

- What kinds of communication and information activities do local people carry out or wish to carry out?

- What communications resources are available to them—media content, technologies, and skills?

- How do they understand the way these resources can be used?

- Who do they communicate with, and why?

- How does a particular medium—like radio or internet—fit into existing *social* networks? Does it expand those networks?

It is important to look at *everything* that could count as a medium of communication. That is, not just press, broadcasting, or telecoms but also roads, buses, and trains, visits to neighbours, gossip, and public and private places where people meet to communicate. It is also important to look at how people *combine* different media.

Communicative ecologies focus our attention on the communication-related aspects of the contexts in which the people we were studying operate. It places media technologies in the context of all the ways of communicating that are significant locally, including face-to-face interaction.

It is recognised that any 'new' connections and networks (social and technical) that develop as a result of the introduction of individual technologies will be far more effective if they are somehow interconnected with existing, locally appropriate systems and structures.

Through this approach we can ask how new media technologies articulate with more traditional ones: how do different media serve different purposes, and how do they combine in people's everyday lives?

approach respects this multicausality and seeks to **build redundancy** into the systems, interventions, and enquiry processes we set up.

- Respect for **diversity and differences** and **seeking inclusion,** which is seen as one of the key challenges of action research. This entails paying attention to relevant issues such as **gender and other equity and social justice issues**.

- Recognising the **power/knowledge differences** inherent in action research projects.

- A **co-evolutionary perspective** on the interaction between technology and society that assumes a reciprocal relationship between the social and the technical spheres. We have argued that it is more fruitful to understand the relationship between constructivist and materialist views about technology and between the cultural and technical domains than to set up unhelpful bipolar positions. We believe that new media action research is most usefully guided by this philosophical position.

- Recognition of the importance of a focus on the distinction between **tacit and codified knowledge** and the interplay between these forms of knowledge.

We explained the alternative co-evolutionary perspective earlier in this chapter, whereas the need to focus on the interplay between tacit and codified knowledge was discussed in Chapter 1. The other elements of our theoretical and conceptual framework are now explained further.

Adopting a Critical Perspective

Our approach involves critically and rigorously questioning various assumptions about both action research and new media. Such an approach recognises the often complex and contradictory nature of both the action research process and new media, with its technology, social, and content layers. We are critical of the assumptions that underpin some approaches to action research, such as, that participation will automatically lead to people's empowerment in terms of having an equal voice and being equally heard by those in more powerful positions. We also reject the assumption that action research mainly involves qualitative research.

As the discussion about technological determinism earlier in this chapter suggests, we also need to critically question assumptions about new media initiatives, particularly their effectiveness and impacts on a community. We suggested that the most fruitful approach here is to assume a reciprocal relationship between the social and the technical. We need to acknowledge that some new media initiatives have failed and that more effective strategies are required to ensure the long-term sustainability and success of many new media initiatives, particularly those implemented in poor and disadvantaged communities. Hearn, Kimber, Lennie, and Simpson (2005) suggested a number of valuable strategies for the sustainability of ICT initiatives undertaken in pursuit of rural and regional development. They include an acknowledgment that *sustainability* means quite different things to various groups involved in action research and community development projects (see also Gurstein, 2003b and the *Journal of Community Informatics*).

Considering the Communicative Ecology

Because social action is embedded in its cultural context, a key principle in action research for new media concerns respect for the cultural context, particularly the *local* cultural context. *Communicative ecology* (Foth & Hearn, 2007; Tacchi, Slater, & Hearn, 2003) is therefore a key concept underpinning our research (see Box 2.2). We believe that the term *ecology* has a lot to offer new media research. Our particular interest in the term stems from our study of people in particular places with access to many different new media. For example, we have studied communication patterns in inner-city apartment buildings (Foth, 2006a, 2006b) and villages in developing countries (Slater, Tacchi, & Lewis, 2002; Tacchi, 2005; Tacchi, Slater, & Hearn, 2003). Case studies of these projects are presented in Chapters 8 and 10.

The communicative ecology is different from 'media ecology' as defined by Neil Postman, inspired by Marshall McLuhan in the early 1970s, and continued through the Media Ecology Association. Media ecology is variously described on the association's website as 'an interdisciplinary field of study,' an 'emerging metadiscipline,' and a 'preparadigmatic science.' According to Postman, 'media ecology looks into the matter of how media of communication affect human perception, understanding, feeling, and value; and how our interaction with media facilitates or impedes our chances of survival' (see the Media Ecology Association website, www.media-ecology.org). A media ecology approach looks at the ways in which media structure our lives, how they influence how we think and feel. A communicative ecology approach encourages us to see each instance of use of media technologies within a complex media environment that is socially and culturally framed. Each community is complex, and each media initiative, event, and relationship will change and shift the power relations at both an individual and community level. The concept of communicative ecologies takes this into account. Putting it bluntly, media ecology suggests a strong technological determinist leaning that communicative ecology actively avoids.

Using an ecological metaphor opens up a number of interesting analytical possibilities. For example, it enables us to analyse the nature of the population or community within each ecology—how the members of this population engage with each other. We can ask what the (often unacknowledged) rules of engagement are, and examine how different features of the ecology rise and fall with time. It also enables us to define the boundaries of any given ecology, and to examine how the coherence of that boundary and the stability of the ecology are maintained. Additionally, it allows us to explore transactions between different ecologies and the direct and indirect impacts that interventions such as action research projects have on these ecologies (e.g., Lennie, 2005). Methodologically, it suggests a holistic perspective that recognises the difficulty of 'quarantining' the focus of our study.

A Holistic Perspective

Because new media systems evolve in the complex context of political, social, economic, and cultural forces, the analysis of new media must adopt multiple perspectives. It is inherently multidisciplinary. There are two ways this complexity can be dealt with intelligibly. First, each perspective can be used as a focus of analysis in its own right. This simplification can allow one aspect of the phenomenon to be addressed in depth while 'holding constant' the other perspectives. Second, we can study the interrelationships between the different perspectives to help to reinstate a more holistic assessment. We do not assume that systems are static, that variables are always easy to define, or that they are related in simple linear ways. This dissuades us from isolating unitary causes or perspectives.

A similar holistic approach is becoming more widely adopted in the fields of planning and community development as a strategy to facilitate sustainable community and economic development. Examples of this are the 'whole systems' approaches to involving the community in sustainable planning and development advocated by Oleari (2000), the 'sustainable livelihood' approach to rural development in south Asia outlined by Rajbhandari (2006), Woog's (1998) use of complexity and systems theory to examine self-organising human activity systems, and Rice and Foote's (2001) systems approach to communication campaigns for improving health conditions of young children in developing countries.

Woog (1998) made the following important point:

> The challenge is to view and work with complex systems in a way
> that recognises that their structural patterns are complex, organic and

unpredictable. They are more suitable to being thought of and worked with as wholes rather than as parts. What we miss in the details we make up for in the reality. (p. 349)

Understanding the Connectedness of Everything

One of the implications of taking a holistic approach is the realisation that most things in any field of action (or communicative ecology) are connected. That is, it is difficult (although not impossible) to hold different variables constant or to observe the impact of one variable in isolation from others. In general we live in a very connected world.

Shifts and effects in one system can cause effects quickly in another section and these systems may not necessarily be co-located geographically.

> Today the world is more like a cacophonous city, connected in a million ways. Continents are crisscrossed with roads and railways, airports and distributions centres. Telephones, computers, faxes, television sets, mobile devices, even electronic tags on consumer goods or clothing can all be connected together, so the world sometimes seems like the marketplace of a medieval city, a buzz of messages, letters, newspapers, complaints and requests, small advertisement and bombastic slogan. (Mulgan, 1998, p. 21)

The explosive growth in information is also associated with the growing importance of connectivity. Connectivity is important because it facilitates the establishment of networks of mutually adjusting and potentially mutually beneficial relationships between the nodes of the network, for example, firms and individuals are the nodes of the communicative ecology.

Of course another term for *ecology* is the *web of life* and another term for *web* is *network*. There is a long tradition of research into networks and social network analysis that began with sociologist Jacob Moreno (1953; see e.g., Rogers & Kincaid, 1981). Network theorist Albert-Laszlo Barabási (2002) described in detail the ubiquity of network structures. A network is simply a linkage of points or nodes such that movement may occur from any one point to any other point. This definition covers both physical networks—the railway system, road network, or telecommunications network—as well as business networks.

From an information science perspective, networks are information resource allocation or information flow mechanisms. Structurally, networks facilitate rapid information transfer by providing horizontal links cutting across institutional boundaries to put people in direct contact with each other.

Networks also help create information as well as transmit it. As each person in the network receives information, it is synthesised and new ideas may spring forth—information easily builds on information. Networks thus share new ideas and help create them. The network is an ideal learning organisation for acquiring relevant, effective information (Rogers & Kincaid, 1981).

A large number of phenomena, ranging from the behaviour of insects to the operation of the internet to the popularity of film stars, can be described as scale-free networks (see e.g., Cohen, Erez, ben-Avraham, & Havlin, 2001; Santos & Pacheco, 2005; Watts, 2003). Scale-free networks are so-called because their fundamental properties do not change as more focal points of activity—nodes—are added (similar to fractals). These types of networks have an important characteristic: the number of connections in the networks is not distributed evenly or as a normal curve, but as a power curve. That is, the number of nodes with a small number of links is very large and the number of nodes that may link is small. Indeed, networks inherently allocate and control resources unequally, as opposed to randomly (the extreme form of noncontrol). Scale-free networks, when represented visually, look like a map of air routes (i.e., a few concentrated hubs with many sparse pathways). The consistent features of scale-free networks are evidence of the self-organising processes at work in such networks—that is, they work via an internal 'logic' that requires no external guidance.

Recognising Multicausality

One of the implications of a connected holistic view is a recognition that any explanation of a phenomenon will not be able to point to single causes and effects. We have often found that doing exactly the same thing on different occasions or in different circumstances has led to different outcomes. For example, the same Web development process might work well on one occasion and fail completely later, or a cell phone product might be phenomenally successful in one country but fail in another. Of course, there may be singular causes at work but in practice it is difficult to disentangle them. In the development of a new media system, code, visual design, interaction design, and content design are all causative. Additionally, they all interact with each other and it is not possible to change one and be sure the other is not changed in any way. Many extraneous factors could also be causative in any given application. It is a guiding principle then, that an action research enquiry respects this multicausality, both in terms of effective design of systems as well as building explanations and undertaking impact evaluations. Although outcomes cannot be related to a 'single cause' determinant they are of course not random either. We may not be able to predict specific outcomes, but we can often develop a deep understanding of the centrally important factors that influence possible outcomes.

Building in Redundancy

Another implication of multicausality is that systems, interventions, and enquiry will be more robust if redundancy is built into each and if there are multiple pathways to success. Although this may seem obvious, it is common for single design approaches, interventions, and enquiry methods to be advocated as being *the* way to do things.

Diversity and Difference

We concur with Greenwood and Levin (2006) who said that diversity 'is one of the most important features of human society' and that the 'diversity of skills, experiences, ethnicities, gender, and politics should be taken as the most valuable source of potential positive change in groups' (p. 11). We use the term *diversity* to mean the construction of particular broad social and cultural categories such as gender, status, and age, whereas the term *difference* is used to mean the multitude of differences that are embedded in diversity categories (Lennie, 2001).

   Taking an approach that recognises and values diversity and difference is important as it enables a more adequate understanding of the problem being addressed, 'provides a basis for crucial insights and new modes of understanding,' and increases the likelihood that innovative ideas or solutions will be put forward (Morgan & Ramirez, 1984, p. 14). Such an approach also enables action researchers to avoid making unhelpful generalisations about particular social groups such as women or young people and to acknowledge the multiple, sometimes conflicting roles, identities, and interests of the various groups involved in an enquiry.

   Our approach also includes an awareness of the way in which gender and other power–knowledge relations affects such things as access to technologies and participation in new media projects and can produce unintended effects.

Power and Knowledge Differences

Rather than take an idealistic view that assumes that all participants in an action research project are the same and equal, we argue that it is more useful to openly acknowledge the differences between participants, and also between participants and researchers, particularly those related to power and knowledge.

Some contemporary research suggests the value of adopting, for example, a Foucauldian model of power in the critical analysis and reflection phases of action research projects (Lennie, Hatcher, & Morgan, 2003). The basic elements of this model are that power is exercised rather than possessed; it is not primarily repressive, but productive, positive, and strategic; and that power is exercised in all our interactions with others and 'analysed as coming from the bottom up' (Humphries, 1994, p. 186). From this perspective, power is something that exists in action, in a network of interconnected relations. It is enacted in everyday social practices, rather than wielded by powerful groups such as corporations. Foucault's work shows 'how objects of knowledge are not natural, but are ordered or constructed by discourses which determine what is "seeable and sayable"' (Jennings & Graham, 1996, p. 171). This power–knowledge nexus highlights the power relations that are enacted in all interactions, whether those involved have an emancipative intent or otherwise.

In this framework, power is intimately connected to knowledge, including the technical knowledge held by new media specialists and the tacit knowledge of community members or workers who use various new media technologies. The shifting and contradictory nature of these power–knowledge relations can be an important focus of critical reflection in an action research project.

Feminist action researcher Marion Martin (1996) suggested that this view of power as a dynamic force can enable us to understand the complex and fluid nature of the power relations inherent in the researcher–participant relationship and in the participatory research process. The Foucauldian model of power is congruent with an emphasis on 'power to' and 'power with' strategies that aim to be empowering for both participants and researchers.

Conventional media and communication studies have evolved a research process that defines relationships between research sponsors, researchers, respondents, and respondent communities. Roles are compartmentalised. In particular, it is only the researchers who are constructed as 'doing' research. As such, domains of knowledge about and perceptions of the research process are therefore differentiated. For example, researchers are often more aware of hypotheses and where the research is heading than participants. Differences in knowledge lead to differences in power and vice versa. Action researchers (Argyris, 1982; Kemmis & McTaggart, 1988; Reason & Bradbury, 2001) argue that this limits the validity of data that researchers are able to access in traditional research. The data that respondents provide is often limited to conscious socially acceptable espousals, or worse, respondents may simply be unable to articulate their experience in terms acceptable to the formal processes of traditional research (Naples & Clark, 1996). For research that seeks to produce action beyond the researchers, this is particularly problematic because action requires critical reflection, insight and emotional risk-taking. The traditional research process limits the production of these precursors to action (Gronhaug & Olson, 1999).

Methodological Principles

Given the broad theoretical and conceptual framework just outlined, we now identify the key methodological principles that guide our approach to new media action research. These principles follow:

- adopting methodological pluralism;

- engaging in constant cycles that link outcomes back to objectives and ongoing learning;

- facilitating participation that respects diversity and differences and accesses all relevant data;

- being aware of the potentially unintended effects of action research;

- taking an open enquiry approach;

- making all aspects of the situation—in principle—open to scrutiny, and making all levels of data visible;

- viewing action research as a political process that requires certain skills to manage well; and

- understanding and respecting time requirements.

Adopting Methodological Pluralism

A pragmatic, mixed-methods approach to social research and evaluation often results in superior research compared with mono-method research (Greene, 2002; Greene & Caracelli, 2002; Johnson & Onwuegbuzie, 2004). A key feature of the action research approach is its methodological pluralism. Johnson and Onwuegbuzie suggested that a mixed-methods approach is the 'third wave' or 'third research movement,' which 'moves past the paradigm wars by offering a logical and practical alternative' (p. 17). Indeed, arguments for triangulation and multiple methods have been presented and explicated for quite some time, from convergent–discriminant matrix and unobtrusive research methods to triangulation and even multiple-paradigm approaches.

Our approach to action research is therefore quite pluralistic with regard to methodology and methods. We agree with Greenwood and Levin (2006), who asserted that action research is 'resolutely a mixed-methods research strategy so long as the particular mix of methods is contextually determined' (p. 98). This means that if the enquiry is assisted by quantitative data in the form of survey or site statistics we will incorporate them. If qualitative or ethnographic data is required, this too can be incorporated. Additionally, with regard to the style of action research (e.g., participatory action research [PAR] vs. action science vs. a design approach), we do not subscribe to the superiority of any one approach (see Foth & Axup, 2006). What brings different approaches together in a meaningful way is the guidance offered by the principles we have outlined here in formulating the enquiry and the design process. In particular, the guiding underlying principle is that action research is always cyclical, with all action able to be evaluated. That is, action research learns from itself.

Engaging in Constant Cycles that Link Outcomes Back to Objectives and Ongoing Learning

Effective participation in technological decision making requires informed choice and debate. Many people feel ill-prepared to participate effectively and to make informed choices without an understanding of technological developments and their potential social impact. Community members want public forums and processes that enable planners, policymakers, and politicians and technologists to hear and act on their community voice (Hearn et al., 1995). However, researchers must be sensitive to every niche of stakeholders found in communicative ecologies in order to be inclusive and ethical (see Ch. 6). Barr (1985) argued for an integrated frame of reference for decision making that incorporates a permanently established mechanism whereby a 'wider cross section of the public can effectively offer an input into the policy decision-making process and later effectively analyse the outcomes' (p. 224).

New media has the potential to offer new forums or processes for participation in open debate, to permit unprecedented access to community opinion and to enable ongoing learning about the effectiveness or otherwise of new technologies. New ways for cooperative communication and community debate through interactive technologies could provide the means of both accessing opinion and broadly dispersing information to the wider community. They could also provide the opportunity to create rewarding relationships with people that were not previously available. We discuss the use of new media tools for collaboration and communication in action research further in Chapters 4 and 6.

People desire wider debates on the future of technology and their social futures. As Lowe (1992) cautioned, the community as a whole too often looks to those who are technically expert for guidance on technological change. When policy decisions rest in the hands of key players with commercial interests or with small lobby groups, the process must be transparent and accountable. This suggests the importance of participation in new media research that can inform the development of such policies.

Facilitating Participation that Respects Diversity and Differences and Accesses All Relevant Data

As identified frequently in the literature, individuals and groups often feel powerless as the narrowly focused economic motives of corporations dictate technology decisions. People express a need for consultative processes that allow suppliers and service providers to know and understand their social needs, and allow those needs to be addressed in the implementation of new media (Hearn et al., 1995).

The importance of participation should not be underestimated, as many have argued (e.g., Hirschheim, 1985). Nothing is inevitable about the social impacts of new technologies, and the recognition of that choice heightens awareness of how those choices create futures. The broad social implications of new media are so pervasive that the community—including service providers, suppliers, and users (especially those with different or special needs)—should make decisions about its social impact as a whole.

As we have already noted, differences in knowledge between participants and researchers engender differences in power. Participants and researchers are also diverse in terms of such things as gender, age, status, ethnicity, ideology, values, and their level of education and information literacy. Although such diversity is clearly important, it can also be problematic in terms of the extent to which all of this diversity can be effectively managed and adequately included in a research project.

Action research seeks to overcome these problems. In theory at least, action research seeks to establish integrated learning and research processes composed of diverse groups of researchers, community members, and other stakeholders (e.g., Bracht, 1999, 2001).

Participation as an ethic has a long tradition in action research (see Reason, 1998), but what is meant by participation varies. One view of participation is that it is completely egalitarian and that all participants can equally take part. However, if we are not careful, along with this egalitarian assumption comes a further assumption that all participants are the same. Of course this is not true. Participants differ in terms of their knowledge base and literacy and their formal and informal power.

Our view of participation therefore comprises a number of principles:

1. All participants are not the same; we need to respect these differences.

2. All participants have a right to exert mutual influence over the research process.

3. In principle, everything in the research process (assumptions, concepts, approaches, and data and interpretations) should be able to be challenged and enquired into by anyone.

4. Diversity is seen as a valuable source of understanding, change, and innovation and the participation of as broad a diversity of interested people should be encouraged as far as possible.

5. The design and facilitation of participation processes need to take Principles 1–4 and the power and knowledge differences between participants and others into account in order to create inclusive spaces in which all participants can give voice to their concerns, issues, and needs. (Chapter 6 suggests a way forward in regard to this principle.)

Although these principles represent the ideal situation, in reality action research is often conducted along a continuum of participation, with some forms of action research, such as PAR, involving and requiring much higher levels of participation than others. Martin (2000) suggested that such a continuum of participation can range from 'cooption' to 'collective action,' and involves varying degrees of control by researchers and professional practitioners.

Being Aware of the Potentially Unintended Effects of Action Research

The Foucauldian model of power outlined in the previous section indicates the dangers of an unreflective ideological commitment to certain emancipative discourses; for example, those forms of action research that seek community empowerment, development, advancement, or social justice of some kind. This suggests the need for an awareness of the potentially negative, unintended, or disempowering impacts of new media action research projects, as well as their positive, intended, empowering effects.

Lennie (2005) showed that, given the complex power, knowledge, and discursive issues involved and other factors, PAR and participatory evaluation methodologies can have contradictory effects. Her analysis of the Learning, Evaluation, Action and Reflection for New technologies, Empowerement and Rural Sustainability (LEARNERS) project, which is discussed further in Chapter 11, demonstrates that although the project had a number of positive impacts in terms of such things as evaluation capacity-building and improved networking among the rural participants, it also had a number of unintended effects. These included a perceived lack of ownership and control of some project activities and various barriers to effective participation, including limited access to new media technologies such as the internet. The LEARNERS project suggests the need to include rigorous analysis of the intended and unintended impacts of action research projects in the new media field.

Taking an Open Enquiry Approach

The principle of open enquiry is useful in new media action research. Organisational researcher Chris Argyris (1982) suggested that open enquiry is a combination of advocating one's position while at the same time managing critical enquiry of it.

We also used the term *open enquiry* in relation to our approach to new media action research and evaluation that is improvement and change-oriented and takes an open, interpretative, and creative approach. As Wadsworth (1991) suggested, this approach enables us to ask 'the previously unasked [and] observe the previously unnoticed' (p. 29). This approach involves asking comparative questions such as 'what's working, what's not working?'; problem-posing and problem-solving questions such as 'how could we improve things?'; implies asking 'what are community needs?'; and 'examines practice in order to extract assumptions and intentions' (p. 34).

Making Everything Open to Scrutiny and Making All Levels of Data Visible

The idea of enquiring into everything is strongly articulated in the work of Argyris (1990). The basic idea is that provided relevant information is available, rational problem solving can be used to solve most problems or construct explanations. However, in any human situation, information is often either not available or made unavailable. This may be because (a) participants are not aware of the relevant information (e.g., why something makes them stressed), (b) they hide or distort embarrassing information (e.g., the fact that a system they made does not actually work), or (c) they omit information (e.g., something that they deem unimportant or not worth mentioning). In addition, it may be that some information is collective in nature and requires assembling (e.g., what a community as a whole thinks about a system). Also, different languages (cultural or technical) and mindsets may make information hard to collect and act on.

Different technical 'facts' can be interpreted in very different ways. Argyris has developed a useful model that provides a map of the levels of meaning that the design and implementation of communication/information systems might invoke (Argyris, 1982; Argyris & Schön, 1978, 1996). This model highlights the subjective responses and defensiveness that can often affect the implementation process. It suggests that a generic approach to implementation will probably ignore important parts of the total complex process.

Take, for example, observations of the number of times an intranet site is visited. Such data would seem to be invaluable to systems designers. However, such behavioural indicators may have a number of interpretations. A systems designer might think that lower usage indicates lower need. On the other hand, it may be that the more expert the user the less often and more efficiently they access the system. The quality of their interaction with the system may be much higher than a prolific user who is less effective. Clearly, behaviour in its own right requires interpretation to make sense of and use the system in a meaningful way. The simple dilemma that underlies many new media design processes is who should provide the interpretation of the facts at issue. This is an issue that has long been acknowledged in the information systems field (e.g., Hirschheim, 1985; Johnson & Rice, 1987; Markus, 1984).

Argyris (1982) and Argyris and Schön (1978, 1996) provided a specific model, developed further in Figure 2.1, which maps the levels of meaning that design and implementation of communication/information systems might invoke.

Each level of meaning has its own specific set of entities and internal principles of syntax and semantics, yet the marginal conditions of one level of meaning are determined by the principles of its next higher level. Polanyi

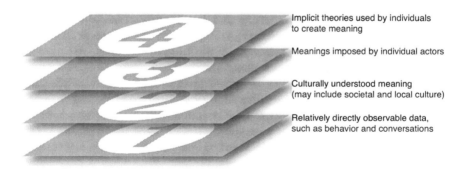

Implicit theories used by individuals to create meaning

Meanings imposed by individual actors

Culturally understood meaning (may include societal and local culture)

Relatively directly observable data, such as behavior and conversations

Figure 2.1. Levels of meaning in a design process.

(1983) termed these the principles of dual control and marginality. Each level of meaning is primarily understood in terms of its own principles, in the context of the next higher level's principles. The complete meaning cannot be grasped and understood by looking individually and independently at any of the lower levels. This is when misunderstandings and misinterpretations happen and the true meaning of communication is camouflaged (Allen, 1996). The holistic perspective is lost by focusing one's perception on details such as words, intonations, and personal interpretations.

The following example illustrates the levels of meaning. A potential user tells a systems designer that the Web interface he or she has designed is unacceptable. The actual words and nonverbals observed constitute Level 1 data. Any member of the user community would understand that the general meaning of the conversation was that the interface was unacceptable. This general meaning, which would be accessible to anyone who shared the language and culture the conversation took place in, constitutes Level 2 data. Additionally, individuals are likely to impose a third specific layer of meaning. For example, the user might say he was honest and forthright; the systems manager might call the same actions blunt and insensitive. This is Level 3 data in Argyris's model. But why should the same physical and cultural data (Levels 1 and 2) result in idiosyncratic meanings at Level 3? Clearly, the answer must lie in the different mindsets of the actors at that point in time. Argyris argued that human actors have 'theories' of their interpersonal world (of which they are largely unaware) that govern the creation of meaning (and therefore resultant behaviour). For example, the client may have a theory like 'the only way I can force the systems manager to change the design is to get upset about it.'

The design of new media systems necessarily invokes change in social systems and requires enquiry into all four levels of meaning. Furthermore, each level of meaning poses its own problems of capture and analysis as well as providing a unique perspective on the overall problem. For example, at Level 1, analysis of communication frequency and length of communication episodes requires sophisticated monitoring and statistical analysis, and can provide information regarding demand and other constraints relevant to a systems designer.

At Level 2, accessing general cultural meanings is also not straightforward, especially when subcultures or different organisations are involved. National culture also can have a large impact on implementation (Narula, 1988; Tacchi et al., 2003). Similarly, the symbolic significance and meaning of pieces of hardware or specialist roles, although self-evident to a given subculture, may not be evident to other interdependent groups or those charged with implementing systems. For example, technical elites may have one set of values regarding legacy systems but users may value them differently.

Level 3 analysis imposes similar problems as Level 2, but additionally must allow for individual idiosyncrasies of meaning. Presumably, the subjective world of individuals needs to be embraced. Importantly, this takes us close to the sphere of action in which implementation must take place. Here biases, perceptions, and other subjective reactions are crucial elements affecting the implementation strategy (Bruce, 1999). This is particularly so when these reactions include embarrassment or threat. Defensiveness by users can render the cleverest technology ineffective. Finally, to intervene in this defensiveness and bring about new patterns of behaviour requires accessing the implicit theories that bring about idiosyncratic meanings. Because these may be difficult to articulate or threatening, this is clearly a difficult task requiring quite intensive interaction with people and possibly highly developed interpersonal and communication skills.

Any single universal approach to design will probably ignore important parts of the total complex process. Although there are notable exceptions (Hirschheim, 1985; Kendall & Kendall, 2005) traditional information systems design processes are often dominated by empirical methods and tend to ignore cultural and human action components of implementation, or to operationalise them in simplistic ways. User participation alone may ignore basic technical requirements. A systematically diverse process within an action research meta-process can be used to enquire into all these levels of meaning, and may overcome these deficits (Hearn et al., 1998). Of course, the essence of such a process is the production of actionable knowledge through learning.

Viewing Action Research as a Political Process that Requires Certain Skills to Manage Well

McTaggart (1991) pointed out that PAR is a political process 'because it involves people in making changes together that will also affect others' (p. 177). As indicated previously, new media action research involves the critical analysis of new media projects, initiatives, and technologies and the communicative ecologies in which they are located. This process of change and analysis can create tensions and conflicts among the various groups involved in these initiatives, which require certain key skills and abilities to effectively and carefully manage.

Greenwood and Levin (2006) described action research as 'a research strategy that generates knowledge claims for the express purpose of taking action to promote social analysis and democratic social change' (p. 5). This social change involves increasing the ability of the community or members of organisations 'to control their own destinies more effectively and to keep improving their capacity to do so within a more sustainable and just environment' (p. 5). They also pointed out that the many different approaches to action research, as outlined in Chapter 1, are often incompatible. For example, some approaches adopt openly ideological positions such as feminism or neo-Marxism, whereas others adopt a more pragmatic philosophy.

This suggests a need for action researchers and participants involved in new media projects to openly declare their particular agendas, values, and perspectives in order to build relations based on mutual understanding, trust, and open communication. However, this ideal is obviously not easy to achieve and requires high-level skills in communication and facilitation. As noted in Chapter 1, action research presents many challenges and ethical issues that must be carefully considered before using this approach.

Understanding and Respecting Time Requirements

An essential practical issue for action research is the time and energy involved in making a commitment to the ongoing research process. That is, the learning orientation that action research advocates is time-intensive—certainly when compared with survey response or other minimally engaging data-collection processes. In some cases, the time available for intense participation, especially by those in positions of legitimate power (CEOs, business people), is limited. This can have the effect of sidelining the practical achievements of the project. However, this is not necessarily true. When the objectives of a project align with the strong interests of the participants significant time can be enlisted from important stakeholders if effort is directed at securing participation.

Conclusion

We began this chapter by considering the relationship between technology and social layers from the positions of technological determinism and the social construction of technology. In contrast to these two approaches, we proposed an alternative co-evolutionary perspective that assumes a reciprocal relationship between the social and the technical. The theoretical and conceptual framework that derives from this position and that guides our approach to new media action research contains the following elements:

- a critical perspective that questions assumptions about both action research and new media;

- consideration of the local communicative ecology of project locations;

- a holistic perspective that recognises the connectedness of everything;

- recognition that any explanation of phenomena, such as the introduction of new technologies, has multiple causes and effects—our approach respects this multicausality and seeks to build redundancy into the systems, interventions, and enquiry processes we set up;

- respecting diversity and differences and seeking inclusion—this entails paying attention to relevant issues such as gender and other equity and social justice issues;

- recognising power and knowledge differences and adopting a Foucauldian model of power;

- an alternative co-evolutionary perspective on the interaction between technology and society; and

- a focus on the distinction between tacit and codified knowledge and the interplay between these forms of knowledge.

We also outlined a number of methodological principles that guide our approach to new media action research. They included adopting methodological pluralism, engaging in constant cycles that link outcomes back to objectives and ongoing learning, taking an open enquiry approach, making everything available for enquiry and making all levels of data visible, and viewing action research as a political process that requires certain skills to manage well.

In the next chapter, we discuss methods that can be used in employing action research for enquiry and design in the new media field while respecting the conceptual framework and methodological principles outlined here.

Chapter 3

Processes, Questions, and Methods

This chapter provides an overview of the fundamental processes and methods that are involved in using action research in new media projects. We begin by explaining the action research cycle and its main steps. We show how this is similar and different to other forms of media research. Some of the common methods that can be used in each step of the action research cycle are described, such as brainstorming and workshops, as well as less common tools such as cultural probes and participatory audiovisual content. Next, we outline the participatory and dialogical processes and skills that are required for effective action research. Finally, we discuss the ethical practices that need to be considered in doing action research, as well as strategies for increasing the rigour of this approach.

Overview of the Action Research Cycle

All research is cyclical in nature, moving from the formulation of the research question, to data collection, analysis of data, and back to the research question. In this regard action research is no different. It proceeds from research questions, issues or concerns to an enquiry process that produces evidence (or data), and then back to a consideration of the research questions or issues (see Fig. 3.1).

Action research differs from other research methodologies in the nature of the enquiry process, which is, in effect, an attempt to take action or provoke change or improvements of some kind (e.g., to design, implement, or evaluate a new media application). As discussed in the previous chapters, action research also seeks to develop actionable knowledge (such as knowledge about the use of new media in reducing poverty or increasing an organisation's effectiveness), and to integrate learning and research into initiatives in a continuous process (see Fig. 3.2).[1]

---

[1]Although these goals are generally similar to those of total quality management, and to some versions of communication audits (see Hargie & Tourish, 2000), there are many philosophical and methodological differences between action research (particularly in its more participatory forms) and these approaches to organisational and communication management.

Figure 3.1. A typical research cycle.

The action operationalises the concept being investigated (e.g., 'social exclusion' or 'collaboration between information system designers') in a kind of quasi-experiment, and also produces evidence about the working of the concepts in question. The type of evidence obtained can vary widely and

Figure 3.2. A basic action research cycle.

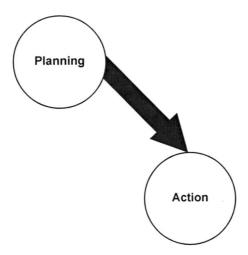

Figure 3.3. Action research Step 1.

can include various forms of qualitative and quantitative data. The action part of action research is also cyclical. For example, taking action typically involves two main activities: planning and action (Fig. 3.3).

Over time, our actions shape our next set of plans (Fig. 3.4).

By *observing* our actions we can generate operational knowledge and learn from our experiences. By *using these observations to reflect* on

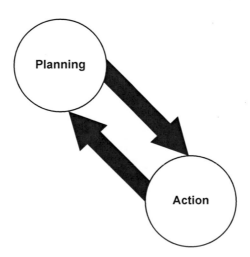

Figure 3.4. Action research Step 2.

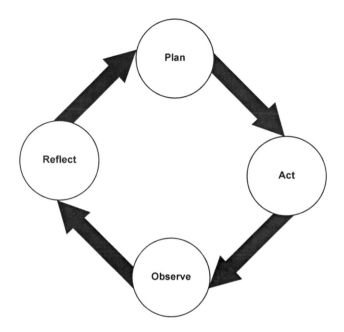

Figure 3.5. The continuous action research cycle.

our actions and experiences we can plan our next actions more effectively (Fig. 3.5).

Box 3.1 describes one example of this process called Appreciative Enquiry (Cooperrider, Whitney, & Stavros, 2003; Cooperrider & Whitney, 2005). This is an action research approach often used in organisations. We show how it can be applied to new media in Chapter 7.

Sometimes the observations and reflections are expressed in local operational terms and thus a more abstracted process is required to translate the 'findings' back to the original research questions. Sometimes these observations and reflections are expressed directly in terms of the research questions; in this case the two cycles effectively collapse into one. In either case, we suggest that it makes sense to always bear in mind the research cycle and the action cycle, as Figure 3.6 shows.

As indicated previously, action research is commonly seen as evolving through ongoing cycles of planning, action, observation, and reflection (see Kemmis & McTaggart, 1988, for more details of this typical series of steps or 'moments'). Others have envisaged routines such as 'look, think, act' (Stringer, 1999) or 'diagnosing, planning action, taking action, and evaluating action' (Coghlan & Brannick, 2001). However, no matter how

---

Box 3.1: Appreciative Enquiry

Appreciative enquiry is an organisational change methodology developed by David Cooperrider and others (Cooperrider et al., 2005; Cooperrider & Whitney, 2005). It is an alternative approach to achieving organisational growth and development and is useful in formulating future-oriented plans in action research projects. It is based on an understanding of organisations as living human systems, socially constructed. In this approach, problem identifiers and bringers are valued as they tell us things could be better: A problem is an expression of a frustrated dream. The social constructionist perspective on which appreciative enquiry is based suggests that, within organisations, what we talk about is what we see, and that we get more of what we pay attention to. Organisations are seen as being made up of many voices, all of which have valid perspectives. Judgments that are made are seen not so much as truth evaluations but as moral judgments.

The five principles of appreciative enquiry:

1. The constructionist principle: We create our world.

2. The poetic principle: An organisation is more like a text than a machine.

3. The simultaneity principle: The question is the intervention.

4. The anticipatory principle: Human systems grow toward positive anticipatory images.

5. The positive principle: It takes energy to achieve change.

The four stages of appreciative enquiry:

1. **Discovery:** Through interviews, surveys, or other means creating and collecting embodied personal stories of the best of times in the context of the organisational area of interest.

2. **Dreaming:** Imagining how life could be if more of the best of times happened more of the time; building a positive anticipatory image based on what is known to be possible (the discoveries).

3. **Design:** Thinking back from the future to how we need to be organised, what we need to be doing now to increase the possibility of attractive futures unfolding.

4. **Destiny:** Doing different things or doing things differently in a coherent and conjoint way, inspired by the work together, energised by the positive energy generated, coordinated by the shared aspiration.

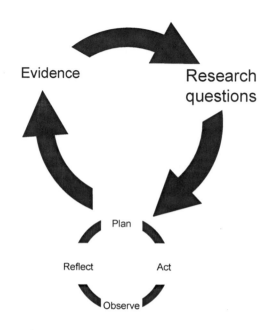

Figure 3.6. Nested action research cycles.

it is conceived, in practice action research is seldom undertaken in an orderly or linear way. As Stringer (1999) suggested, it can include 'working backward through the routines, repeating processes, revising procedures, rethinking interpretations, leapfrogging steps or stages, and sometimes making radical changes in direction' (p. 19).

Although action research can be a complex procedure, we use Figure 3.6 as the basic model of action research to explain procedures for each part of the nested cycle. It is important to clearly identify the most effective and appropriate techniques and methods for particular action research questions or projects (Crane & Richardson, 2000). Using a mixed-methods approach that combines a range of methods, and the systematic collection of data adds rigour to action research projects and increases the trustworthiness of the findings (Lennie, 2006). More details about many of these methods can be found in Tacchi, Slater, and Hearn (2003) and UNESCO (2007), and in standard social research methods texts such as Babbie (2001), Denzin and Lincoln (2005), Neuman (2006), Patton (2002), Seale (2004), Stoecker (2005), Strauss (1998) and Yin (2003). Dillman (2007) and Hine (2005) provide useful information about online research methods such as internet surveys. We outline some of these methods later in the chapter.

Identifying Research Questions

An action research project typically begins with a group of people (media designers, teachers, community members, etc.) acknowledging a shared concern or issue. From their critical educational perspective, Kemmis and McTaggart (1988) described action research as arising from a 'thematic concern (or educational issue, or broad educational question)' (p. 9). The thematic concern defines the major area in which the group decides to focus its improvement or change strategies. In a new media project, questions related to thematic concerns could include the following:

• How do different members of an online network influence and learn from each other?

• How can culture and creativity combined with new media technologies become a seedbed for innovation among young people?

• How can new media be used to enable poor people in developing countries to find a voice to be heard?

The main challenge in facilitating the outer cycle of action research, described earlier, lies in being able to combine the language and concepts that define the community of practice of researchers (i.e., the codified knowledge of the research community) with the local (tacit) operational language of the participants and other stakeholders. Explicit attention needs to be paid to this when formulating research questions, when translating these questions into action, and when seeking to reflect on the outcomes of action in terms of the original questions. Processes are needed to assist in this translation so that it becomes a mutually educative endeavour. Essentially, however, the overarching principles are those that guide the formulation of clear research questions in any evidence-based enquiry.

Understanding the context of a project is an important part of developing a holistic appreciation of the research questions. Coghlan and Brannick (2001) suggested that the action research cycle should begin with asking questions such as 'Why is this project necessary or desirable? What are the [external] economic, political, and social forces driving change? What are the [internal] cultural and structural forces driving change?' (p. 7). Similarly, Stringer (1999) argued that the first task of an action research process 're-quires participants to become familiar with the complexity that surrounds them' (p. 44). Facilitators need to 'construct systematically a picture of the situation in which they are working to locate the individuals and groups with whom they will work and to formulate a preliminary understanding of their situation.' A concept we like to use in media-related initiatives is the *communicative ecology* (the system of media and information flows in local community), which was discussed in detail in Chapter 2.

Some of the methods that can be useful here include the following:

• community mapping (see Box 3.2);

• scanning the local context;

Box 3.2: Community Mapping

Community mapping is a useful tool for exploring and discussing the location and use of community services and facilities. It can highlight the location of low socioeconomic groups in relation to services and facilities. These maps can include transport links, shops, schools and hospitals, information and communication technologies, and entertainment facilities and meeting places. Rich pictures (Monk & Howard, 1998) are a useful technique to illustrate the map of a community.

Conducting community mapping is an excellent way of finding out how different groups experience the same space. Do men and women see their local areas differently? What about different age groups, different ethnic groups or religions? This can be very important if you want to gain a deep understanding of a place or community. For example, if a woman is not allowed access to an area because of her gender, this space may not appear on her map. It is important to note these differences.

People will prioritise what is important to them, so it is useful to gather a few maps of the same area from different groups in the community.

The mapping process can be started by asking questions such as:
• Where are the shops?
• Where do you catch the bus?
• Where do people gather?
• Where is the best land?
• Where are the poorest houses?

There are many other questions that can be asked in order to construct these maps, depending on what you are trying to explore. Community characteristics that appear obvious to one person or group, may not be obvious to another person or group and can form an important starting point for exploring local issues.

Adapted from Tacchi et al. (2007). Further useful information on community mapping, needs assessments and program sustainability can be found in Bracht (1999) and Rice and Atkin (2001).

- workshops where communicative ecologies are explored;

- cultural probes (see Box 3.3); and

- existing public information such as government statistics and census data.

Box 3.3: Cultural Probes

This innovative method is a particularly useful technique for new media designers. It can enable them to understand a local culture, explore people's attitudes toward their environment and their use of new media, and provides opportunities to 'discover new pleasures, new forms of sociability, and new cultural forms' (Gaver, Dunne, & Pacenti, 1999, p. 25).

As Gaver et al. explained, a *cultural probe* is a package containing items such as maps and dot stickers, postcards, a disposable camera, a photograph album, and a media use diary, which was provided to individual research participants. Requests for particular information or pictures were included with each item but 'oblique wording' and 'evocative images' were used on items such as postcards to allow participants 'as much room to respond as possible' (p. 23) Participants used the probe to record information and then mail it back to the design team. The designers did not analyse this data but used it to develop 'an impressionistic account' of participants' beliefs and desires, their 'aesthetic preferences and cultural concerns' (p. 25). Gaver et al. see their role as 'provocateurs' and the cultural probes they designed for each location were envisaged as interventions that would affect the elders in their project 'while eliciting informative responses from them' (p. 25).

The cultural probes were personally presented to groups of participants so that they could explain their intentions, answer questions and encourage the elders to 'take an informal, experimental approach to the materials' (p. 26). While the probes were important to understanding the research sites, they did not directly lead to the design scenarios they produced for each site. Rather, they both inspired their designs and let them 'ground them in the detailed textures of the local cultures' (p. 29). The cultural probes provoked participants to think about the roles they play and the pleasures they experience. One of the strengths of this technique was the continuous personal conversation that was established with the groups involved.

Planning the Action

Once the key research questions and concerns are identified and some understanding of the context is developed, the next key step or 'moment' in the action research cycle involves collaboratively planning the action (e.g., designing, implementing or evaluating a new media project) and deciding how to respond to research questions or issues. The plan must be flexible and critically informed in terms of the potential constraints and risks involved (Kemmis & McTaggart, 1988). Plans will be refined as new understandings emerge. Crane and Richardson (2000) suggested that planning involves three main stages: (a) clarifying the questions being asked, (b) identifying the actions to be tried out, and (c) developing the action plan. The plan outlines details such as 'what, who, when, where, and how' and involves 'designing a framework to guide action' (Crane & Richardson, 2000, p. 2.5). When making a research plan it is also useful to ask:

• Why are we doing this research?

• What information are we seeking?

• What methods are best suited to each research activity?

• How will we use the research results?

Asking these questions creates a healthy environment for the research that benefits project development, and ensures that research is properly planned and always relevant. The effectiveness of the action research project will, to a large extent, depend on how well it is planned.

Part of planning may be to establish the *purpose* and *goals* of an information and communication technologies initiative or project. Every initiative takes a direction and produces outcomes. Defining the purpose of an initiative publicly identifies what the initiative is about. Defining more specific goals helps the initiative to stay on track. These goals can be used to assess whether an initiative has been successful. In other words, goals describe what should happen as a result of the initiative.

How are the goals of the initiative defined? Usually everyone involved or affected by the initiative (the stakeholders) have a view on what they think the goals of an initiative should be. Potential stakeholders could include community members, funding agencies, government agencies, community organisations, and private companies.

Many initiatives will have goals defined for them by their funding agency, such as those associated with the UN Millennium Development Goals (United Nations, 2002) or government policies on youth engagement. Whether these goals can be achieved may depend in part on whether other stakeholders agree with these goals. Therefore, goals need to be clearly defined and negotiated among the different stakeholders. If all of those involved in the initiative are also involved in discussions around the purpose and goals, and they understand them, they are more likely to work towards achieving them.

Useful methods for planning action include the following:

- brainstorming ideas for project activities such as the design of a website (see Box 3.7 for a brief explanation of brainstorming);

- stakeholder analysis (see Dick, 1997, Mitroff, 1983) and developing engagement strategies—working out who needs to be involved in the action and in what ways;

- clarifying stakeholder roles—working out who will do what in the project; and

- planning strategies and developing a timeline for actions.

Taking Action

Action is about 'systematically and creatively' implementing the plan and testing research questions in practice. It involves communicating with those involved, involving people in the process, keeping track of what happens, then possibly asking people to vote on any actions and changes to plans and processes (Crane & Richardson, 2000). Kemmis and McTaggart (1988) suggested beginning with simple changes and small action research cycles involving small groups of people, then, later widening participation to larger groups. This requires an awareness of the following:

- the practices of those involved in the initiative;

- the ways in which they are attempting to achieve their purpose and goals on a day-to-day basis, as an organisation, and in relation to stakeholders, including the communities they seek to serve; and

- an awareness of the initiative's internal structures and systems, including the ways in which the initiative's resources are being used.

Often it can be useful to document action as it happens, using methods such as fieldnotes and diaries, video- or taperecordings, and photographs. Participants can be encouraged to create audiovisual, audio or visual content on the actions or the issues they feel require action to be taken (see Box 3.4).

Observing

The aim of observation is to accurately describe and document the effects of the action (e.g., conducting a digital storytelling workshop with young indigenous people). This involves collecting evidence about the action. Observation provides a sound basis for critical reflection 'by producing a widely accepted understanding of what actually happened' (Crane & Richardson, 2000, p. 2.9). Rigorously collecting and analysing data is essential to producing a trustworthy account of the action. As with monitoring, observation can be an ongoing activity. Useful observation tools and methods include the following:

• participant observation and fieldnotes;

• participatory audiovisual content creation (see Box 3.4);

Box 3.4: Participatory Audiovisual Content

This technique can often provide a significant amount of comparative data, which can be used in further research by planners, media content creators, or community members. This method is particularly useful when working with people who are illiterate as they can create a piece of audiovisual content to express themselves and put their concerns and needs across.

Participatory content creation can be used in at least two ways:

1. Images and sounds of a service such as a school, a telecentre, or a radio station can be recorded. These can then be used to spark discussions, perhaps of problems, with other members of the community as well as with outsiders to the community or organisation. A range of perspectives can be explored in this way, and overlapping and contrasting experiences can be highlighted and further explored. It can help those without a voice to be heard by others in or outside of their local context.

2. This method is a good way of finding out more about differences resulting from gender, age, ethnicity, and so on. Giving a camera and microphone to a group of women may provide access to issues and areas that male researchers might not be able to access. It allows female participants to show the researcher what is important to them without the researcher being present. Using this technique requires lending the equipment and training people how to use it, but it can lead to very positive results and is a form of content creation in its own right that might appeal to many audiences.

Adapted from Tacchi et al. (2007). See also Burgess (2006), Freidus and Hlubinka (2002), Klaebe and Foth (2006), and Lambert (2002).

- observation proformas (a checklist of the specific activities or behaviours you are interested in observing, with spaces to record details and possibly an evaluative measure of some kind);

- visual ethnography (see Box 3.5);

- wall charts;

- informal interviews;

- focus groups; and

- minutes of meetings and community forums.

In new media projects computer logs and browsing histories can also be rich sources of data that can tell us what websites people have visited, when, and how often.

Box 3.5: Visual Ethnography

Visual ethnography is the use of photography, film, video, and hypermedia in ethnographic and social research. Visual images and technologies can be effectively combined to form an integrated process throughout the different stages of an action research project, from planning and implementing the project and engaging in fieldwork to analysis and representation (Pink, 2006). Pink suggested that visual research methods should be rooted in a critical understanding of local and academic visual cultures, the visual media and technologies, and the ethical issues they raise.

Margolis (2006) identified three meanings of visual ethnography:

1. **Using cameras and other devices to gather data:** Film and video cameras are seen as particularly well suited as data-gathering technologies for projects that involve small-group interactions, ethnography, participant observation, oral histories, and so on. Video cameras can also be put into places where a researcher would not be welcome or to remove the observer effect.

2. **Using sociological knowledge to study visual culture:** Art, photographs, film, video, facial expressions, computer icons, landscape, architecture, machines, and so on are parts of the complex visual communication system produced by members of societies. Visual images are primary evidence of human productive activity and their use and understanding is governed by socially established symbolic codes that can be deconstructed or analysed using various methods, including ethnographic tools.

3. **Using visual technology to communicate by producing films and videos:** Documentaries, dramas, and experimental videos can be used to assess what they mean to viewers. Computer graphics can be used to represent complex social relationships, and research participants can be taught how to make films or videos about their lives and experiences.

Reflecting

Reflection is a process of making sense of problems, issues, and processes; interpreting a variety of information and perspectives; and negotiating meanings. The context of an action research project should be taken into account when making interpretations. Reflection 'informs improvements to practice and affirms or challenges particular ways of doing things' (Crane & Richardson, 2000, p. 2.11).

Regular critical reflection is an important component of evaluating action research projects (Lennie, 2006). Ideally, action research projects should include a meta-learning process that involves 'diagnosing, planning, taking action and evaluating how the action research project itself is going and what you are learning' (Coghlan & Brannick, 2001, p. 19). Tools and methods for reflecting on action and undertaking meta-learning and evaluation include:

- brainstorming;

- personal reflection diaries;

- video or audiorecordings of participants' reflections;

- facilitated group discussions held after project events such as workshops;

- short feedback questionnaires;

- research question evaluation workshops (see Box 3.6); and

- web logs and online discussion boards (see Ch. 4).

Feedback forms can be made an integral part of a user's visit to places such as telecentres and media training rooms by making them part of logging in to computers, or signing up for classes. The questions asked on such forms should be carefully considered and fit within the overall research process. Log books can be set up in nonintrusive ways for staff to record their main activities, the kinds of people with whom they have dealt, and so on. Log books often list only the most basic information about activities throughout the day; it takes only a little more information to make it a rich source. Visitor books and suggestion boxes can be made available and participants can be encouraged to use them. These feedback mechanisms are often a normal part of the functioning of organisations. The idea is simply to learn from, and develop, the ways in which an action research project can be most effectively documented.

The purpose of this step is in effect a realistic and researched *evaluation* of how the initiative is working to achieve its purpose and goals,

---

Box 3.6: Research Question Evaluation Workshops

The final phase of the action research process can benefit from deliberative reflection on the guiding agenda of the research. This helps to refocus participants on the original objectives and rationale, to try to formulate general principles, and relate participant learnings to a broader set of concepts. It may also make explicit the 'mental casual models' that researchers and participants are using to explain what has happened. In some cases, these can be compared with formal models of the problem situation.

Such a workshop also provides an opportunity to marshal various kinds of evidence from participants' experiences to either support or challenge the different interpretations of events. Experiential narratives are often useful here. In addition, formally collected data may also be incorporated in the process. Questions that help stimulate a critical discussion could be: How do we know A caused B? Was this true for anyone else? Is there a general principle at work here? What was going on when that happened?

The Most Significant Change technique (R. Davies & Dart, 2005) is a useful variant of this process.

---

through reflection and self-awareness, and through researching those on whom you seek to have an impact. Action research can be used to uncover how well the initiative is doing according to local communities, local users, initiative staff and volunteers, donors, and other external agencies. Both formative and summative forms of evaluation are useful here. Formative evaluations, which gather ongoing information about project processes and implementation, problems, and progress, are useful when the aim is to help develop a project. In contrast, summative evaluations are appropriate when the aim is to evaluate and document the outcomes and implementation of a project (Robson, 2000).[2]

Informed by the research findings, the fourth question requires a re-evaluation of the purpose and goals, a review of processes and practices, and an analysis of effectiveness, achievements, and shortfalls. It requires renewed planning and actions that will draw on the research, reflection, and evaluation undertaken and improve the overall effectiveness of the initiative. It will take into account the resources that can be accessed and those that could potentially be accessed. This whole process should allow for the development and ongoing adjustment of short-, medium- and long-term plans.

---

[2]Robson (2000) pointed out that 'in practice it is rare to find either a purely formative or purely summative evaluation' (p. 51).

This process of planning, acting, observing, and reflecting is continuous. However, at each stage the new media initiative is better informed and is developing from a position of growing strength (Tacchi et al., 2007).

If the research questions are abstract or conceptual it may be important to formally review the findings of the action research in terms of the original research questions using a process such as the one described in Box 3.6.

This step of examining the evidence for the research questions completes the cycle described in Figure 3.6.

Participatory Methods and Dialogical Skills

In Chapters 1 and 2, we explained that action research assumes that social action is socially constructed and therefore, in order to isolate and understand various forms of social action, stakeholders are involved in articulating what these social actions are, who they impact upon, and what they mean in various contexts. Underlying all the methods of action research is the generic 'method' of being in dialogue with those involved in the research to generate an understanding and articulation of 'what is going on.' Thus, all parts of the cycles—formulating research questions, taking action, observing and reflecting on action, and evaluation—are, in principle, one dialogical activity.

Some generic dialogical processes underpin all parts of the action research process. Another way of expressing this dialogic encounter is the term *participatory*. The many participatory imperatives in action research (such as participatory action research [PAR]) are very well documented (see e.g., McTaggart, 1991; Reason, 1994). Thus, dialogic skills and tools are employed in all parts of the action research process, ideally (although perhaps in different ways) by both the researchers and participants. To be effective, these skills and tools require certain 'literacies' related to participation in the action research process. The core literacies are what Dick (2002) referred to as first-person, second-person, and third-person skills. First-person skills are about giving information—they are required to articulate one's position clearly and, if necessary, assertively. Second-person skills are about getting necessary information—that is, listening carefully and actively enquiring into the other's viewpoint. Third-person skills are the skills of facilitating others to give and receive information. These three skills are used all the time in the action research process, and are guided by a principle of open enquiry, which Argyris (1982) suggested is a combination of advocating one's position while at the same time managing critical enquiry of it.

In addition to these skills are some generic 'information-exchange' processes that are often used in action research. These are brainstorming, nominal group technique, and the Delphi method (see Box 3.7). As indicated earlier, brainstorming is a very common tool for assembling unedited or unevaluated group information (ideas, opinions, fantasies) and in the

---

Box 3.7: Brainstorming, Nominal Group Technique, and the Delphi Method

The aim of *brainstorming* is to come up with as many creative ideas as possible in a short time. The idea is to free up the imagination and come up with new ideas about goals, the project, or anything that is important to the group. The facilitator ensures that all participants can contribute and that all ideas, no matter how 'way-out,' are recorded.

Typical brainstorming ground rules are as follows:

• All ideas are encouraged and recorded without comment or criticism.

• Creative thinking is encouraged—way-out ideas can lead to creative new approaches.

• Quantity rather than quality is pursued. A challenging but attainable goal is set.

• Participants are asked to build on the ideas of others, and to look for combinations arising from ideas already put forward.

Discussion and evaluation takes place after the list of ideas has been created. Ideas can be eliminated or combined and the list refined. The group is now ready to set priorities, choose suggestions, plan activities and brainstorm further topics (Coovor, Deacon, Esser, & Moore, 1985; Dick, 1991; see also Paulus & Nijstad, 2003).

The nominal group technique differs from brainstorming in that group members are given time for individual thought before the information collection and recording process begins. Each person contributes one idea in turn that has not already been publicly recorded. As with brainstorming, censorship and criticism are discouraged and the focus is on the public list of ideas rather than on the individuals and group discussion. Dick (1991) suggested that this technique may be more effective than brainstorming as it better enables equality between group members, ideas are unlikely to be lost, it is simpler, and does not require an experienced facilitator. However, brainstorming has its own advantages (Dick, 1991).

The Delphi method has been most commonly used for future forecasting by a panel of experts. However, it can also be used for other problem-solving and task-oriented activities that depend on information that participants collectively hold. A simple Delphi involves asking panel members several questions, then collating and summarising their replies. The summary is then sent out to begin the next cycle. The core of this method is its cyclical nature and its treatment of 'idiosyncratic information' (Dick, 1991). The level of consensus between panel members usually increases with each round. The main elements of the Delphi method can be combined with techniques such as brainstorming and nominal group technique and used in large- or small-group settings (Dick, 1991; see also Linstone & Turoff, 1975).

new media research context is very useful in the design process. Nominal group techniques and the Delphi method are more structured forms of group idea generation, which again can be used throughout the research phase to elicit research questions, design or action alternatives, facilitate critical reflections, and so on. These generic information-exchange methods are often used in workshop settings.

All research traditions typically utilise some form of social encounter to obtain information from participants, for example, the one-on-one interview, the survey process, or participant observation. Action research often uses participant workshops as its core process, although, as we have already suggested, any other methods (both qualitative and quantitative) can be integrated into the process. Workshops encourage dialogic encounters and can be designed around the generic methods described previously. Other techniques such as interviews, observations, focus groups, and diaries can also be used to generate information, but these are typically fed back into the workshop format at some point in the process.

Ethics in Action Research and New Media Projects

Given the close personal relationships that are often formed between those involved in action research projects, and the level of engagement with participants that is required, it is vital to use ethical principles and practices in the action research process. The following are key strategies for conducting action research in an ethical manner (adapted from Tacchi, Slater, & Hearn, 2003).

Explain yourself: Before conducting any research activity such as an interview, group discussion, or survey, researchers should explain briefly but clearly why they are doing the research, what they are trying to find out, and how they will use the material. This is sometimes impossible in everyday participant observation and sometimes also during meetings, but if a researcher is asked about his or her role, it should be explained. Participants should be given the opportunity to ask the researcher questions about the research, its findings, and potentials.

Respecting confidences: A researcher will need to assure all interviewees that what they say will be kept confidential and is nonattributable, if they so desire. The researcher needs to honour that assurance by not using people's real names or identities when communicating their material (e.g., in reports). All research data such as recordings, transcriptions, and field-notes must be kept safe.

Treating people sensitively: During research activities, a researcher may bring out strong emotions and confidences, and form close relationships. These need to be treated sensitively. It is the researcher's responsibility to respect the research relationships they develop. In all research activities, they must be careful not to be intrusive or disruptive.

Exploring sensitive issues: Researchers need to be prepared to find ways to explore sensitive issues in their research. Respecting people's opinions and viewpoints is important in this enterprise, even if the researcher strongly disagrees with them. The researcher needs to first understand people's perspectives and beliefs about such things before considering whether and how an initiative might challenge them.

Never put people at risk or endanger their well-being: Reporting on what people say and do can have real consequences for them (and for the initiative). The researcher should think carefully about the possible implications for participants. No research is more important than people's lives or livelihoods. Researchers also need to maintain an awareness of dangerous situations and the importance of ensuring their own safety.

Increasing the Rigour of Action Research

Avison et al. (2001) suggested that the double challenge of action and research creates many difficulties and may partly explain why 'many information systems [IS] researchers have been reluctant to use this qualitative research method in the past' (p. 28). However, although they see action research as a valuable methodology in the IS field, they argue that the rigour of action research projects requires improvement. Greenwood (2002) has made similar criticisms.

Action researchers reject scientific ideals such as objectivity in favour of a holistic approach that acknowledges and takes into account the diverse perspectives, values and interpretations, and contexts of participants and research facilitators. However, as Lennie (2006) argued, rigour need not be lost in this approach. Increasing the rigour and trustworthiness of action research projects increases the likelihood that results are seen as credible and are used to continually improve and better manage new media initiatives. Lennie outlined a range of strategies that can be used to increase the rigour and trustworthiness of PAR and participatory evaluation projects. They include:

• using participation and communication methods that develop rapport and relations of mutual trust and open communication;

- using multiple theories and methodologies, multiple sources of data, and multiple methods of data collection;

- undertaking ongoing meta-evaluation and critical reflection;

- using rigorous data analysis and reporting processes; and

- asking participants to critically assess and review action research case studies and reports.

Conclusion

New media action research requires careful and systematic planning, along with effective communication, participation, and engagement techniques and skills in facilitation and dialogical processes. Action research cycles should begin by developing a good understanding of the context of a new media project. The ideal is to build a research culture in which critical reflection and meta-learning and evaluation become an everyday, built-in component of new media initiatives. We advocate using a mixed-methods approach to data collection, and suggested some of the commonly and less commonly used methods that can be effectively used in new media action research projects.

Although PAR and evaluation methodologies have many strengths, they also raise many complex theoretical, methodological, and ethical issues and challenges. These issues have implications for the quality of new media action research projects and the trustworthiness of their results. Therefore, we outlined a range of strategies to increase the rigour and trustworthiness of action research projects. The use of such strategies would address Greenwood's (2002) call for action researchers to 'hold ourselves accountable to higher standards' (p. 117).

Chapter 4

New Media Tools for Collaboration

Action research is collaborative in nature. It usually involves a variety of stakeholders, who may include community members, volunteers, funding bodies, customers, or clients (and sometimes the clients of clients), government representatives, and academics from disciplines, faculties and institutions other than your own. Effective collaboration in and with these different clusters and teams ensures that the research is carried not by the few but by the many in order to encourage collective ownership of the project, its findings and associated interventions, and subsequent change processes. It also fosters a multidisciplinary approach with the potential for a range of different or symbiotic solutions to be found in a given situation. One advantage of this multidisciplinarity is the opportunity for peer support and the mutual stimulation of ideas and creativity, which can emerge in one discipline and then be taken up in a different context in another discipline enriched by its own methods and approaches.

However, the level of complexity in establishing rapport and maintaining continuity of communication and progress increases exponentially the more stakeholders are involved and the more diverse their backgrounds and interests are. Chapter 1 described the objective of action research to generate a learning and research process that integrates various stakeholders in mutual knowledge sharing and exchange. Translating the theory of collaboration into practice presents a number of operational issues and challenges. For example, a small exploratory study at Queensland University of Technology in 2004 showed that 79% of respondents collaborated with other researchers within their faculty, 61% collaborated across faculties within their university, 52% with researchers across states within their country, and 42% collaborated with researchers internationally. Collaboration—at our, as well as at other, universities and institutions worldwide—is increasingly seen as crucial for ensuring quality and impact in rigorous research projects. However, many respondents expressed concern that many barriers exist to their collaborative research processes. Some of the most common issues are:

- insufficient awareness of potential partners;

- negotiating and managing individual time constraints and work practices;

- difficulties maintaining research momentum because of communication fragmentation across multiple communication platforms (phone, mail, e-mail, etc.);

- language barriers (both across languages and disciplines);

- infrequent face-to-face contact;

- lack of accessible, easy-to-use and maintain technology platforms to support collaboration;

- poor support and training options to help the technically challenged;

- insufficient methods to properly account for individual's intellectual property contributions; and

- costs associated with technology support as well as travel.

Collaboration for applied and rigorous enquiry and research in the era of the Network Society is not an option but an imperative (Keane, 2004). At the same time as the technological advances in information and communication technology (ICT) are driving the internal processes that led to the genesis of the Network Society, there is a wealth of opportunities to use these innovations for the purpose of enabling and supporting collaboration. Interdisciplinary and interinstitutional collaboration and linkages between academia, industry, and the community sectors can all benefit from the creation of, and access to, online repositories, new media tools, digital communication devices, and shared workspaces. Yet the promise of these systems and tools and their implications for what is increasingly called e-research is yet to be fully realised in practice. This holds true especially outside their original disciplinary base of science and engineering, that is, in the broad fields of the creative arts, humanities, and social sciences (Dutton, Carusi, & Peltu, 2006).

Action researchers face an increasingly pressing need in this area for a collaboration tool that can handle digital content and multimedia artifacts (data, results, literature, documents in progress, posts for comment, communication, creative works, etc.). The effective design and implementation of such a tool has the potential to:

- accelerate action research cycles through faster peer communication;

- make research more responsive, transparent, and accountable;

- increase and better distribute access to digital content and multimedia artifacts, and facilitate cross referencing and triangulation of different data sources, helping to tackle complex cross-disciplinary analysis;

- allow multiple levels of creative, curatorial, and analytical work to proceed simultaneously;

- link data and artifacts remotely to different analytical tools and the teams who specialise in them; and

- facilitate communication across institutional boundaries between action researchers, fieldworkers, participants, research sponsors, and other stakeholders.

In this chapter, we first review some of the key literature that deals with collaboration research, that is, the study of collaborative practices especially in the fields of knowledge management and computer-supported cooperative work (CSCW). We briefly discuss how some of these findings can be transferred from a business context to an academic context, highlighting the particular needs and requirements of action researchers. We then describe some of the tools widely available to enable and support collaborative research and discuss their advantages. Following this overview, a number of case studies are presented to illustrate the practice of using these tools for action research and collaboration as well as associated ethical and administrative issues.

Collaboration Research

Collaboration research is the study of practices that enable people to work together effectively for a shared purpose or common goal. In this section, we review some of the contributions from two relevant fields of research in order to inform our thinking around new media tools that enable collaborative action research. Although most of these works presume the context of a commercial or business workplace, some of the underlying findings and principles can be adopted for our purposes. In turn, we look at the fields of CSCW and knowledge management.

Computer-Supported Cooperative Work

CSCW is the field of study examining how people work together using computer technology. Hiltz and Turoff (1993) described many issues not only for academic collaboration but also for policymakers. Much of the early discussion about e-mail and computer conferencing involved research collaborators as well as community groups. Preece et al. (2002) provided a useful taxonomy for the social mechanisms in communication and collaboration processes. They distinguished between conversational, coordination, and awareness mechanisms. Using this model, it is possible to classify various collaborative technologies that support each mechanism. Technology to support *conversational* mechanisms is also referred to as computer-mediated communication (CMC) technology, which is further classified into synchronous (phone, real-time online chat, instant messaging) and asynchronous (e-mail, discussion boards) modes of communication.

As action researchers immerse themselves with participants and stakeholders in order to connect with them and encourage them to directly participate in the project as co-investigators, conversation and dialogue are paramount. Establishing good rapport and trust and negotiating and mediating between the different needs of various stakeholders requires sensitivity and diplomacy, which is easily jeopardised by the lack of physical presence in remote communications. One of the respondents to the survey mentioned earlier said: 'a mix of means of communication is always important in my experience, so that online [collaboration] works better once you have had face-to-face meetings.' However, individuals have their own communication preferences, and Preece et al. (2002) argued that 'not having to physically face people may increase shy people's confidence and self-esteem to converse more in "virtual" public' (p. 112). Offering multiple communication channels will cater for both cases and action researchers have to select strategies that correspond with the personality types found within their community. Large open discussion fora or time-intensive workshops can be off-putting for some participants, which may result in some voices remaining unheard. Some new media tools can give voice to previously unheard community members by ensuring the availability of communication channels that are fine-grained enough to recognise marginalised voices. On the other hand, the traffic on online discussion fora or e-mail lists can become very fast and complex. Despite attempts by Donath (2002), Smith (2002), and others to provide software applications to help manage large virtual spaces, in the context of action research projects, it is usually advisable to keep conversations informal and intimate in order to elicit a maximum of explicit and tacit knowledge sources.

Apart from the distinction between synchronous and asynchronous modes of communication, we also distinguish between collective and network modes of communication and interaction (Foth, 2006b). A discussion forum for example allows for broadcast-style one-to-many and many-to-many modes of communication. In a face-to-face meeting, an individual stands up to air his or her opinion and the remaining attendees collectively listen.

Another individual may respond in the same public manner. The process in an online discussion board is very similar, and some people may be intimidated by such public interaction either on- or offline. Network modes of communication on the other hand follow a peer-to-peer approach to communication that is more sensitive to individual communication preferences and can offer more privacy and confidentiality. New media tools that can be used in this way are e-mail, short messaging service, and instant messengers (Foth & Brereton, 2004; Muller, Raven, Kogan, Millen, & Carey, 2003).

Conversational mechanisms are certainly one of the key interaction paradigms. The other mechanisms Preece et al. (2002) distinguish are *coordination* (e.g., calendars, diaries and time tables) and *awareness* (e.g., staff directories and the ambient awareness status provided by instant messengers). Tools to visualise awareness information (e.g., Erickson, Halverson, Kellogg, Laff, & Wolf, 2002) have an increasingly important role to play in providing information not only about availability and present location but also about the existence of prospective collaborators in the first place. New media tools allow us to work on multiple projects simultaneously, resulting in a complex web of interconnected links and ties. The potential resources and capabilities available through tapping into such professional networks represent 'network capital' (Quan-Haase, Wellman, Witte, & Hampton, 2002), but 'connectivity seems to go to the connected: greater social benefit from the internet accrues to those already well situated socially' (Hampton & Wellman, 2003, p. 283). Awareness tools help untangle professional networks and increase accessibility.

Knowledge Management

The roots of knowledge management go back to organisational management and information systems studies. Whereas CSCW focuses primarily on the human–computer interaction design issues of the technology that supports collaboration, knowledge management's interest in collaborative activities is concerned with the way people work together effectively to discover, generate, and share knowledge. Responding to recent innovations in network communications technology that enable distributed and heterogeneous peer-to-peer modes of communication and collaboration, Bonabeau and Meyer (2001) identified flexibility, robustness, and self-organisation as three of the key strategies for successfully breaking down operational processes and appropriately allocating work tasks to staff. These objectives are also applicable in action research processes, which require smart ways of maintaining momentum considering their usually nonprofit *modus operandi*.

Collaboration is all about the sharing of information, knowledge, skills, and expertise. Cross and Borgatti (2004) conducted a study that found four characteristics that facilitate successful information seeking and sharing:

1. an awareness of another's relevant expertise;

2. being able to gain timely access to that person;

3. the willingness of a potential knowledge source to actively engage in problem solving; and,

4. a safe relationship to promote creativity.

Cross and Borgatti argued that 'knowing who knows what does not ensure that valuable knowledge can be drawn out of a network' (p. 152) and suggested that all four principles are interrelated and equally important. Although their study was conducted in an organisational context, these principles hold true for action research projects as well, as Gustavsen (2003b) pointed out—commenting here on the status quo in the field of action research:

> To learn from practices, research needs to develop social relationships; internally within the research community as well as in relation to other actors. 'The new production of knowledge' as identified by Gibbons and colleagues (Gibbons et al., 1994) is above all a network activity, and research cannot stay outside this process and remain as isolated individuals looking at the world from up above. (pp. 162–163)

The network activity to which Gustavsen alludes has been conceptualised in the notion of 'communities of practice' (Millen & Fontaine, 2003; Millen, Fontaine, & Muller, 2002; Nissen, Kamel, & Sengupta, 2000; Wenger, McDermott, & Snyder, 2002), which bring together professionals and practitioners across organisational hierarchies for the purpose of sharing domain knowledge and exchanging expertise and case-specific experiences. Reason and Bradbury (2001) view action research as playing a crucial part in establishing communities of enquiry within communities of practice, which seek to uncover not just the symptomatic and apparent issues and problems in the community but the actual causes and underlying circumstances. New media tools and systems can help facilitate these collaborative enquiries.

Tools and Systems

Trying to establish and maintain rapport with a diverse range of researchers, co-investigators, participants, and other stakeholders representing different social networks and interests in the community may look like a daunting task. However, introducing flat and informal communication structures at the base and allowing participants to self-report and self-document the process of action and reflection helps in sharing responsibility and fosters a sense of achievement and collective ownership. Furthermore, new media tools can help communities working collaboratively on a shared enquiry and toward a common goal. This section focuses on the internet and web applications, although other new media technologies, such as radio or cell phones, may be appropriated.

The internet is a technical network of computer networks that is no longer used by commercial enterprises for e-business and e-commerce alone. With the emergence of social software such as wikis, discussion boards, news and recommendation systems, community networks, e-mail lists, and blogs (cf. Bashaw & Gifford, 2004; Rheingold, 2002; Surman & Diceman, 2004), the internet follows a very people-centred trend as a platform that allows 'ordinary' humans (nonexperts) to create and sustain interactive social networks (Burgess, Foth, & Klaebe, 2006; Davies, 2003; Wellman et al., 2003). Some of these tools, especially e-mail and instant messaging, may already be in use in some communities, and it is essential for action researchers to be aware of existing and preferred communication channels that are used by members of the community to exchange information and to network (Foth & Brereton, 2004).

Some tools that are valuable in supporting or supplementing existing communication strategies are available in easy-to-install and maintain, free open source packages such as Drupal (http://drupal.org) and Confluence (http://www.atlassian.com/software/confluence/). These software applications create secure online environments with networking features to support the formation of interconnected action research clusters. It is possible to build a tiered infrastructure: A separate instance of the online environment can be set up for each cluster with flexible levels of access privileges. Additionally, they allow people to use everyday tools and applications with interfaces they may already be familiar with from other contexts.

Technology can visualise or illustrate ideas and concepts that may be too difficult to describe in words alone. Explicit speech and language and written reports may not appropriately capture action research true to the original context. As indicated in Chapter 1, the debate about recognising the importance of tacit knowledge (Polanyi, 1983) is an ongoing theme in action research, design, and community literature (Hearn & Foth, 2005; Rust, 2004). The demand for practical tools and methods to elicit, document, and interpret expressions of tacit knowledge may be met through acts of sociocultural animation that provide community members with opportunities for creative expression (Foth, 2006d). With readily available tools for amateur and nonprofessional users to create images, music, and videos, digital storytelling (Burgess, 2006; Burgess et al., 2006; Falzone, 2004; Freidus & Hlubinka, 2002) is an excellent method to mobilise the tacit, nonverbal, nonwritten, emotional, metaphorical, playful dimensions of activity and knowledge in action research and to capture the 'richness of events' as postulated by Arnkil (2004). Moreover, technical networks allow for the distribution and exchange of the products of creative expression along social networks that blur the boundaries between producers and consumers and stimulate critical reflection and discussion across the meta-network of the community.

A Case Example

The following case study illustrates the use of new media tools for collaboration in action research. *ICTs for Poverty Reduction* is sponsored by UNESCO and focuses on the innovative use of information and communication technologies to empower people living in poverty (Foth & Tacchi, 2004; Slater & Tacchi, 2004; Tacchi, 2004; see also Ch. 8, this volume). Research is integrated into a number of community multimedia centres in south Asia to help those projects develop effectively while at the same time investigating—through site-specific research and through comparison—how ICTs can contribute to poverty-reduction strategies. The focus is less on technology itself than on its innovative and creative use, in various combinations, in specific locations. Each site has a project worker trained in action research who is responsible for ensuring the research is undertaken and fed into each project's development. Ongoing training, support, and supervision happens online through e-mail, a research website and chat, as well as face-to-face through workshops and site visits.

One of the main challenges for the researchers overseeing this comparative, creative, and collaborative research project is the way in which its success relies on the ability to use the very same new technologies that are being researched. A Web-based interface has been established to enable the remote and widely dispersed researchers to communicate and collaborate with the lead researchers, to archive and discuss research data, and to provide a space where a research network capable of generating significant findings can be developed and maintained. The research process itself has resulted in a level of understanding about how new networked technology can be applied and adapted in creative ways for this kind of dispersed research project. The collaborative community website has been running since late 2002. The site is a first step toward building a set of tools to support the exchange and communication between the lead researchers who train and support the action researchers located at different community-based media initiative sites. It is intended to optimise such exchange for rigorous and productive research.

This secure[1] site is hosted in Australia and used by 43 members who include lead researchers, local action researchers, project coordinators, and the UNESCO team. Members access the site from New Delhi, Kolkata, Baduria, Bangalore, Budikote, Chennai and other places in Tamil Nadu, Darjeeling, and Uttaranchal in India; Sitakund in Bangladesh; Tansen and Lumbini in Nepal, Jakar in Bhutan, Uva and other places in Sri Lanka; Brisbane in Australia; and London in the United Kingdom.

The current website allows the team to explore the potential of an online space for the archiving of research data from across the local initiatives; it enables the lead researchers to support and train local researchers; and it allows for exchanges and discussions on the data being collected and the development and application of the research. The research website provides the core of the online interaction with local networks of fieldworkers, supplemented by e-mails and online chats using instant messaging. The four main sections of the site are a user directory, an online journal, a discussion board, and a file-sharing area. These are discussed in turn.

Realising the idea of networking community members has to start with offering ways for community members to find out about each other and to raise awareness of the informal networks as well as skills and experiences that are present across the community. Integrated into an asset-based community development approach (Kretzmann & McKnight, 1993), the generation and population of an *online community directory* presents an opportunity to create a 'white pages' list with contact details of participants and stakeholders that may increase levels of community efficacy (Carroll & Reese, 2003). The directory can be categorised according to individual and group (i.e., social network) membership. Combined with separate mailing lists for each of these entities, the directory acts as a starting point for networking the networks and can be used to broadcast or specifically channel information between participants and feed results back to the community at large.

---

[1]In keeping with our ethical principles (outlined in Ch. 3) of respecting confidences and ensuring all research data is kept safe, the website is restricted to project members only. However, within the site we adhere to our principle (outlined in Ch. 2) of making everything available for enquiries and making all levels of data visible and accessible.

The process of critical enquiry and reflection on an individual level is supported through *online journals or blogs* to write up, or paste in, fieldnotes that are an important research tool in this project. Each researcher has his or her own journal to submit postings. These act as a personal diary that participants use to record notes, events, experiences, and observations, and copy and paste information into from e-mail, instant messaging, or chat communication. Journals support both private and public entries, the latter can be used to share thoughts and reflection with other participants who can then comment on these public entries. The online journal is also a means of documenting progress that is driven by community participants. Instead of interview recordings and meeting minutes that require a dedicated transcriber or secretary, journals involve users in the documentation process itself, which in turn helps to share ownership and responsibility, support transparency and accountability, and maintain rigour by collecting rich accounts of personal reflections.

Individual journals or blogs ultimately count for very little; the value and importance of blogging is in the way it transcends website boundaries and enables the diffusion of information, and the distribution of discussion and collaboration across a broad range of individual sites running very different systems. Value accumulates at the level of the overall 'blogosphere' (encompassing all blogs) rather than the individual blog: a very problematic phenomenon for institutions still working along a very industrial model where the faculty (or factory) gates are heavily policed. However, creativity and collaboration is increasingly distributed across networks. In the future, platforms will interface effectively with a wide variety of other systems, using tools from trackback and content syndication at the most basic end (Hammersley, 2003) to more sophisticated approaches that may ultimately employ some of the concepts arising out of the various semantic Web initiatives.

Whereas the journal is the preferred communication tool on the individual and social network level, the *discussion board* provides a communicative outlet for the collective meta-network of enquiry and practice. As shown in Figure 4.1, it is divided into multiple discussion forums according to research themes or community issues, and documents network as well as collective action and progress. Postings are of research data such as interview transcripts, and also, analysis and draft papers. Results from the individual and group reflections are fed into the discussion forums for wider circulation and debate. A discussion board is a very public, broadcast-style medium and some members of the community may not feel confident enough to contribute to a large unknown audience online—or offline for that matter. Hence, it is crucial to combine it with more private and

Projects

Darjeeling Himalaya Internet Railway Darjeeling, West Bengal, India	46	98	Sat Dec 04, 2004 4:31 pm Karma ➜🗋
Empowering Resource Poor Women to Use ICT Tamil Nadu, India	20	35	Thu Jan 20, 2005 3:59 pm Savithri ➜🗋
ICT Learning Centre for Women Seelampur, East Delhi, India	33	52	Thu Jun 02, 2005 6:33 pm sarita ➜🗋
Jakar Community Multimedia Centre Jakar, Bhutan	7	12	Mon Jul 12, 2004 4:47 pm Savithri ➜🗋
Nabanna: Networking Women and Indigenous Knowledge Baduria, North 24 Parganas District, West Bengal, India	39	132	Fri Jun 03, 2005 3:25 pm Savithri ➜🗋
Namma Dhwani - Local ICT Network Budikote, Kolar District, Karnataka, India	37	128	Thu Apr 21, 2005 5:21 pm Savithri ➜🗋
Tansen Local ICT Network Tansen, Palpa District, Nepal	67	182	Fri Jun 03, 2005 3:11 pm Savithri ➜🗋
Uva Community Media Network Uva Province, Sri Lanka	23	73	Thu Mar 24, 2005 2:35 pm Savithri ➜🗋
Youth-Led Digital Opportunities Sitakund, Chittagong District, Bangladesh	11	19	Thu Mar 31, 2005 8:33 pm Savithri ➜🗋
Uttaranchal Himalaya Trust Community Radio Initiative	52	94	Thu Jan 06, 2005 10:26 am Jo ➜🗋
Lumbini Lumbini Information and Communication Cooperative Ltd., Nepal	48	153	Tue May 31, 2005 8:25 pm Savithri ➜🗋
Lumbini World Heritage part of the Lumini project	4	14	Mon May 16, 2005 4:30 pm Savithri ➜🗋
Madan Pokhara CMC	20	64	Sat Jun 04, 2005 6:38 pm Madanpokhara ➜🗋

Local Information Networks

what is LIN? description of this project	5	9	Thu Apr 14, 2005 10:01 pm Savithri ➜🗋
LIN case study methodology methodology discussions	2	3	Fri Mar 04, 2005 1:42 pm Megan ➜🗋

Figure 4.1. Discussion board divided into forum sections and topics.

intimate communication facilities such as journals but also e-mail, instant messaging, and offline face-to-face interaction.

The last major function that plays a crucial role in this project is a *file-sharing area* that is used to collect, store, and archive all sorts of digital artifacts including written documents such as reports, meeting minutes, invitations, and audiovisual files such as images, maps, photos, diagrams, recordings, songs, and videos. The file-sharing area becomes a gallery to showcase the wealth of knowledge, skills, and experience, and the progress made by the community. In this sense, it functions as a central online repository that reflects the virtual composition of the project's community memory.

Those familiar with using face-to-face methods of reflection and communication may be skeptical about the extent to which average participants would have the literacy and inclination to use online tools such as those described here. However, as discussed in more detail in Chapter 8, the sites in question have been contributing research data for more than three years, with participants who rank as relatively poor in global terms. The research has proved important locally for individual project development and at the same time comparison of research across the meta-network has helped the research team to learn from each other's experiences. The data is posted on the website in different sections and other action researchers comment on and critique the data, thus adding new dimensions to the analysis and new directions to the project. More than this, the process of training all the researchers in the same methodology (Tacchi, Slater, & Hearn, 2003; Tacchi et al., 2007), and storing and discussing research data in a centralised location has given us the opportunity to compare and contrast research, and develop significant insights into the potential role of ICTs in poverty reduction.

Issues

While exploring how new media tools can be of assistance in establishing collaborative work practices and maintaining research momentum, we must also acknowledge that the provision of technology itself is not sufficient to ensure successful collaboration. Other factors have to be taken into consideration in order to use collaborative tools effectively. Many technical solutions require access as a prerequisite. At the very time information technology (IT) departments in universities, governments, nongovernmental organisations, and businesses are tightening network security to produce safe computing environments, the needs of collaborating researchers seem to be moving in the opposite direction. Open access and cross-institutional networks would allow researchers to communicate and collaborate freely. Yet, this is not easily possible in today's environment, which leads to tension between open collaboration and tight security.

The tools described in this chapter highlight a need for methods to overcome the difficulty of hosting highly collaborative research tools working with multimedia and creative content within and across university networks. As the demand grows for interinstitutional and international research collaborations that deal with digital content (especially but not exclusively creative works) along with the desire to use new technologies to explore and research the use of the same, it is problematic to find that academics are unable to fully explore the interactive potential and speed of communication that these new technologies offer. Finding a way to overcome these obstacles will mark a significant breakthrough for truly collaborative research. However, apart from a couple of progressive university

IT labs, at present such systems must often be hosted through commercial providers, outside of university networks, because:

- university publishing policy requires moderation of user-generated content that is incompatible with the practice of open online collaborative spaces;

- tight university network security policies make it difficult for people to host material on computers connected to the university network without university-issued log-in privileges;

- up- and downstream bandwidth requirements and hosting costs cannot compete with commercial plans; and,

- the installation of nonstandard applications and operating systems is discouraged and hinders free exploration and testing of cutting-edge applications.

What are the best network designs and implementations to support research collaboration? What network policies will ensure appropriate network security while enabling optimal collaboration? The legal risks that may apply to organisations hosting collaborative workspaces need to be identified, and risk-management plans developed. The benefits and risks of open access to research data, files, and results need to be explored, as well as—beyond access—issues of effective usage (Gurstein, 2003) involving training and embedding technology in the communicative ecology of the community.

Additionally, the use and development of open source software (Bashaw & Gifford, 2004; Lessig, 2005; Surman & Diceman, 2004) for collaborative action research is of relevance here. Open source is particularly important because of the potential for re-use of technology and the ability of organisations to customise the software as needed for any given deployment. A framework that was not available in an open source model would cause difficulties for technological transfer to other universities, project teams, and external organisations. Furthermore, the open source model allows for continual innovation and evolution of the framework, and those benefits can be passed on to all users of the framework. However, open source software requires a significant level of administrative maintenance similar to proprietary solutions, involving updates, compatibility checks, tweaking of features, implementation on old or changing servers, and managing version control of multiple components or modules.

Furthermore, interactivity, although bringing benefits for collaborative research and creativity, carries with it some legal risks for the host of the collaborative space. The host can, in some cases, be held liable for the wrongdoings of its users. This is particularly relevant in areas like defamation and copyright infringement. Any organisation that plans to deploy an interactive collaborative workspace needs to be aware of the inherent risks involved, as well as strategies to mitigate these risks. These strategies may include an appropriate level of moderation of content, peer-approval processes, and, particularly in the Australian context, compliance with the new 'safe-harbour' requirements for carriage service providers inserted into Division 2AA of the *Copyright Act 1968* (Commonwealth) by the *U.S. Free Trade Agreement Implementation Act 2004* (Commonwealth).

The copyright licensing models chosen for disseminating research content are vitally important when establishing an online collaborative tool. It is important to consider the extent to which the information submitted by action researchers can be made available to the general public, if at all, and on what terms. Creative Commons is an organisation that provides simple and flexible copyright licences that enable information to be easily shared and collaboratively developed (Lessig, 2004). In appropriate cases, these licences may be used to govern the terms on which information is made available both to action researchers and the general public. Important issues to consider in this regard include protection for sensitive information, reciprocity of shared developments, and distinctions between commercial and noncommercial uses of information.

Conclusion

Rigorous action research increasingly requires a commitment to meaningful collaboration with a cross-disciplinary team of researchers and a diverse range of stakeholders. In this chapter, we have traced some of the theoretical influences that go back to research in the fields of CSCW and knowledge management. Although the scope of applicability in these areas is usually limited to commercial business contexts, the practical findings hold valuable insights from which action researchers can benefit as well.

Arguably, the use of new media tools for collaboration in action research offers vast potential to provide a more inclusive and democratic environment that responds to the call for more participatory (and thus collaborative) research, postulated by Reason (1998) and others. Some of the tools described here offer a chance to engage with fine-grained, capillary communicative structure of communities and provide a means to spread information and feed research findings back to the community. The rapidly progressing development of new media technology requires a constant review of new trends and solutions. Nonetheless, our case study of community multimedia centres in south Asia illustrates that simple, open-ended tools that allow informal social dialogue, a degree of appropriation, and user-led innovation are the most successful. More advanced and sophisticated tools may be less successful because they tend to be too complex to be easily customised by the community (Gaved & Foth, 2006). The final section of the chapter reminds us that in any case of technology adoption and deployment for action research projects, issues of access, technology literacy, maintenance continuity, and intellectual property need to be considered.

Part II

Advanced Approaches to Action Research and New Media

Chapter 5

Ethnographic Action Research

This chapter introduces ethnographic action research (EAR) and its use in the ongoing monitoring and evaluation of new media initiatives in cross-cultural development contexts. Since its development in 2002, EAR has undergone a process of continual refinement via projects conducted in various south and southeast Asian countries.

EAR is similar to participatory action research (PAR), with three key distinctions or characteristics that we elaborate in this chapter as we describe how it is practiced. First, the *ethnographic* refers not only to the key methods that are used (none of which is exclusive to EAR), but also to the *ethnographic approach* that is a fundamental plank of EAR and the way it is both integrated into the development of media initiatives and is ongoing. EAR is designed to build the capacity of media initiatives to monitor and evaluate, and consequently to alter practices as part of their ongoing development. The EAR researcher is a member of the media initiative team, usually with other roles and responsibilities within the initiative itself. Second, EAR works with the conceptual framework of the communicative ecology (see Ch. 2). This involves paying keen attention to the wider context of information and communication flows and channels—formal and informal, technical and social—and monitoring opportunities for both intervention and the changes that result. Finally, the media itself are used as tools for action research, for exploring issues in a community as well as archiving, managing, and collecting data and facilitating online networks of EAR researchers. Although we suggest it is the combination of these key characteristics that makes EAR a recognisable and distinct form of action research, any or all of them might be usefully taken up and employed without the others, and no doubt are in a variety of ways that we are unaware of.

In this chapter, we overview the background to the development of EAR: how it emerged, what perceived needs it was responding to, and what it consists of. We then briefly outline the current application of EAR in south and southeast Asia and the various theories of empowerment, inclusion, and new media use that underpin EAR. Next, we outline the basic principles of EAR and the key questions that guide this approach. Following a discussion about ethnography and embedded media, we describe the mix of methods that are typically used in an EAR project and the various uses of media that can be made in these projects. Finally, some of the limitations and ethical issues and challenges that need to be taken into account in using this methodology are considered.

Background

Media and communication studies have argued for some time that by giving 'ordinary' people access to media and other information and communication technologies (ICTs), and encouraging them to create their own local content, they are better able to become 'active citizens' (Rodriguez, 2004). Power relationships shift when people achieve usually privileged access to media (Couldry, 2000), and yet, these power relations remain dynamic, permanently shifting and changing (Rodriguez, 2001). Development and poverty-reduction agencies are interested in the idea that community-based media and ICT initiatives can help to empower ordinary people. Media and other ICTs are regularly employed in initiatives that seek to reduce poverty in developing country contexts. Large donor organisations are constantly seeking to improve knowledge and policies for ICT for development.

UNESCO, in particular, views information, communication, and knowledge as core to human progress and well-being, and sees traditional and new media as providing opportunities for higher levels of development across the world. This opportunity holds challenges, not least due to the fact that many people and nations 'do not have effective and equitable access to the means for producing, disseminating and using information and, therefore, to development opportunities' (UNESCO, 2005, p. 191). Despite a proliferation of research and activity, an appropriate methodology had not been developed that addressed some of the fundamental concerns in this field—poverty itself and the impact of media initiatives on it.

Although ICTs are often promoted as effective for development and social change, many ICT projects have failed. In recognition of the need for more subtle and holistic impact and evaluation measures and methodologies, new sets of indicators are being developed that are consistent with a focus on community dialogue and broader social change, rather than individualistic behaviour change (Parks, 2005). This is echoed in the field of health promotion where concentration on individual behaviour change is misplaced once it is recognised that more permanent and larger scale change can be achieved by social change at the community level, and where evaluation needs to be aware of the specific issues of a community-based programme (Bracht 1999; Thompson & Kinne, 1999). EAR was first developed in response to this need for a more subtle and holistic approach, through initial support from the British government's Department for International Development (DfID) in 2002, and from UNESCO who continue to support, use and promote it, mostly in south Asia but also in Africa, and most recently through support from the United Nations Development Programme (UNDP) for use in Indonesia (see Ch. 8).

The development of EAR started with a small research project in Sri Lanka. Funded by DfID, it was designed to explore the usefulness of ethnography in the development of a transferable methodology for monitoring and evaluating media and communication for development initiatives (Slater et al., 2002; Tacchi, Slater, & Hearn, 2003). This took place in a context where significant funding was given to ICT and poverty-reduction activities, but the usual baseline survey approach to monitoring and evaluation and impact assessment was unsatisfactory. Indicators were hard to determine, and it was felt that the real achievements of such initiatives were not picked up in quantitative approaches to evaluation. Anecdotal evidence of interesting social change abounded. It was thought that ethnography might help to capture the kinds of changes that surveys and impact assessment failed to take account of.

To explore this, an ethnographic study was undertaken of the Kothmale Community Radio and Internet Project (KCRIP) in Central Province, Sri Lanka. The Kothmale community radio station had been operating since the 1980s, whereas the internet centre was a fairly recent addition (since 2000). KCRIP provided an interesting example of a 'community multimedia centre' that was anecdotally having a lot of positive outcomes, but little rigorous research and no regular monitoring and evaluation was taking place to provide evidence. The combination of the internet centre and the radio station was of particular interest in an area where most people had access to radio, but very few to other electronic communication technologies such as telephones, computers, and the internet.

A fairly standard ethnographic approach was used that tried to take account of the short duration of the field trip (one month). The project involved a team of three researchers from the United Kingdom and Australia and local research assistants and translators. We used a form of participant observation in that we 'hung around' at the centre and in the surrounding areas. Our main source of qualitative data was through a series of in-depth interviews in a range of locations (including households, shops, temples, the radio station and computer centre itself, and local schools), which we conducted with translators and local research assistants. We also used a short survey administered in 200 households by the research assistants.

A full analysis of the research findings can be read elsewhere (Slater et al., 2002). Suffice to say, this research allowed us to come up with some interesting descriptions of the activities of KCRIP and some of the characteristics of local communities and their media uses and information sources. What it failed to do was give us a methodology that was useful for the ongoing development of KCRIP itself. Although the evaluation at Kothmale came up with interesting and important findings in academic terms and in terms of how the project might adapt and develop, there were two significant problems that directly led to the development of EAR.

First, one month's ethnographic fieldwork does not constitute a fully fledged ethnography as understood by anthropologists—long-term immersion in the site of study. We partly overcame this limitation through using a team of researchers and local research assistants, but the limitation remained. There were so many more lines of enquiry that we were unable to pursue to deepen our understanding of KCRIP and its context. So, as an ethnography itself, the research was weak, but promising in the insights it allowed for.

The second and far more significant problem was that rather than simply coming up with research findings and recommendations, we wanted those involved in KCRIP to be empowered to apply them. Despite enormous interest from KCRIP staff and volunteers in our findings, there was no real ownership of the evaluation on the part of KCRIP, and no obvious route to making use of the findings. We recognised the need to develop a methodology that aimed to overcome both of these problems—integrating an ethnographic research approach into media initiatives and their development, training project workers themselves to undertake long-term ethnographic work, and drawing on the strengths of participatory and action research traditions.

It is clear then that EAR developed from recognition that an ethnographic approach provided important and useful insights that could help media initiatives to develop effectively, alongside the acknowledgment that on its own it was unlikely to be applied in any useful and useable way. Ethnography offered an interesting approach in a field where both donor organisations and practitioners are questioning the appropriateness of the quantitative indicators that major donors themselves have been using to measure poverty, health, education, nutrition, and other areas of development (Cracknell, 2000). It is argued that the benefits that poor people themselves give priority to are often more closely linked to qualitative indicators such as the right to involvement in national life, and the movement toward greater social equality; aspects of life that quantitative indicators are unlikely to identify and measure. This is clearly articulated in the work of Sen (2000, 2002), and Communication for Social Change, who are working to develop indicators for social change (www.communicationforsocialchange.org). This issue is complicated further by the different ways in which poverty itself is understood and operationalised at an etic rather than emic level (Laderchi, Saith, & Stewart, 2003; Lister, 2004).

Current Use of EAR in South and Southeast Asia

The most recent development in the practice of EAR illustrates how we are currently using it in the field. This is a major research project called Finding a Voice: Making Technological Change Socially Effective and Culturally Empowering, which is being conducted between 2006 and 2009 in India, Nepal, Sri Lanka, and Indonesia. Finding a Voice explores the use of combinations of old media (radio, TV, video, print, etc.) and new and emerging media (internet, digital formats and technologies, wireless, etc.) for development. A more detailed account of this project is provided in a case study presented in Chapter 8.

A network of 15 ICT centres is taking part in the research project, dispersed across the four countries. Part of the project aims to explore how different combinations of media work together. We are working with the network of centres to develop and provide training and support in the use of media and ICTs in the creation and distribution of locally produced content. Each centre has an EAR researcher working as an integral part of the centre. The EAR researcher has been trained through workshops in the region and is further supported online and face to face, and given follow up training by an Australian team of researchers.

Essentially, the EAR methodology combines participatory techniques and an ethnographic approach in an action research framework. Ethnography and participatory techniques are used to guide the research process and action research is used to link the research back in to the initiative through the development and planning of new activities.

The aim is that the initiative develops a *research culture* through which knowledge and reflection are made integral to ongoing development. The research aims, methods, and analysis arise from, and then feed back into, a rich understanding of the particular place. EAR researchers are encouraged to involve participants and workers both as informants and as fellow researchers. It provides a way of listening carefully to what people know from their own experiences and then brings this local knowledge into the ongoing processes of planning and acting. The key methods that are used include participatory techniques; observation, participant observation and fieldnotes; in-depth interviews; short surveys; and diaries, feedback mechanisms, and other forms of 'self-documentation.' We describe the basic principles of EAR and the methods that are typically used in more detail later in this chapter. The EAR methodology is set out in detail in a handbook (Tacchi, Slater, & Hearn, 2003; Tacchi et al., 2007).

ICTs, Inclusion, and Development

Although the concept of *poverty* has been problematised and expanded to include issues of inclusion, capacities, vulnerabilities, and deprivation alongside more traditional income poverty (de Haan, 1999; Sen, 2000), the relevance of ICTs in this wider understanding of poverty still requires interrogation. Social exclusion and inclusion is clearly of relevance in the wider debates around the 'digital divide,' especially considering Castells' view of the connected and networked world: where dominant values and interests are connected and distances between them minimised, while what is not connected or networked is in danger of becoming devalued or excluded (Castells, 1996). But how to link ICTs with development is still contested. Simply providing access to technologies is increasingly seen as inadequate to bridge the divide (Mansell, 2002). And simply providing access to information available through these technologies is increasingly challenged as not enough when local content creation—genuine participation—is ignored (Feek, 2004; Tacchi, 2005).

Mansell (2002) emphasised our lack of understanding about the impacts of new media technologies in the context of developing nations, which in part is a consequence of the priority given to the promotion of ICT diffusion in pursuit of more diverse access. This is tied closely with assumptions about what access will do in terms of empowering those who are disadvantaged. There has been little debate regarding the developments of new media and an examination of alternatives 'that are consistent with a goal of empowering the majority of citizens in their interactions with the new media' (Mansell, 2002, p. 408). Currently in practice there is an overemphasis on macro-level issues of technology access and social exclusion rather than micro-issues of the capabilities people require to function in a society where internet-based communication interactions are increasingly favoured.

These issues were brought out strongly by Rice et al. (2001) as they interrogated six bodies of literature to critically examine the concept of access and its many dimensions in relation to information and communication. They showed how access is highly consequential and multidimensional; that it is not simply about the physical but also about the cognitive, affective, political, economic, and cultural. Issues of access are found to be pervasive and complex (Rice et al., 2001):

Access lurks in our definitions of request or query, in a users ability to identify a need, in the very awareness that information systems are available and in trusting that information useful in addressing that need exists and is retrievable through an information system.

Access lurks in the social and cultural contexts of information seeking . . . which are tied to the degree to which an individual is an insider to a given information system's culture . . . and therefore to the rules required to gain access to the information potentially available through it. (p. 26)

Research has clearly shown that community-based media that mixes new and older media technologies provides an effective vehicle for development (Feek, 2004). However, Dagron (2001) asked: 'If community media is the answer, what is the question?' (p. 24). He suggested that the answer may well be the question; that if the questions were discussed with the communities in which media initiatives are placed and if a 'permanent and nonexclusive dialogue' is established among all stakeholders, then the question itself may become irrelevant. Questions and answers must be worked out in each community, in its own context, in a participatory way. For effective and sustainable community media initiatives there needs to be mechanisms for ongoing dialogue and participation in the development of the initiative itself, along with recognition that each community has its own particular context that needs to be understood.

EAR provides a vehicle for such processes that consider not only the communication initiative being developed, but also the existing 'communicative ecologies': the flows and channels of communication and information that include all forms of mediation and knowledge and information transfer. Additionally, it provides a template for developing sustainability plans that recognise and respond to the needs, desires, and resources available within each specific community. Communicative ecology places ICTs (which include radio, computers, cell phones, print media, etc.) in the context of all the ways of communicating that are significant locally, including face-to-face interaction, and recognises that any 'new' connections and networks (social and technological) that develop as a result of the introduction of individual ICTs will be far more effective if they are somehow interconnected with existing, locally appropriate systems and structures (Foth & Hearn, 2007; Slater & Tacchi, 2004).

In the Finding a Voice project, all of the EAR researchers began their research by starting to build an understanding of the communicative ecologies in the communities their media centres serve. These understandings will gradually deepen and the EAR researchers will observe changes in the communicative ecologies as a result of their media interventions.

This allows them to monitor changes that happen as a result of their interventions. It also helps researchers identify and understand the existing information and communication flows and channels—formal and informal, social and technological—their interventions can tap into and leverage off (see Ch. 8 for some examples of EAR researchers' work on communicative ecologies).

As a first step in understanding the significance of the ways in which information flows, and who has access and is able to use which communication technologies, EAR researchers themselves are asked to map their own communicative ecologies at their first training workshop. They are asked to think about what factors affect the communication choices they make.

The key questions that need to be asked in order to understand local communicative ecologies are as follows:

• What kinds of communication and information activities do local people carry out or wish to carry out?

• What communications resources are available to them—media content, technologies, and skills?

• How do they understand the way these resources can be used?

• Who do they communicate with, and why?

• How does a particular medium—such as radio or internet—fit into existing social networks?

• Does it expand those networks? How can a media centre connect to its users' social networks?

While thinking about their own communicative ecology, EAR researchers are asked to map their own social network by drawing a rich picture (Monk & Howard, 1998)—the people, activities, relationships, and media they are linked to on a weekly basis—and to indicate the different sorts of information they get from different people and places (health, education, entertainment, family, social events, and local and national news). They are asked to think about the different factors that place them in different social networks.

This exercise serves to demonstrate the differences among people who may think initially that they are similar. Gender differences, the impact of the lack of infrastructure, the differences between urban and rural settings, and the impact of differential pricing structures are among the issues that often emerge from this exercise.

Basic Principles of Ethnographic Action Research

EAR combines three research approaches: ethnography, participatory techniques, and action research.

Ethnography is a qualitative research approach that uses a range of methods and has traditionally been used to understand different cultures in detail. Participatory techniques are used to help both researchers and participants understand complex issues in an inclusive and participatory manner. Action research is an approach that is used to develop new knowledge and new activities through new understandings of situations. Ethnography and participatory techniques are used to guide the research process, whereas action research is used to link the research back in to the initiative through the development and planning of new activities in ongoing cycles.

As the Finding a Voice project demonstrates, EAR combines research with project development. It has been designed primarily to be applied to community-based information and communication or media projects. EAR can help to evaluate and monitor ICT projects, but it does more than this. To be really effective, EAR should be a built-in component of a media project that is integrated into the project itself, adequately resourced and ongoing. It allows for the fully transparent development of a project, for ongoing monitoring and evaluation that will affect the ways in which the project develops, and it helps to build flexibility into projects so that they can adapt to local needs and changing situations. It is an approach that recognises and documents successes *and* failures, opportunities *and* challenges, recognising that in order to overcome obstacles those obstacles need to be fully understood, and that it is only through addressing failures that projects can learn. Both success and failure in project implementation are therefore recognised as important building blocks in a project's development.

Ethnography and Embedded Media Development

EAR researchers in the Finding a Voice research project are integral members of each media centre's wider team, and they often have other tasks. Whereas one person is identified in each centre as responsible for ensuring EAR is carried out, EAR tasks are often shared by media centre team members and volunteers. EAR researchers are local residents, sometimes with no background in research. They are trained to conduct EAR for the benefit of their local centre's development. This is an ongoing position. EAR is part of the media centre, not external to it. It is a built-in component of a media centre that is integrated into the centre itself. Ideally, it allows for the fully transparent development of a centre, for ongoing monitoring and evaluation that will affect the ways in which the centre develops, and helps to build flexibility into centres so that they can adapt to local needs and changing situations.

The EAR researcher is given two particular and related tasks: Develop a research culture within the media centre and work as a sociocultural animator.

Research Culture

Rather than considering research as an activity that happens to a development initiative by external evaluators at specified points in time (e.g., at the beginning of a donor-funded activity and one year later), EAR integrates research into the project's continuous cycle of planning and acting. The organisation can change, adapt, and respond on the basis of informed reflection. Instead of simply measuring impacts at certain points in time, EAR means that media centre staff and volunteers continuously reflect on and produce knowledge about how they are working. In order for the media centre's staff and participants to feel ownership of this process, and to see its value, an EAR researcher aims to develop a research culture through which knowledge and reflection are constantly fed back in ways that help development. EAR incorporates common features of action research. It involves a range of people planning, doing, observing, and reflecting throughout all stages of the research and media centre activities and development. It seeks to ensure that media centres are linked to the aspirations and circumstances of people locally by making sure those people and their viewpoints are integral to the development of the project.

Research is focused on how problems and opportunities are defined by people locally and allows research methods and the centre itself to creatively adapt to the local situation. A division between researcher and research subjects is avoided. Rather, EAR involves many different roles and different kinds of conversations. Hence, participants can be engaged both as informants and as fellow researchers. It provides a systematic means for listening carefully to what people know from their experience, helping to structure this more clearly, and bringing it into the processes of planning and acting.

Sociocultural Animation

Thus, the researcher's role is more than simply being attached to a media centre to carry out research. An EAR researcher may undertake a variety of roles within a centre, and research responsibility may be shared between different members of staff and volunteers. In any case, the researcher should be an integral part of a team, not an outsider only there to judge how well they are doing. One way of describing the role of the EAR researcher (or researchers) is through the term *sociocultural animator*. Foth (2006d) described sociocultural animation as 'a way of mobilising the social and cultural participation of individuals and community members so that they become actively engaged in their personal development and in the development of their community' (p. 640). In this role, they encourage awareness among all staff and volunteers of the local social and cultural environment. Not only will the researcher encourage project workers themselves to be active in the shaping and evaluation of the projects, he or she will encourage project workers to engage in interaction with local people and groups, to look to local people and groups as participants, and to include their ways of making sense of the world and themselves in their evaluations of projects. Animation in this sense suggests viewing project workers, local communities, groups, and individuals as active agents.

The findings from EAR activities can be fed into a media project's development in several ways. The researchers can play a role in making sure research is both appropriate and understood by all concerned. They can do this through discussion with staff and stakeholders, through the verbal reporting of research findings, through written reports, through participation in planning and evaluation meetings, general centre meetings, and staff meetings. It is a resource that will only be effective for a media centre if it is integrated into that centre's activities. If everyone involved understands that EAR is there to help them as a valuable resource that they can call on when needed, a 'research culture' can develop and EAR is more likely to be effective.

Key Methods Used in EAR Projects

EAR researchers use a range of key methods to uncover and explore different kinds of knowledge. Each research plan uses at least three methods from the EAR 'toolbox' (Tacchi, Slater, & Hearn, 2003; Tacchi et al., 2007). The key methods include the following.

- **Observation, participant observation, and fieldnotes.** This is the kind of data-collecting activity that EAR researchers continuously undertake. It can be undertaken by anyone involved in an initiative simply by reflecting on what they observe and recording this in the form of fieldnotes. EAR researchers encourage this as they work toward developing a research culture. Fieldnotes record as much as possible of what EAR researchers see and hear, and also record their own reactions and ideas as they happen.

- **In-depth interviews.** In the EAR context, these are detailed conversations with a range of people, guided by an interview schedule—a list of a few major topics to be covered in each interview—while leaving sufficient room to respond to what is interesting in the conversation.

- **Participatory techniques.** Techniques such as mapping, sequencing, and comparing are aimed at getting EAR researchers started in collecting data and quickly gaining an understanding of the local area, local people, and local issues, including local communicative ecologies (see some examples in Ch. 8). These techniques are consistent with methods used in PAR for example. They complement the ethnographic tools and although they are a useful way of starting EAR work, they can also be drawn on at any time later to explore issues in different ways, and to test findings or ideas generated using different tools. They can also be used for consensus-building.

- **Short questionnaire-based surveys.** All of the tools above generate detailed information on a small number of participants. Short questionnaire-based surveys can allow researchers to generate less detailed information from larger numbers of people and to collect relevant quantitative data.

- **Diaries, feedback mechanisms, and other 'self-documentation.'** All kinds of participants—staff, users, and community members—can express themselves on a range of social or personal issues; keep logs of their activities; or document their lives through text, audiorecordings, photographs, or drawings. Centres can also use feedback forms, visitors' books, logbooks, suggestion boxes, and other ways to obtain feedback.

Examples of the way in which these methods are used in combination with the key approaches used to study the communicative ecologies of media and development initiatives are provided in Chapter 8.

The Uses of Media in EAR Projects

A distinctive characteristic of EAR is the use of media as a tool for action research itself. In the Finding a Voice research project, media are central to the activities being studied, but ICTs are also used as a mechanism or tool for research training, management, and data archiving and analysis itself.

Engaging local people in the creation of media content can allow insights into the pressing issues of a community as well as give insights into everyday lives that are barely visible. The World Bank's *Voices of the Poor* study (Narayan, Chambers, Shah, & Petesch, 2000) demonstrates that directly listening to the voices of the poor, in whatever mediated format, does allow different perspectives and different understandings to develop.

Online communication and networking tools are also being used to establish a support network of action researchers across continents. The Finding a Voice project was developed from earlier work with a network of community media centres in south Asia, supported by UNESCO (see Ch. 8; Tacchi, 2005). Since late 2002, a collaborative, members-only community website has supported the associated network of action researchers (see Ch. 4; Foth & Tacchi, 2004). The website has allowed researchers in Brisbane, Delhi, and London to support and enhance the training of local action researchers located across south and southeast Asia. It allows discussions on the data being collected and the development and application of the research. Interaction through this website is supplemented by emails and online chats using instant messaging.

A range of individual communication and networking tools can also be used to support action research. These tools include:

- a user directory that enables the networking of community networks;

- weblogs that enable researchers to write up, or paste in, fieldnotes;

- discussion boards, which provide multiple discussion forums for the collective meta-network of enquiry and practice;

- file-sharing areas that can be used to collect, store, and archive all kinds of digital artifacts, including written documents and audiovisual files; and

- publication of audiovisual material collected via Third Generation mobile phones and mobile music players by uploading this material to a website and then distributing a feed via podcasting.

These networking and communication tools were described in more detail in Chapter 4.

Limitations, Issues, and Challenges in Using EAR

Although EAR has proved effective in a number of major media and development projects, it has some limitations and issues that need to be taken into account, as with all participatory research and evaluation methodologies.

While participation and self-help as concepts in poverty reduction appear to have significant rhetorical power, there are some complexities to consider. Weinberger (2000) looked at women's participation in Southern

Chad and Pakistani Kashmir. She found a 'middle-class effect' of participation: It was mainly those from the middle classes who participated, those who are more articulate and vocal in the first place. Streeten (2002) pointed out that certain groups—the poorest (e.g., women, the young, and the disabled)—have the least power and opportunity in participation initiatives. This is further supported by findings from research conducted in Kothmale, Sri Lanka. Women and Tamil communities had far less opportunities to engage with a project that was designed for all the local communities, although participation was possible for some women and for many young people (Slater et al., 2002). It is also clear in UNESCO-supported community ICT initiatives in south Asia that the 'less poor' participate more than the 'extreme poor' (Slater & Tacchi, 2004).

Long-term immersion in the field of study, and working within a research culture that understands the role of research and allows it to feed into activities is highly important. Getting widespread participation, especially from the poorest local communities, is a real challenge for community ICT and media centres, and a focus of training and support input in the current Finding a Voice project. Participation needs to be supported actively. It is only sustained research that helps initiatives to adapt and change in light of growing understandings that participation itself can be evaluated and adjusted, as each local circumstance requires.

MacColl et al. (2005) identified a number of ethical issues that they encountered when using EAR for understanding and facilitating distributed collaboration in the Australian context. These issues may also apply in the development context. They included the difficulty in obtaining informed consent from participants because of the wide-ranging nature of the observations conducted by the researchers, and the possibility that the risk of harm to participants and the agents of change may be increased because 'change is fundamentally risky' (MacColl et al., 2005, p. 3). They also found that sharing observational data raised confidentiality and anonymity issues as a result of the small number of people involved in the project.

Many researchers have highlighted the political nature of participatory forms of research and evaluation (Humphries, 1996; Lennie, 2006). However, although power is a central issue in participatory evaluation, it is often ignored (Gregory, 2000). As noted in Chapter 2, this suggests a need to openly address issues related to the conflicting agendas and perspectives, and the power relations among those involved in EAR projects that can hinder the effectiveness of this approach. Before embarking on EAR projects, appropriate strategies clearly need to be developed to minimise potential risks or conflicts between the various organisations and people involved.

Conclusion

PAR is widely used in development situations. EAR differs from PAR in three key ways that have been outlined in this chapter. First, the *ethnographic* in ethnographic action research refers not simply to the kinds of methods that are promoted through this approach. It references the embedded and sustained, long-term engagement in the site of study, and indeed the capacity-building component that means that it is media centre staff and volunteers themselves who undertake and manage the action research process.

Through working with the conceptual framework of the communicative ecology, attention is paid to the wider context of information flows and channels, the barriers and the opportunities that exist and can be created. Using EAR, media for development initiatives can develop in ways that recognise and respond to local social, political, cultural, and economic contexts and that see each media technology as just one in a wider communicative ecology that predates their intervention and is at the same time altered by it.

Creative use of the media also allows media centres to gain insights into the lives of those they seek to change for the better. It can help to build dialogue and understanding of those whose lives are rarely the focus of attention. Additionally, media tools can be used in action research practices to help share, store, manage, and analyse data, and provide support for action researchers who are geographically remote from one another.

As with all participatory research and evaluation methodologies, EAR has certain limitations and issues such as those related to inclusion, power, and ethics that need to be considered before starting an EAR project.

Chapter 6

Network Action Research

Networks, social networks, technical networks, the process of networking, and the design of network applications have a deep impact on almost all areas of society including science, economy, and community. Scientists such as Barabási (2003) and Watts (2003) offer an extensive overview of how processes such as market transactions, business operations, viral infections, and social behaviour between people can be described as networks. Castells (2000b) coined the term *Network Society* for the changing *zeitgeist* of this era. Based on the notion that network concepts are a fundamental paradigm for achieving a deeper understanding in various areas of science and technology, scholars acknowledge the increasing significance of technologically mediated networks in the epistemology of their home discipline, such as in the arts and humanities (Keane, 2004), urban studies (Mitchell, 2003), and community development (Gilchrist, 2004). Technology and networks, especially the internet, have become part of everyday life—at least in more developed parts of the world (Wellman & Haythornthwaite, 2002). The ubiquity of the internet and the spread of cell phones and other network technologies afford communication patterns that change the character and quality of community interaction and engagement.

In this chapter, we suggest that action researchers would benefit from a debate around issues related to the network qualities of community and the implications it has for action research. We expose the relevance and capacity of using action research in the nexus of people, place, and technology and discuss the shifting quality of community as networks, as well as the challenges for action researchers that emerge from this shift. Network action research is proposed as a methodological variation that has the potential to address some of those challenges. To provide empirical support, we introduce an example drawn from an investigation of social networks in inner-city apartment buildings. Another example, taken from a multi-site research project on information and communication technology (ICT) for poverty reduction, was provided in Chapter 4. The purpose of this chapter is to introduce and illustrate with examples a methodological variation of action research, rather than report the research projects in detail.

People, Place, and Technology in Social Networks

The traditional view that the effects of globalisation have been made possible through the global spread of information and communication networks has been refined by a notion that Robertson (1995) and later Wellman and his colleagues (Hampton, 2001; Wellman, 2001, 2002) popularised with the term *glocalization*. The internet and other forms of global networks enable the exchange of business information and the real-time communication between corporate players across nations, but there is a noticeable trend toward using the global network for *local* interaction (Fallows, 2004; Horrigan, 2001; Horrigan, Rainie, & Fox, 2001; Rice, 2002) and *social* interaction (Huysman & Wulf, 2004; Thurlow, Lengel, & Tomic, 2004; Wellman et al., 2003). The majority of communication and interaction facilitated by global networks can be categorised as social and informal, and takes place within the geographic vicinity of the actors. The majority of phone calls and e-mails connect people within the same city, company, or community (Wellman, 2001).

Although the widespread significance of localness in online communication and interaction is just starting to be fully realised, websites such as community networks have been used for some time in various forms to enable local interaction, to provide local information, and to support local activism (Harrison & Stephen, 1999; Schuler, 1996). These systems are usually implemented by re-appropriating existing technology that was originally designed with a different—usually commercial—context in mind. However, technology designers and developers are quick to create purpose-built solutions that integrate place-based functions and features (Rheingold, 2002). Cell phone manufacturers and network carriers are in the process of implementing location-aware services that range from interactive directory assistance that suggests nearby cafés and restaurants, to sending discount vouchers for a store that the cell phone owner is physically close to via short message service (SMS). Location-aware applications and so-called 'locative' media on the internet have started to emerge, such as local grass-roots amateur journalism sites (www.indymedia.org) and neighbourhood discussion boards that indicate the user's physical distance from the origin of the discussion (www.upmystreet.com). Similarly, the popular location-based mapping services by a major search engine (maps.google.com) evidences the rise of local interaction mediated by networked technology.

Research that situates itself within the nexus of people, place, and technology has to cope with the complex sum of the individual characteristics that each variable brings to the study. The human dimension of 'people' contributes a fuzzy and indeterministic quality, 'place' adds the imperative to ground and delimit intervention in the local context, and notions of 'technology' expand considerations around design, access, effective and ethical usage, training, maintenance, and sustainability. The flexible, practice-led, and local nature of action research makes it a well-suited starting point that easily adapts to changing situations in this multifaceted and cross-disciplinary environment (see Ch. 1). At the same time, the characteristics that make action research, in a sense, predestined for this purpose also call for an appropriation and customisation of methods for the specific context it is applied in. As already noted in Chapter 1, action research is an umbrella paradigm, a family of approaches of enquiry, or as Dick (2003) called it, a 'meta-methodology' that allows a variety of underlying methods to be used under its guiding principles.

Several methodologies, some of them influenced by or related to action research, have been proposed to study the interrelationship between people and technology, including the following:

- network ethnography (Howard, 2002);

- virtual ethnography (Hine, 2000);

- ethnographic action research (see Ch. 5, this volume);

- action research in user-centred product development (Brandt, 2003);

- participatory design (Greenbaum & Kyng, 1991; Schuler & Namioka, 1993); and,

- interaction design (Cooper, 1999; Cooper & Reimann, 2003).

This chapter points in the direction of significant developments and challenges for these human-centred methodologies and proposes a variation of action research that integrates key aspects of people, place, and technology research. It is both *network* action research and *networking* action research in that it uses technology to network participants and stakeholders in an action research project and takes into account the shifting quality of community as networks.

The Shifting Quality of Community as Networks and Emerging Challenges for Action Researchers

The focus on people in action research often requires a debate and definition of the term *community*.[1] Over the years, social scientists have come up with

---

[1]See Katz, Rice, Acord, Dasgupta, and David (2004) for a review of concepts of community and implications of new media.

a plethora of definitions for community with 'people' being the only common denominator. Tönnies's (1887) image of community as *Gemeinschaft* resembles small-scale neighbourhood-based, village-like collective groups of residents that show a high level of social capital. The communication and social interaction in this type of community is mainly from door to door and from place to place (Wellman, 2001). However, with the introduction of readily available and cheap means of transportation and the rise of ICT, people are able to connect with a diverse range of other communication partners outside the immediate vicinity of the neighbourhood and beyond their own physical reach. Within the concept of the 'space of flows,' Castells (2001) speaks of private 'portfolios of sociability' that people create and maintain, which now not only include family and kinship ties but also a variety of other social ties—both strong and weak—with friends, co-workers, peers, and other acquaintances. The composition of the portfolio is flexible, varies according to personal circumstances, and is adjusted and shaped through the use of cell phones, e-mail and SMS. The use of such communication devices affords personalisation of social interaction to a degree that enables people to shift from door-to-door and place-to-place relationships to person-to-person and role-to-role relationships (Wellman, 2001, 2002).

People operate a variety of roles in diverse networks. The roles and social identities that people act in and switch between seamlessly can include family roles, job positions, committee and volunteer memberships, and informal roles as friends, supporters, counselors, neighbours, and so on. Each of these roles is a node that is linked to a wider social network in which the person may also fulfill bridging functions between networks. These networks make up a communicative ecology that is very unlike a collective *Gemeinschaft* and resembles more a swarm (Satchell, 2003) or an urban tribe (Watters, 2003b). As such, they present a challenge to collectivist images of community that are sometimes found in action research.

Action researchers try to reach out and interact with members of a community in order to animate participation and engagement in cycles of planning, acting, observing, and reflecting. The shifting quality of community as networks means that action researchers need to be aware of the networked, dynamic, and fluid communicative behaviour of community members. The imperative of action research to nurture the community action cycle with the results of enquiry and reflection requires a process of information dissemination that works within and across networks. Therefore, the capacity of community members to operate as nodes and along links of social networks has direct implications for the communication strategies that action researchers and community participants apply in their day-to-day operations.

A collective approach may entail the distribution of information flyers and newsletters, liaison with community leaders, and setting up community steering committees, focus groups, and information evenings for the wider community. Although action research projects that follow such procedures can certainly demonstrate the rigour and academic validity of their interventions, actions, and findings, the question remains whether the community engagement process is in fact representative of the community at large. It also needs to be demonstrated that 'communities of enquiry within communities of practice' (Reason & Bradbury, 2001) have been formed that are indicative not just of the symptomatic and apparent issues and problems in the community but of the actual causes and underlying circumstances.

Table 6.1 provides an overview of the emerging challenges that arise from a conventional approach toward action research that regards community

Table 6.1. Action Research Challenges and Responses from a Network Action Research Approach

Emerging Challenges of a Collective Approach Toward Action Research	Responses From a Network Approach Toward Action Research
How can action researchers ensure that the views of community leaders and members of focus groups are in fact representative of all community members?	Network action research maps existing informal social networks and seeks to integrate them into the communication mix.
Are recruiting and communication strategies suitable for all personality types found within the community? Will some members of the community be intimidated by large open discussion forums or put off by time-intensive workshops? Will their voices therefore remain unheard?	Instead of one-to-many and many-to-many 'broadcast-style' information-exchange media, network action research harnesses informal peer-to-peer channels that provide a more private, intimate, and ethnographic way of communicating and engaging with community members.
Will previously unheard community voices remain unheard because collective communication strategies are not fine-grained enough to recognise marginalised voices?	Network action research taps into the capillary communicative structure of communities and provides a means to channel information 'upwards.'
Members of social clusters and their immediate surrounds usually show a very homogenous set of political opinions and attitudes. Yet, is there a process to mediate between opinion leaders that also informs discussion by integrating less well-represented but perhaps crucial and ethical points of view?	Network action research is wary of the fact that the most motivated volunteers are the best-suited participants and encourages other community members to make themselves heard by allowing them to participate despite little effort or time commitment.

continued on next page

Table 6.1. *Continued*

Emerging Challenges of a Collective Approach toward Action Research	Responses from a Network Approach toward Action Research
How can action researchers ensure that the open learning and enquiry process and subsequent results that community leaders and volunteers are encouraged to engage in will spread through the community at large and reach members that are not actively participating in the project?	Network action research taps into the capillary communicative structure of communities and provides a means to channel information 'downwards.'
What factors influence participation and engagement and how could levels of participation and engagement be increased through different outreach and communication strategies?	Network action research is woven into existing communicative structures that are already in place for existing purposes, so it usually does not require an additional commitment of time and energy.
Does the action research process try to elicit tacit knowledge from community members by allowing them to act and reflect in their natural work and living environment instead of reporting on their action outside of it? Can they easily and conveniently participate in the project while pursuing their day-to-day activities?	Network action research allows members to participate in their natural work and living environment. It also encourages creative expression beyond the written word or verbal speech, thus allowing a wider range of data formats and tacit forms of knowledge to be included.

as collective only and thus ignores the network dimension of community interaction. This view is contrasted with potential responses by a network approach toward action research.

These are just some of the questions that action researchers face on an ongoing basis. Network action research is not the Holy Grail that will answer them all, but it is a valuable approach to consider, which can suggest appropriate network strategies that may contribute a first step toward a solution to some of these issues. To some extent, this approach is also related to knowledge management (see Ch. 4) as it has many of the same goals—although largely in organisational contexts. In the frame of communities of practice, it also applies to nonprofit groups, cross-organisational communities, online communities, and the like; it also focuses on how new media may foster increased awareness, contact, collaboration, and collective benefit through shared knowledge. As discussed in Chapters 3 and 4, communication and collaboration are key in action research, and network action research may bring about an addition to or variation of existing communication strategies that are more suitable for working with communities and other social formations in the Network Society.

Operationalising Network Action Research

The following section describes ways to operationalise network action research. Network action research does not mean that the entire research momentum is driven by technology. Technology is increasingly becoming part of everyday life, and action researchers certainly have to take this into account, but some communities may still be in the process of coming to terms with issues of new media and ICT access and usage, particularly those in rural or disadvantaged areas. However, in any case, it is necessary to first focus on *strategies* that acknowledge the human-to-human ties and social networks that are formed and sustained in the community through existing means of communication, and then look at how *tools* (see Ch. 4, with case studies in Chs. 5 and 8) may be employed to support those strategies. Strategies are illustrated in a case study of interventions to social networks in an inner-city apartment complex in Australia.

Strategies

The following strategies are illustrated with examples drawn from a case study that examines the social and technical dimension of networks in inner-city apartment buildings (Foth, 2006a, 2006b; Foth & Hearn, 2007). The site for this case study is a residential building complex in a major capital of Australia that comprises 94 one-, two-, and three-bedroom units with approximately 160 tenants. This case study ran between late 2002 and early 2006. The tenants in the building are mostly international students between 17 and 24 years of age who study at nearby tertiary institutions. They come from a variety of national and cultural backgrounds including Asia (mostly Singapore, Japan, China, Taiwan, Korea, India, Saudi Arabia, and Oman), North America, and Europe (mostly Scandinavia, Germany, and the United Kingdom).

The agenda of the action research approach in this case was guided by specific objectives to analyse and understand the social fabric of residents in urban neighbourhoods and how new media and ICT, especially internet-based tools and applications, can be used to facilitate neighbourhood connections and social networks between residents. The study also looked at (a) the process of installing and customising existing, mostly open source tools to facilitate community-building and to establish an online community network, and—in a later stage—(b) the design and development process, both online and offline, to create purpose-built solutions that take into account the specific requirements of a place-based community, as opposed to a virtual community.

The research in the case study looked at each subnetwork. Initially through an online survey and follow-up interviews, it involved participants in a critical reflection of how their current activities can be improved and possibly contribute to making the apartment complex a better place for everyone to live. Barbecue nights are organised to welcome new residents and to provide an informal opportunity for all residents to meet each other. The goal is to raise awareness of what different residents contribute to the community and how this implicit pool of interests, skills, and cultural backgrounds can be harnessed by the community. This process also involved reflecting on the variety of social networks present in the building and their activities, and promoting openness and social permeability to join other networks.

The term *community* is often used as a convenient container by researchers and external stakeholders to collectively refer to a more or less well-defined group of people. However, members of this so-called community may or may not feel inclined to play an active part in it. Or they may also refer to this group that they are apparently a part of, as community, without being able to specify in any more detail what constitutes membership in this community.[2] The residents of this case study may be part of a neighbourhood community for the purpose of defining and delimiting a research group, but they may not know their neighbours or feel a sense of belonging to the building, street, block, or suburb in which they live. Moreover, in interviews it became clear that they feel more strongly about the social networks they actively create and maintain themselves that include social ties to others who may not be part of the neighbourhood community.

The guiding principle of network action research moves away from a pure homogeneous model of community and acknowledges the fluid, dynamic, swarming, chaotic qualities of social networks that are present in communities. The primary objective of network action research is to map the existing (formal and informal) networks that operate within the community

---

[2]Another typical example is the term *government* that is informally used to refer to local, state, or national government agencies and entities of state power. Similar to the term *community*, the usage of the term ignores the intricate networks of public agencies and associated power relationships that are mostly hidden or too complex to easily explain in the daily usage of the term.

and initiate small participatory action research projects within each of them. The task of the action researcher is then to link each of these subnetworks of enquiry to form a larger networked community of practice.

Several smaller social networks already existed at the case study site. Some residents know each other through attending the same classes at university. Others meet to play table tennis, pool, or soccer. The local area network in the building facilitates multi-user network games to be played by some tenants across floors and apartments. Some participants also reported that they like to share video games, DVDs, and CDs with other residents in the building. As well, most two- and three-bedroom apartments in the building are shared, thus their inhabitants represent small networks of roommates who may in turn be connected to other residents in the building through other kinds of social ties.

The communicative structure that network action research acts upon resembles less the conventional image of community that is collective, highly structured and formalised, and more the image of an 'anthill' that appears to be chaotic and unstructured from the outside, but is highly efficient and networked on the inside. The process of critical enquiry, reflection, and action takes place in multiple instances within multiple networks. Instead of multiple volunteers participating in one action research project, network action research encourages participants to initiate multiple action research subprojects, which are networked to form a larger action research project on the level of the meta-network. Figure 6.1 illustrates this concept by contrasting the communicative ecology of conventional action research initiatives with that of network action research.

The principles and processes of fostering social (nontechnical) networking in communities have been well documented by Gilchrist (2004). Some of these principles include establishing a warm rapport with representatives of all networks that are present in the community, creating opportunities for networking to occur, forming bridging links between those networks, and negotiating access and trust in order to encourage participation through flat, comforting and informal communication procedures that easily feed information across other networks and into the meta-network with a minimum amount of distracting informational noise. The action researcher's task in this context is to monitor the communicative ecology of the community and provide additional meta-networking nodes that act as an interface between different stakeholders to allow the free flow of information and experience exchange.

The action researcher involves the community of residents in a mapping exercise to create a rough inventory of the social networks that live in the building. Some of these social networks do not have a strong self-awareness and members may be affiliated with a network *ex-officio* due

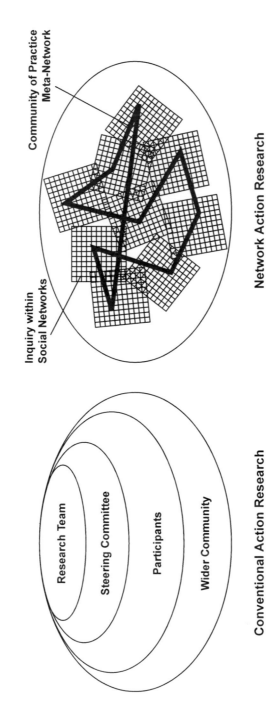

Figure 6.1. Communicative structures in conventional versus network action research.

to their national origin or study program without feeling a strong sense of belonging. Some examples of the social networks identified within the communicative ecology of the apartment building are as follows:

• National groupings are the most obvious form of informal syndication. Some residents, especially from the United States, move into the building as part of a group booking by the university. They then form networks on the basis of their common national origin, which provide peer support that helps them during the initial phase of orientation or even culture shock. Apart from the Americans, other strong groupings in the building are the Singaporeans and the Scandinavians.

• Study clusters are based on similar degree programs and academic disciplines, such as information technology (IT), engineering, and business. Participants explained that they think study groups would be beneficial to set up to prepare for exams and assignments and to exchange study notes, however, without help it is difficult to identify other residents who study in similar fields.

• A number of residents who either study IT or are highly computer literate volunteer to support other residents in hardware and software issues and look after the maintenance of the building's IT infrastructure. This group is paramount in developing an online community network that provides a resident directory and facilitates interaction and networking among residents as well as between residents and the on-site managers. This group is also well connected technically through online games and instant messenger applications.

• Other networks form around interest-based commonalities, such as the 'rugby league fans' or the 'movie buffs' who have repurposed the common room as a social space to watch sports broadcasts and host themed movie nights (e.g., the theme of the first series was 'movies made in Australia').

Selected members of these and other social networks become action researchers in their own right who pursue their individual project initiatives (study groups, movie nights, travel excursions, website design, etc.) by looking at the situation and context not just from one top–down global perspective, but from their personal perspective within their own terms of reference (see Chap. 1). The personal understanding that every participant brings to the networked effort ensures that participants see the relevance of their commitment at all times and that their reflection and action is not seen as additional work but an ongoing way to improve their quality of life. They also connect with the lead researcher to form a broader network of enquiry through individual face-to-face interaction, e-mails, and social gatherings. This meta-network drives the concerted effort toward cycles of community action and reflection and is the key to operationalising network action research.

Figure 6.2 is a rough sketch of a rich picture (Monk & Howard, 1998) of some of the networks in the communicative ecology of the building. It is important to note that the membership depicted here is an abstraction; it is overlapping and residents are in fact members of multiple networks. A tenant from Singapore who studies IT and enjoys watching movies would be—for the purpose of describing the research process—a member of four or more social networks in the communicative ecology of the building. The large grid in the background symbolises the cross-network linkages within and between social clusters that are much more capillary and fine-grained in reality. The selected action researcher of each cluster brings their knowledge of the micro-perspective and thus enlarges the social awareness of the macro-situation. The thought bubbles represent concerns or issues of a particular network. The action researcher establishes a rapport with each social network to form the meta-network of enquiry. Instead of imposing formal communication procedures, network action research utilises existing communicative structures in place within each network to facilitate an exchange of information between the meta-network and subnetworks and within subnetworks.

The dialogic nature of network action research recognises the hybrid qualities of networked individualism (Castells, 2001; Wellman, 2001, 2002; Wellman et al., 2003) as well as the social capital in and value of informal social gatherings such as a chat between roommates, neighbours, or friends over a cup of tea, or the small talk between parents while waiting to pick up their children from school. If community members are aware of the options available to them to feed results easily back into the meta-network, these types of interaction can be integrated in critical enquiry and reflection and harnessed for the benefit of a more representative, agile, current, and inclusive action research process. Although some scholars such as Putnam (2000) seem to underestimate the value of informal communication and engagement, others acknowledge the power that is evident in weak ties and informal social networks (Fischer, 2005; Florida, 2003; Granovetter, 1973; Sobel, 2002; Watters, 2003a).

Instead of relying solely on formal structures such as focus groups, steering committees, and workshops, a network action researcher seeks to also map, maintain, and harness informal social networks and thus fulfils the role of a community or neighbourhood worker who not only connects the community with researchers and sponsors but also networks the networks

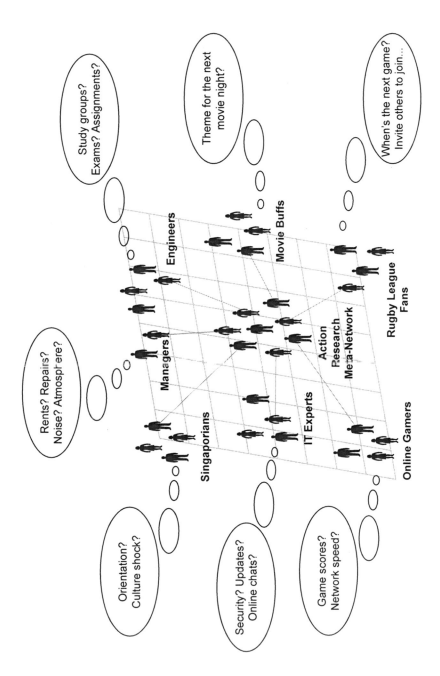

Figure 6.2. Rich picture of social networks and action research meta-network.

in an effort to develop the infrastructure necessary for sustainability and ongoing learning networks. These tasks and activities may resemble the labour-intensive groundwork that an ethnographer performs in the initial phases of community immersion, asset mapping, and trust-building (Tacchi, Slater, & Hearn, 2003). The use of technology tools may come to our aid and should be assessed to supplement existing communication channels and to document progress. Tools to operationalise network action research are discussed in more detail in Chapter 4, with a case study illustrating their use in Chapter 8.

Ethics

Network action research is a variation that is suitable to applying action research principles in virtual networks (cf. Howard, 2002), but it is also a way of conducting action research in place-based communities by acknowledging, mapping, and tapping into the social networks inherent in the local community. As such, network action research calls for a dual awareness of both the human and the technical dimension of social networks. Recognising, interpreting, and acting on the networked quality of the communicative ecology found in these communities will help action researchers to adhere to broader ethical imperatives that form the basis for any kind of action research initiative (Reason, 1998).

Instead of rigid and formal communication structures, the dispersed and intricate quality of operationalising network action research seeks to provide more natural and convenient means to engage the entire community. However, this process of engagement is not collectivistic in that it would try to capture everyone with the same message through the same channel; rather, it is about introducing a more democratic process that supports reflection and action outside the traditional knowledge generating institutions, entities, and individuals.

The bridge from critical enquiry and reflection toward action requires informed decision making and a way to allow the wider community to take responsibility for the decisions made. With the backing of the meta-network and tools that raise awareness about issues faced by the community at large, the networking quality brings about much more transparent procedures. It helps to focus on the dialectic thread in the informal, messy and sometimes chaotic day-to-day operations within the social networks that remains visible and meaningful.

Some action research methods such as workshops and community meetings can require a certain amount of confidence and willingness from community members in order to actively participate and be heard. Such methods have the potential to exclude or disempower disenfranchised members of the community who should have a say in the action research process to ensure that their needs and issues are adequately addressed. The more organic structures that network action research advocates allow minorities and less confident community groups to participate in ways that they may feel more familiar and comfortable with. Informality, flat hierarchy and the strategic channelling of information also enables participants to remain anonymous and to keep their input confidential to a degree that a public hearing or group discussion cannot.

Additionally, attributes of the communication strategies of network action research assist in maintaining a credible level of accountability and rigour by making the research process, observations and interpretations public, and discussable and challengeable by community participants. The history, process, and causal interrelationships are visible and illustrated through oral, written, and audiovisual narratives that provide a rich backdrop from which action and research reports can be derived. Some forms of action research are sometimes confused with consulting services. Having a rich ethnographic repository available that is generated by community participants through the process sets network action research clearly apart from consulting.

Conclusion

Action research puts a strong focus on people-centred and participatory methods and emphasises the evaluation of practical outcomes and achievements as measures of quality and rigour as opposed to publication outcomes and the ability to transfer and theorise research findings. Technology is practice-oriented and has in recent years advanced to offer more ergonomic interfaces, broader human interaction, and better user-centred applications. Many technologies that support human communication and social interaction have become ubiquitous in most developed parts of the world with associated effects on community and sociability. Yet, literature that reports on the potential methodological challenges and opportunities that recent technological advancements and societal changes pose for action research is rare.

Network action research is a methodological variation of action research that responds to the shifting quality of community interaction and is enacted by the same set of tools that initiated, and sustains, the societal shift toward networks in the first place. However, as Gilchrist (2004) rightly pointed out, 'networks in themselves do not guarantee improved decision making or better access to information' (p. 66), but—when keeping the imperative of inclusive and diverse networks in mind—they do provide an opportunity to interact with community members in a more contemporary and rewarding fashion that is more compatible with networked individualism.

It is important to understand network action research not as a technical methodology, but as a way to recognise the significance of human networks within communities and society. Technology can be a great aid to support the process, but this is not as essential as understanding and implementing the different strategic approach that network action research follows to facilitate critical enquiry, reflection, and action.

Chapter 7

Anticipatory Action Research

There is much research that examines the effects of new media or evaluates new media systems, but there is relatively little research into ways of testing the future social and cultural implications of the introduction of new media: in anticipating the opportunities and negative consequences of future media.[1] Most of the literature concerning the effects of technology on society (and the concurrent social shaping of technology) is historical, rather than forward-looking. The premise of anticipatory action research (AAR) is that by anticipating the ways in which innovations in new media might impact on existing social structures we can plan, prepare, make choices, and take responsibility for these future impacts.

Of course, as the future is not predetermined, we are left in a position where we can only anticipate certain likely impacts based on our current understanding, experiences, and structures. In fact, it is probable that many more impacts than those currently being debated in the literature will emerge. Meanwhile, it is appropriate to anticipate some of the likely impacts on users and potential users while the technology is still emerging. This would allow the **appropriate** design and policy development to take place, taking advantage of the desirable features of new media, while avoiding undesirable social impacts and the legislative problems encountered overseas.

Specifically, AAR applied to new media can accomplish the following:

- AAR allows designers, planners, and policymakers to anticipate the problems and opportunities that may lie ahead with the introduction of new media.

---

[1]There have been some notable exceptions, for example, Hiemstra (1983) and Hirschheim (1985).

119

- It promotes participation by users, service providers, and suppliers in the assessment of new technologies in order to anticipate issues, opportunities, and problems.

- AAR tests co-learning relationships among technical experts, systems and applications designers, users and researchers.

- AAR facilitates socially desirable processes and change in partnership with those organisations developing new media.

We begin this chapter by considering both traditional scenario-based future-oriented methodologies and more recently developed methodologies that can be used to generate new and alternative futures. The theoretical basis of anticipatory studies of new media is then discussed, focusing on the intentional and unintentional consequences of the introduction of information and communication technology systems (ICTs). Research into cell phone use is used to illustrate these intended and unintended effects, particularly studies that consider the social and cultural factors involved. A case study is provided that demonstrates how AAR could be used to assist a telecommunications provider and other groups understand, co-learn and co-develop applications and services for cell phones. The various steps involved in conducting a three-day workshop for this purpose are described. Finally, we suggest some uses of AAR in identifying emerging social innovations in cell phone use.

Future-Oriented Methodologies

There are many processes of human deliberation or enquiry that are future-oriented. Planning is perhaps the most taken for granted of these. Planning (and by implication designing) is an attempt to assert some control over the future. To the extent that one also collects information in the service of making plans then, future-oriented research is involved. In fact, there are many sophisticated future-oriented research/planning/action methodologies.

Technological forecasting (Martino, 2003) has a long tradition and different approaches can be discerned. Martino uses the term *technology futures analysis* to describe a range of methods that have been used for forecasting, road-mapping, foresight, and assessment of new technologies. These include quantitatively oriented analyses, qualitative approaches, and participatory techniques. Participatory approaches are very similar in operation to action research. Similarly scenario-building has also been employed in many fields (Van Notten, Rotmans, Van Asselt, & Rothman, 2003). These approaches may be qualitative or quantitative, or both. For example, Kok and van Delden (2004) combined narratives and quantitative models in building scenarios to combat the desertification of Spain. They ran a series of workshops with a variety of stakeholders to build a number of narrative scenarios (e.g., convulsive change, water shortage). Actual variables that could be measured were then derived from these scenarios and quantitative modeling undertaken. Modeling allowed decisions about land use and other factors to be deliberated.

The design of technologies increasingly focuses on what are often called *use scenarios*. Use scenarios are concrete descriptions of activities that users do as part of their life that can be used to drive the ongoing design and evaluation of new media and ICT systems. They have proved valuable research and design tools because, as narratives, they can move from general work process to detailed and specific interaction in a coherent and systematic way (Carroll, 2000; Manning, 2003). Use scenarios are often informed by qualitative research. For example, cultural probes (Gaver et al., 1999) are a method to elicit research data relevant for technology design in environments that are usually challenging to observe. Probes are functional products with open-ended functionality that support user-led innovation and capture examples of social interactions. They offer an authentic insight into the user environment. As explained in Chapter 3, participants may be given a variety of objects such as disposable cameras, notebooks, audiorecorders, maps, photo albums, and postcards to record aspects of their social life and environment. Although seemingly simple tools, use scenarios and cultural probes require a deep understanding of the environment they are representing, if they are to be useful (Carroll, 2000; Kristoffersen et al., 1998). Empirically informed use scenarios can nevertheless function as vehicles for supporting the creative meeting between users and designers. They can indicate the usefulness of a system relative to the background of the social environment, and they can be used to generate new metaphors and concepts that can drive the development of new kinds of social and mobile applications.

It is the generation of new metaphors and models of the future that underlies an important methodological distinction in the family of future-oriented methods. That is, some approaches seek to know and design the future through prediction based on extrapolation of past trends and events, whereas others seek to generate new and alternative futures (see Ramos, 2006). There are two important methods that exemplify the latter, namely Cooperrider's appreciative enquiry and Inayatullah's causal-layered analysis (CLA).

As explained in Chapter 3, appreciative enquiry is an organisational change methodology developed by David Cooperrider and others (Cooperrider et al., 2003; Cooperrider & Whitney, 2005; see also Thatchenkery & Chowdhry, 2007). It offers an alternative approach to achieving organisational growth and development to the more prevalent problem-solving methodologies. It is based in an understanding of organisations as living human systems, socially constructed; everything human is present in organisations, including emotion. Within the appreciative enquiry approach, problem identifiers and bringers are to be valued as they tell us things could be better: a problem is an expression of a frustrated dream. The social constructionist perspective on which appreciative enquiry is based suggests that, within organisations, what we talk about is what we see and we get more of what we pay attention to. Organisations are seen as being made up of many voices, all of which have valid perspectives. Appreciative enquiry moves from initial data collection to identify positive images of the future through to design and enactment of that future.

Inayatullah (1990, 1999, 2004) developed CLA as a future-and action-oriented approach to try to move beyond shallow surface analyses of problems. CLA is based on the assumption that the way in which one frames a problem changes the policy solution and the actors responsible for creating transformation. The method is based around enquiry in a number of levels of any problem. The levels included in CLA begin with the 'shallow' (trends, issues, etc.) and proceed through institutional, cultural, worldview, and mythic levels. CLA asks us to go beyond conventional framing of issues. However, it does not privilege a particular level. Moving up and down layers allows integration, analysis, and synthesis, and horizontally we can integrate different discourses, ways of knowing, and worldviews, thereby increasing the richness of the analysis. What often results are differences that can be easily captured in alternative scenarios; each scenario in itself, to some extent, can represent a different way of knowing. However, CLA orders the scenarios in vertical space. For example, taking the issue of the digital divide in schools can lead to a range of scenarios. A short-term scenario of increasing the number of ICTs in some schools is of a different order than a scenario that examines changes to curricula to build literacy or a scenario that invests in regional infrastructure or telecentres, or one that questions the value of ICTs and schooling in the first place.

More generally, Inayatullah (2006) suggested 'anticipatory action learning' occurs where:

• the goal is to create alternatives by questioning the future;

• objective and subjective may both be true;

- interaction between meanings and actions are the most crucial;

- language is constituted through creating communities of meaning and doing;

- the future is not fixed but continuously being revisited;

- reality is process-based;

- learning is based on programmed knowledge and questioning [the future] plus ways of knowing;

- learning occurs from doing, from experimentation;

- participation occurs—all participants are asked how they see the future; and

- a research agenda is developed with respondents—the future is mutually defined.

Applying these ideas to new media research then, we can define AAR for new media as a participant-oriented approach to research that seeks to generate action and knowledge within ongoing social contexts that involve the development and deployment of new media. The methodology also calls on action research processes that are designed to help participants (including sponsors and researchers) conceptualise the issues, problems, and opportunities that are capable of anticipation through the interaction of a range of expertise and needs. Hence, the information is shared between experts and nonexperts in a co-learning situation. AAR will normally proceed to implement insights that are generated, perhaps by input into design processes.

Theoretical Basis of Anticipatory Studies of New Media

In Chapter 2 we discussed the relationship between new media and society in terms of a number of principles, arguing for a co-evolutionary view. Even with this complex view of causality in the relationship between technological and social change, it is still possible to describe changes to social and individual domains that follow after changes to technologies, without asserting any causality in the strict sense of the word. An awareness that social change is implicated in technological change is particularly important for those responsible for introducing new technology.

Many theoretical models of social and technological change (Hearn & Mandeville, 2005; Rogers, 1962, 2003; Sproull & Keisler, 1991; Volti, 2006) speak of the 'consequences of technological change.' This enables us to speak meaningfully of anticipatory studies of new media. Importantly, as Hearn and Mandeville (2005) demonstrated, investment by organisations in ICTs may have intentional or unintentional consequences. For example, they suggest that ICTs can enhance productivity in five key ways.

1. ICTs can reduce the transaction costs of the enterprise.

2. ICTs can expand and enhance the relationship of the enterprise to its stakeholders.

3. ICTs 'informate' the processes of the enterprise making them 'smarter' and thus more robust, accurate, or attractive to clients.

4. ICTs stimulate completely new products or services for the enterprise.

5. ICTs enhance the reputation of the enterprise as progressive (regardless of the results of 1–4).

However, they also propose that ICTs can also have the opposite effect.

1. ICTs can increase the transaction costs of the enterprise.

2. ICTs can negatively affect the relationship of the enterprise to its stakeholders.

3. ICTs make the processes of the enterprise needlessly complex, in effect 'dumber,' and, therefore, less robust and attractive.

4. ICTs can eliminate existing products or services for the enterprise.

5. ICTs can damage the reputation of the enterprise as technocratic (regardless of the results of 1–4).

For example, despite the cost, the addition of information to a product or service—informating—can potentially make it more robust, attractive, or timely, and thus more competitive (Hearn & Mandeville, 2005). The control of plant growth by ICT-directed nourishment systems in order to better match market demand is an example of the way that basic industrial-age products have been made 'smarter' (Hearn & Mandeville, 2005). Market research is an example of a less direct way that informating can occur. Speciality retailers, for example, can track customer tastes via information technology and match the inventory of individual stores (Baily, 2004).

However, Hearn and Mandeville (2005) also highlighted the potential for information intensity to add significant costs to an enterprise without improving quality or lowering cost. The collection and analysis of information—for the sake of quality assurance, improved decision making, or simply because it is made possible by ICTs—can significantly increase transaction costs. Additionally, cheap information storage can add to the complexity of an organisation, its processes, and individual decision making, if information is simply collected rather then sorted. Increased informating can also lead to increased monitoring and surveillance.

Hearn and Mandeville (2005) also suggested that the costs of this info-glut scenario can be long term and difficult to assess. For example, the service sector's long-run productivity stagnation may be, in part, a function of this phenomenon. ICTs can hamper service quality in sectors (e.g., education) where the human element and expert personal interactions are still crucial.

Combining the idea of intended and unintended consequences with our model of the three layers of the communicative ecology (described in Ch. 2) gives us the matrix shown in Table 7.1., which draws on the example of the introduction of the domain name system.

Case Study

Recent research into cell phones can be used to illustrate how new media have both intended and unintended effects and to show how an AAR approach can be employed in both the design of cell applications, as well as shaping social and policy innovations around it (see e.g., Castells, Fernandez-Ardevol, LinchaunQui, & Araba, 2006; Goggin, 2006; Horst & Miller, 2006; May & Hearn, 2005; McGuigan, 2005).

Table 7.1. Model for thinking about consequences of new media: The case of the domain name system (adapted from Maher, 2006)

	Intended Consequences	Unintended Consequences
Technical	Domain names invented to make numerical internet provider easier to keep track of	Complex ASII coding regimes now required to deal with addresses from different languages
Content	Sort content into a fixed, simple, and flat categorisation scheme	Difficulty of establishing separate content categories (e.g., for porn)
Social	Establish simple internet governance regime	Create a new commodity boom and bust

Adapted from Maher (2006)

Cell phone penetration in most developed countries exceeds 80% of the population and in Australia, for example, the industry has a larger economic impact than free-to-air television, newspapers, and the publishing industry combined (Australian Mobile Telecommunications Association, 2004). Throughout the 1990s telecommunications carriers began to bring new services 'online.' Many of these new services have had dramatic social consequences. Plant's 2004 multi-nation study for Motorola is a notable investigation. Plant's study found that people as individuals and in groups are using cell phones in significant and unintended ways in their social and cultural lives, with the nature of the use very much related to the cultural and social specificities of their lives and the conditions in which they live. Horst and Miller (2006) found low-income Jamaicans use the cell phone to establish extensive networks, a practice identified as 'link-up,' mirroring a pattern that may be found in a wider range of Jamaican networking strategies, including the creation of spiritual and church communities, the search for sexual partners, and the coping strategies adopted by low-income households.

Ling's (2004) qualitative and observational research covers several countries, concluding that the cell phone has significantly affected notions of accessibility, safety and security, coordination of social and business activities in the everyday, and use of public places. Katz and Aakhus (2002) suggested that a number of implicit and explicit factors come in to play that determine cell use in a culture: social factors such as social roles, personal needs, reference group attraction/avoidance, networks of social ties, and synergies of additional participants in the network combine with technological aspects such as the phone's model, features, ease of use, and social appropriateness for use. Castells et al. (2006) presented global findings that contrast use in developing versus developed countries. They argued that the main difference between rich and poor users is that, among rich people cell telephony is a complementary technology, whereas for the poor it is an affordable substitute for the expensive, and sometimes nonexistent, fixed telephony. They chronicle many unintended social consequences, including changes to the way social networks are chosen, the development of instant communities of practice (flash mobs) for entertainment or activism, and the blurring of everyday-life roles.

Case Study of the Use of AAR for Mobile Phone Applications and Services

Given this background to the development of the cell phone, the following case study illustrates how AAR could be used to assist a telecommunication provider, and various user groups to understand, co-learn, and co-develop applications and services for cell phones.[2]

---

[2]The design here is an amalgam of a number of studies conducted by Greg Hearn.

The core of the AAR approach to this problem would be designed as a three-day intensive co-learning experience that essentially represented a microcosm of the various stakeholders in the evolution of new applications for the cell phone. For example, one would expect designers, telecommunications engineers, a demographic spread of consumers, special interest group representatives such as the disabled or particular ethnic groups, cell phone content developers, and retailers. Obtaining participants for this type of research is not always easy because there is a large time commitment involved. In contrast to randomly sampling with relatively shallow measurement (and time commitment) this approach uses purposive sampling and intensive involvement. Often, the stakeholders represent sections of the community of interest with a real stake and interest in the outcomes of the study. (Note: It is often by working through and with real social organisations that it is possible to recruit participants willing to be involved.)

Over the course of the three-day workshop, information about proposed applications and designs would be presented and the informed views of technical and systems experts presented to users in such a way as to facilitate the following:

- sharing of information and ideas;

- identification of the different standpoints of various stakeholders;

- construction of notions of possible futures;

- responses of potential consumers; and

- anticipation of social acceptance or rejection of new information services.

A typical workshop would consist of the steps described here.

1. **Identify personal and societal goals.** The workshops begin by encouraging participants to discuss their personal and societal goals both for the immediate future as well as the longer term future (the benchmark for 'the future' is usually 10 years time). These goals will later help the participants to define how future technology, including telecommunications services, may help them to achieve their goals and how technology may threaten these goals. These may be generated and shared using the collaborative tools described in Chapter 4.

2. **Remember the recent history of technology.** The recent history of technology is often discussed next. Participants recall the introduction over the past 20 years of microwave ovens; fax machines; cell telephones; colour television; smaller, more portable computers; photocopiers; Tupperware; computerised telephone exchanges; satellites; CDs as well

as social innovations such as the Anti-Discrimination Act; the Disabled Persons Act; and 'married women allowed to work in the public service.' This process is designed to illustrate the rapid development and adoption of technology and social innovations.

3. **Imagine future technology.** In small groups, the participants are then asked to 'imagine' what future technology, including new cell phone applications, might be like. The rationale of this stage is to invoke a more particular future context in the light of which the future new media might be examined.

4. **Information sessions.** An information session is typically conducted by representatives from cell phone companies and other service providers. This session explains new media, describes some of its applications, and offers an opportunity for questions and answers.

5. **Design the ideal system.** Once the future technological world is described and discussed, consideration is given to developing an ideal set of technologies that would help the participants achieve their goals as identified in the first session. New applications, features, and services are then discussed.

6. **Explore the issues.** The previous sessions are designed to lead to a more specific debate of the issues, potential problems, and opportunities associated with the implementation of new media. This final phase provides participants with an opportunity to reflect on the workshop as a whole and to consolidate and express insights and concerns. It represents a final forum for public debate.

7. **Analyse and process.** A unified thematic reporting of all seminars is often the most sensible way to characterise the seminars to nonparticipants. As Anderson (1987) argued, the narrative form is one effective way to portray the rich and complex information that emerges from qualitative research and is often used in scenario development (see Kok & van Delden, 2004). The thematic descriptions are constructed by the research team as conglomerations of all workshops, via a process of categorising themes from transcripts and notes. This categorisation is achieved via discussion and debate within the research team and is therefore clearly an interpretive process. Bias is at least partly constrained, however, by the reality of conflicting or different perspectives within the research team.

As well, these 'readable characterisations' are typically forwarded to a panel of participants to confirm them as faithful representations.

It is important to note that this process is interpretive only in terms of categorisation of themes, points, and issues. As a strict procedural rule, the researchers add no new insights or points during the assembly process. Furthermore, every point that is considered to be important enough to be included in transcripts by seminar participants is included in these descriptions. Therefore, the descriptions consist as much as possible of the exact words recorded in the workshop. They are edited to provide for continuity and to eliminate duplication. The narrative descriptions can then be used to build quantitative models or to inform the development of specific use scenarios (Carroll, 2000; Manning, 2003). For example, narratives often refer to constructs that can then be formally defined, measured, and modeled in relation to other variables. Use scenarios are concrete descriptions of activities that users do as part of their life that can be used to drive the ongoing design and evaluation of new media and ICT systems. They have proved valuable research and design tools because, as narratives, they can move from general work process to detailed and specific interaction in a coherent and systematic way. They can function as vehicles for supporting the creative meeting between users and designers, and they can be used to generate new metaphors and concepts that can drive the development of new kinds of new media applications.

Of course the claims that are made for the impact of a single, three-day event need to be kept in perspective. Changes in participants' understanding and intentions are but a small part of the overall flux of factors that shape the design of new telecommunications services. The participants are only a tiny microcosm of the universe of relevant shapers of policy and design in this field. A major challenge for AAR is the question of how to spread the outcomes achieved with the direct participants to a broader set of stakeholders. In terms of the diffusion of the results, the strength of action research becomes a potential weakness. The outcomes are experientially based and are therefore powerfully understood and integrated by participants. However, the experiential nature of outcomes also means that others without the experience are less likely to accept them when compared to diffusion of scientific outcomes, for example, that rely on authority and logic. In this regard we find the potential of new media to 'spread the experience and reflection' as a frontier worth exploring through wikis, blogs, and so on—as per the discussion in Chapter 4.

Uses of AAR

As waves of innovation in technology come upon us, there is an important need for research that helps to prepare for the future and even to influence it. AAR can be used, for example, to identify emerging spaces of social innovation in order to further enhance socially responsible, social innovations in cell phone use in terms of the following:

- Applications: e.g., short message service, multimedia message service, games, information services, direct marketing, e-mail, internet, location-based services, e-democracy, downloads, consumer assistance, business, education, and medical applications.

- Interfaces: e.g., gestural or voice control, better visual design.

- Aesthetics: e.g., the 'aestheticisation in everyday life' through fashion, membership, identity; and the 'insertion' of increasingly miniaturised technologies into bodies and the everyday.

- Cutting-edge technologies: e.g., temporal ad hoc networks; 'spontaneous and opportunistic human behaviour and practice'; 'practical telepathy'; de-compartmentalisation of media technologies for voice, camera, printing, recording and sharing, and data.

Conclusion

AAR for new media was defined as a participant-oriented approach to research, which seeks to generate action and knowledge within ongoing social contexts that involve the development of new media. AAR proposes that by anticipating the ways in which innovations in new media could impact on existing social structures we can plan, prepare, make choices, and take responsibility for these future impacts. We suggested that it is most effective to anticipate some of the likely impacts on users and potential users while a technology is still emerging. This allows the development of appropriate design and policies that take advantage of the desirable features of new media, while avoiding undesirable social impacts and potential legislative problems. We considered that, applied to new media, AAR can accomplish the following:

- It can allow designers, planners, and policymakers to anticipate the problems and opportunities that may lie ahead with the introduction of new media.

- Participation by users, service providers, and suppliers in the assessment of new technologies in order to anticipate issues, opportunities, and problems is promoted.

- Co-learning relationships among technical experts, systems and applications designers, users, and researchers are tested.

- AAR facilitates socially desirable processes and changes in partnership with those organisations developing new media.

A number of future-oriented methodologies were reviewed, including technological forecasting, scenario-building, and use scenarios. Use scenarios and methods such as cultural probes were considered valuable research and design tools because, as narratives, they can move from general work process to detailed and specific interaction in a coherent and systematic way. They can also support creative meeting processes between users and designers, and generate new metaphors and concepts that can drive the development of new kinds of social and mobile applications of new media.

Appreciative enquiry and CLA were seen as important new methodologies because they use participatory methods to generate new and alternative futures, and allow organisations and problems to be probed at a much deeper level than usual. CLA enables us to go beyond the conventional framing of issues and to integrate different discourses, ways of knowing and worldviews, thereby increasing the richness of the analysis. Inayatullah's anticipatory action learning methodology is valuable because it requires action research processes that assist participants to conceptualise the issues, problems, and opportunities that are capable of anticipation through the interaction of a range of expertise and needs, and involves experts and nonexperts sharing information in a co-learning situation.

We demonstrated the value of anticipatory studies of new media in identifying the intentional and unintentional consequences of the introduction of ICTs such as cell phones, including effects on cost and greater information overload and complexity. Our case study demonstrated how AAR could be used to assist service providers and other groups to understand, co-learn, and co-develop new media applications and services. This co-learning experience would facilitate:

- sharing of information and ideas;

- identification of the different standpoints of various stakeholders;

- construction of notions of possible futures;

- responses of potential consumers; and

- anticipation of social acceptance or rejection of new media and information services.

Although AAR has many strengths, we also acknowledged its limitations and challenges. They include how to spread the outcomes achieved with participants to a broader set of stakeholders, and how to facilitate acceptance of outcomes by those who were not part of the intensive AAR experience. This highlights the importance of informed choice in technological decision making and the need for appropriate processes that allow technology suppliers and service providers to know and understand the social needs of community members and participants and to enable those needs to be addressed in the design and implementation of technology.

Part III

Case Studies and Application

Chapter 8

Alleviating Poverty Through ICTs in South and Southeast Asia

Action research often lays claim to emancipative aspirations. Certainly, it at least embraces work in contexts that may be challenging in terms of distributive justice or access to material or informational resources. This chapter illustrates the use of action research for new (and traditional) media in just such a context. Contemporary development and globalisation discourse tends to consider information, communication, and technology as important elements of social and economic inclusion. The problem of a *digital divide* is considered a social one. However, the assumption that access to information and communication technologies (ICTs) may bring benefits to poor people is primarily based on the perceived socioeconomic benefits of ICT proliferation and use in developed, rather than developing contexts.

There is evidence that ICTs hold both negative and positive possibilities in terms of benefiting the information poor, and it is the larger political, economic, social, cultural, and gender contexts of many of these situations that can lead to unequal and in some cases limited benefits from ICT use. It is necessary to pay careful attention to the local social networks alongside the local technological networks; combined they might be seen as 'local information networks' (Nair, Jennaway, & Skuse, 2006).

After introducing two ICT projects conducted in south and southeast Asia, this chapter begins with a discussion of these issues. The concept of *digital divide* is critiqued and we consider the key issues and gaps that emerge for ICTs and poverty reduction, with an emphasis on voice. We outline three different understandings of the potential role of voice in understanding ICTs and poverty: (a) in local content creation and voice poverty; (b) in terms of research methods, monitoring and evaluation, and impact assessment; and (c) in terms of access and use, mixing old and new media, and advocacy. In the remainder of the chapter, we present examples of the use of ethnographic action research (EAR) in the two research projects.

The ictPR Project

In mid-2002 UNESCO called for proposals for innovative applications of ICTs for poverty reduction in south Asia. The project they funded was called ICTs for Poverty Reduction (ictPR), and the research was conducted by researchers from Queensland University of Technology (QUT) and the London School of Economics (see Slater & Tacchi, 2004) from late 2002 to 2004. Nine local initiatives were supported—five in India and one each in Bangladesh, Sri Lanka, Nepal, and Bhutan. Of the nine project sites, eight contributed research data to a centralised research website, which continued beyond the funded period. Each local initiative had a local researcher who was trained in EAR (Tacchi, Slater, & Hearn, 2003). As explained in Chapter 5, this methodology takes an ethnographic approach to action research, through the use of methods such as participant observation, in-depth interviews, and writing fieldnotes. Research is fed into the development of local initiatives in an ongoing cycle of *plan, do, reflect.* EAR is therefore a methodology that combines research with project development. It has been designed particularly for ICT for development projects, and was largely developed and refined through its first application and testing in ictPR.

A basic principle of EAR is that in order to understand the potential and real impacts of individual ICTs in any given situation, you need to place this experience within a broader understanding of the ways in which communication and access to, and the use of, information is structured in people's lives. Each instance of communication or information use takes place within an already existing communicative ecology, and each place has its own unique communicative ecology. Each local use of a media technology takes place in complex information and communication environments. These environments are linked to other media and social and cultural networks that need to be understood if particular instances of use are to be analysed and learned from. Using ethnographic methods, the ictPR EAR researchers conducted research within this holistic framework. They sought to understand their project and improve it, based on a good understanding of the wider contexts in which they worked.

Although not totally successful in each case, this research has proved important for individual project development locally. At the same time, comparison of research data across the sites helped us to learn from each other's experiences. More than this, the process of training all the researchers in the same methodology, and storing and discussing research data in a centralised location, provided the opportunity to compare and contrast data, and develop significant insights into the potential role of ICTs in poverty reduction. These insights are based on data from across the sites, which use a range of media mixes, approaches, resources and organisational structures. Indeed, the implementation of the methodology has varied across projects, with some spending considerable time conducting research prior to the intervention, and others taking a far more action research approach, testing and adapting (experimenting) through the implementation of the project and project development methodology at the same time.

The ictPR initiatives encompassed a wide range of technological, social, and organisational combinations. This allowed us to investigate some of the different directions that community ICTs can take, as well as the ways in which different media and media mixes could be related to poverty reduction. To demonstrate the range of applications of ICTs, we briefly describe two of the nine initiatives:

Nabanna: Networking Rural Women and Knowledge (Baduria, West Bengal, India) uses grassroots processes to build information-sharing networks among low-income, rural women. Networking is done face to face and through Web and print-based mechanisms, linking women and their groups from different parts of the municipality.

Namma Dhwani Local ICT Network (Budikote, Karnataka, India) combines a radio studio, an audio cable network that delivers radio to local households, and a telecentre with computers and other multimedia tools. It is run by and centred on a network of women's self-help groups and linked to a local development resource centre. Radio programming addresses local information and communication needs, drawing on productions by local volunteers as well as a variety of multimedia resources, like websites and CD-ROMs.

UNESCO supplied all nine initiatives with computers and internet access. Although some quickly integrated internet use into their work, others struggled with this process because of connectivity or other technical challenges. All of the sites were also supplied with digital cameras, multifunctional printers, and digital pen drives, and in some cases webcams and microphones.

The Finding a Voice Project

The research project Finding a Voice: Making Technological Change Socially Effective and Culturally Empowering builds on the ictPR project. It is funded by the Australian Research Council, UNESCO, and the UN Development Program (UNDP). It began in 2006 and will run through 2009 and is taking place in India, Nepal, Sri Lanka, and Indonesia. The project is a partnership between researchers at QUT, the University of Adelaide, UNESCO (south Asia), and UNDP (Indonesia). The research is investigating how processes for participatory local content creation might be developed and implemented in each study site, and what the consequences of this might be. It is focusing on how to encourage ordinary people to engage in local content creation using new and emerging technologies like computers, internet, and cell phones as well as more traditional media like radio and video. Other key research questions are as follow:

- How can all of these media work together in the community multimedia and telecentres developed by UNESCO and UNDP across south Asia and Indonesia?

- How can these technologies and centres be used more effectively for poverty reduction?

- How can media be used creatively for positive social change?

- What role can trained EAR researchers play in extending the use of ICTs to the poorest?

A network of 15 ICT centres (or group of centres) has been established across four countries—Sri Lanka, Nepal, India, and Indonesia. Just as in the ictPR project, the centres are not all the same, but all have computers and internet connectivity. Some are community computer centres (sometimes called telecentres), whereas others are community radio stations, or video centres with access to local cable TV networks. Additionally, two community libraries in Nepal are part of the network. Here we briefly describe two of the initiatives, both of which were also part of the earlier ictPR project.

Tansen Community Media Centre (Tansen, Nepal) works with local youth from poor families and traditionally marginalised caste groups, training them in audiovisual production and computer and internet skills. The centre is made up of a digital production studio and a computer/internet access centre and is linked to a local cable TV network. Participants' audio and audiovisual programming is aired on the cable TV network and local community radio stations.

ICT Learning Centre for Women (Seelampur, New Delhi, India) is an open learning centre for girls and women located at an inner-city madarsa (Islamic school) in a high-density, low-income area of New Delhi. A range of interactive multimedia content has been developed and used to support vocational and life-skills training and to build awareness of health issues and livelihood opportunities.

As with the ictPR research, we are exploring how different combinations of media work together. We are working with the network of centres to develop and provide training and support in the use of media and ICTs in the creation and distribution of locally produced content. We are developing these activities and collecting data on them through a team of locally embedded EAR researchers.

Poverty Reduction and the Role of ICTs

The concept *digital divide* has increasingly been questioned. This concept—which simply describes the access or lack of access to computers and digital information—is less useful than *digital inequality* (DiMaggio & Hargittai, 2001; Selwyn, 2004) or *digital inclusion* as a means of describing the relationships among ICTs, cultural agency, and social contexts. There are complex interrelationships between social and technological networks, and issues of access versus effective use or *engagement* (Warschauer, 2003). Within the development arena, a gap exists between technology and development that some researchers argue is a more fitting focus of our attention than digital divides between developed and developing countries. This gap is caused by the rapid evolution and expansion of technologies and technological determinist responses from development agencies (West & Selian, 2005). However, reasoned and pragmatic approaches to and discussions of ICTs and development have emerged that do consider both context and relevance and these are being addressed by many agencies, including UNESCO.

A major problem has been with the way digital divide policy debates have tended to focus almost exclusively on macro issues, assuming that new media is beneficial to all citizens and the only barrier to closing the gap is lack of physical access. Many studies have shown this is overly simplistic and there is growing recognition that access is not only about physical access but needs to be broadened to include awareness, engagement and use, motivations to use technologies, barriers to use, and, more broadly, issues of participation in networks, societies, and cultures (DiMaggio & Hargittai, 2001; Jenkins, 2006; Katz & Rice, 2002; Rice et al., 2001; Selwyn, 2004; Warschauer, 2003). Furthermore, although new technologies can provide new and interesting ways for civic, political, and community involvement, they may also widen existing gaps 'further blocking access to those already without access' (Rice & Haythornthwaite, 2006, p. 93).

However, a comparison of U.S. and European Union (EU) policy documents through a computer-assisted text analysis demonstrated a clear tendency in both U.S. and EU policy to frame the digital divide and issues of access in economic and market-based terms (Stewart, Gil-Egui, Tian, & Pileggi, 2006). Additionally, dominant technological configurations of new media are promoted in intergovernmental discussions and assumed to be the most effective, whereas other configurations are rarely presented (Mansell, 2002). The focus tends to be on markets, governance, and regulation, whereas micro-level issues aim for broad productivity gains such as employment and income rather than broader capability concepts such as democratic participation, strengthening civil society, and promotion of rights. We can perhaps learn from Warschauer (2003), who focused on ICT for social inclusion (and used the term *digital inclusion* rather than *digital divide*), and attempts to reorient the concept of the digital divide away from a focus on gaps to be bridged by providing computers and internet access, to a focus on 'social development issues to be addressed through the effective integration of ICTs into communities, institutions, and societies' (Warschauer, 2003, p. 9).

An important point is to find out how to integrate ICTs into communities. Does effective integration mean more than simply providing training in computing and allowing people to use the internet to access information from elsewhere? If so, can they be integrated in ways that prioritise local content creation at the community level? Can they be used to enable people to find their voice and, importantly, to be heard? Despite the interactive potential of new media technologies, dominant configurations tend to follow a broadcast model of one to many. Interactivity is rarely explored innovatively and two-way flows of information are rarely promoted. We cannot assume that access to information delivered via new technologies equates to effective use—delivery of information does not mean that people are thereby informed in any meaningful way. Integration of ICTs into communities and people's engagement with those ICTs requires the development of a new media literacy if the objective is to provide not only access, but the ability to analyse, critically evaluate, and use ICTs and the information and knowledge it can carry, along with the ability to create content (Livingstone, 2004).

If we accept that ICTs have a role to play in poverty reduction and development, the key issues that emerge for ICTs and development today are nicely summarised by Feek (2003) into a series of 10 issues and gaps. Table 8.1 combines four of the issues and gaps identified in Feek's review of work on the applications of ICTs to processes of human development with the key issues raised through the ictPR research project (Slater & Tacchi, 2004).

The first issue can be seen as one of *inclusion and freedom of expression*. The range and variety of the voices that are heard in the Information Society along with the information that is available and circulated should surely be scrutinised (Article 19, 2005) if we are pushing new ICTs with little or no cognizance of existing and functioning communicative ecologies (see Ch. 2, this volume) and information networks, both social and technological. If

Table 8.1. Issues and Gaps in ICTs and Poverty-Reduction Projects

Issue	Gap
Voice vs. information: emphasis on 'pushing' information, not enough attention on the use of ICTs to communicate a range of different 'voices' related to any issue.	Insufficient use of ICTs to increase 'voice' in development and communication of ideas, information, and perspectives.
Technical vs. content: emphasis on technical infrastructure rather than content—the development and communication of ideas, information, and thinking specific to particular contexts, by and for those people.	Insufficient attention to prioritising local content development.
Discreet vs. integrated communication: tendency is to view new ICTs as separate from older ones. Strategies and programs that mix them may hold more promise.	Insufficient incorporation of new ICTs with older communication technologies.
Potential vs. proof: program managers and agencies have insufficient tools to evaluate weaknesses in program design and make adjustments mid-stream.	Insufficient attention to ongoing and embedded evaluation of the impact of new ICTs.

given a voice, what do poor people say about their experiences of poverty, and their needs?

The second issue draws attention to the need for a shift in thinking away from ICTs as merely infrastructure for the delivery of information, to creative tools and communication channels that can be used to create *and distribute local content.* Research shows that strengthening participation in content creation is a particularly high priority in poor countries (FAO, 2003; Slater & Tacchi, 2004), where the introduction of new technologies can increase, rather than reduce, inequality (Mansell & Wehn, 2003; F. Rodriguez & Wilson, 1999; UNDP, 2001).

The third issue is one of *mixing technologies.* The tendency is to view new ICTs as separate from older ones while strategies and programs that mix them can be seen to hold more promise. There is insufficient incorporation of new ICTs with older communication technologies, such as radio.

The fourth issue is that of *embedded and ongoing evaluation.* We argue that the way indicators are developed and impacts are measured needs to be rethought, and that the capacity of local ICT initiatives to conduct continuous evaluation needs to be built. The examples presented in this chapter illustrate the value of using EAR to address the need for embedded and ongoing participatory research and evaluation in ICTs for poverty alleviation initiatives.

ICTs, Poverty and Voice

Voice, Freedom of Expression and Local Content Creation

Development theory and practice has long recognised the importance of social context, communication, and participation in facilitating poor people to realise a broad range of human rights—to development, education, health, and well-being (Servaes, 1999). Voicing their needs is now seen as fundamental to most processes of human development (Chambers, 1995; De Haan, 1999; Gardner & Lewis, 1996). The rapid emergence and new articulations of ICTs in marginalised communities therefore suggest a need to understand and develop culturally appropriate interfaces not simply for creating channels for information to be delivered to marginalised people, but for the local creation of local content if there is to be meaningful uptake of ICTs among the most marginalised and disadvantaged in developing countries.

New media technologies are said to combine producer and user roles rather than separate them, for example, in the notion of the *produser* (Bruns, 2006). Participation is a key factor in what Henry Jenkins (2006) called a new 'participatory culture.' This is particularly interesting in relation to questions of engagement, self-representation, and social, political, and cultural participation. The idea that new technologies can enable new forms of 'vernacular creativity' (Burgess, 2006) through the use of computers, software, and peripherals such as digital cameras apparently places everyone with access—physical, economic, cognitive, affective, political, cultural, and other relevant forms of access along with requisite skills—(Rice et al., 2001) in the position of a potential producer. Livingstone (2004) suggested that of the four components of media literacy—access, analysis, critical evaluation, and content creation—the latter two are the most critical to a democratic agenda.

One of the problems with newer ICTs is the lack of formats for local content creation that do not depend on traditional literacies. So, although community radio, for example, has many formats for programmes, a tele-centre made up of a room full of computers and peripherals provides few obvious options for creative activities that do not require high levels of traditional literacy and computer literacy—the danger of reinforcing the participation gap is clear here. Technologies themselves, when introduced into a community, can widen gaps between rich and poor members because these technologies do not come bundled with 'factors that cannot be leapfrogged: namely, education and training, basic human and service infrastructure, and the human interaction essential to development and security' (West & Selian, 2005, p. 3). So, it is not simply about introducing technologies and encouraging content creation and voice, the process needs to allow for active inclusion, education, and capacity-building, and needs to be creative and imaginative in its use of technologies, as well as relevant and context specific.

Voices of the Poor: Participatory Approaches to Monitoring and Evaluation

Given the aspects of social change that might be significant outcomes of ICT for development initiatives, the lack of embedded and ongoing evaluation becomes a real issue. Sen's long-term analysis of development and poverty and his emphasis on capabilities has permeated the work of UN agencies, development departments, and donors (Sen, 2000, 2002). However, monitoring and evaluation is not well geared to capture changes in capabilities and substantive freedoms, given its orientation to the measurement of *impacts* that are more related to increasingly outmoded indicators of poverty and income deprivation alone. Not only do we need to rethink how we set indicators and measure impact, we need to build the capacity of local ICT initiatives to conduct ongoing evaluation (formative, summative, and ongoing), in such a way that they can adapt to research findings that they both own and understand. We need to be able to develop new indicators to track aspects such as risk, vulnerability, social exclusion, access to social and cultural capital, and the ability to have a voice and to be heard.

For the Finding a Voice research project, a local EAR researcher working within a community radio station and community learning centre (CLC) in Nepal recently reported on an impromptu group meeting in a rural area of Nepal with a group of women attending an informal education class in the local CLC. He asked these women what it meant to be poor in this place, and asked them who the poor were. The women, all older than age 30, identified themselves as poor for a range of reasons, including having no land, having to work very hard in others' fields for little pay, having no education and low levels of literacy so that they are unable to benefit from what society has to offer—including what they saw as not being full citizens because they are not able to avail themselves of services such as sending their children to school. For these women, all of this results in them having no trust in society, and in high levels of social exclusion:

[The women told me that] not having an education is poverty because it is related to the opportunity for work, equal wages, and social stigma in the society. Not having any source of income is poverty. The issue of citizenship is also the cause of poverty. Their community is living in this place since 70 years but they are not getting the citizenship. When the election comes they are encouraged to vote and the political parties manage to allow a vote for them, but later when the election ends they come back to the same position. When they wanted to send their children to government school, the school needs a birth certificate of the children and for that the family member must have the Nepali citizenship and due to these problems they do not send their children to school. (Deepak Koirala fieldnote December 12, 2006, Madhawaliya CLC, Nepal)

Participatory methods encompass a plethora of approaches to both research and action, and the EAR researcher cited here used one such approach: letting the women themselves tell us, from their own lived experience, what poverty is, and what it feels like. The World Bank's Voices of the Poor research project (Narayan et al., 2000) drew particularly on the Participatory Poverty Assessment method, and was based on the premise that the poor themselves are the true experts on poverty. Narayan and Petesch (2002) stressed that participatory research methods are interactive, open-ended, exploratory, and most importantly a partnership between local people and researchers, working together to identify problems, collect data, conduct analysis, and develop follow-up actions. Interestingly, the study had to be undertaken on a very large scale (Voices of the Poor collected together the voices of 60,000 poor men and women, from 60 countries) to be taken seriously in the generally quantitative research paradigm of the World Bank.

Mixing Media: Having a Voice and Being Heard

In communication for development, older communication technologies such as radio and TV have a continuing relevance. Whereas newer ICTs have in some ways simply created confusion about development priorities (West & Salian, 2005), older media technologies have a much clearer and more developed role. Community media and particularly community radio have well-established models and formats. Access to and participation in new ICTs such as the internet and the World Wide Web (WWW) are more problematic (cell phones are an exception in many places; see Horst & Miller, 2006). West and Salian argue that the development of new

ICT initiatives, such as telecentres, should not occur at the expense 'of reinforcing the continued functioning and maintenance of older, proven modes of communication' (West & Salian, 2005, p. 38), while Dagron (2001) argued that although the potential of the internet is great in development communication, the most promising developments happen where it is combined with radio.

Despite the promise of new media as participatory, on their own these media tend to stand out as difficult to access, and even more difficult to engage with in many contexts. James (2004) argued that a model based on *intermediaries* has far more chance for success than the flawed and often stagnant model of the fixed-location telecentre (a room containing computers). By intermediaries, James referred to both people and media—so in the case of the Kothmale Community Radio and Internet Project in Sri Lanka (an often cited example of a rural radio station that has internet-connected computers, and is one of the Finding a Voice study sites), it is both the radio presenter (the person) who mediates between the information gathered from the WWW, and the radio itself as the medium that delivers that information to a large number of people (Slater et al., 2002). Girard (2003) also strongly advocated using the medium of radio to access the power of new ICTs and the internet.

The Use of EAR in South and Southeast Asian ICT Initiatives

EAR and the concept of communicative ecologies has been used by local EAR researchers across the networks of community multimedia centres (CMCs) in south and southeast Asia that make up the ictPR and Finding a Voice research projects. The concept of the communicative ecology was explained in Chapter 2. Here we look at how, in practice, it is utilised and the kinds of insights it helps the EAR researchers to develop.

Local EAR researcher Sita Adhikari works as the EAR researcher in two rural community libraries in Nepal for the Finding a Voice project. These libraries each have a computer with internet connections. Sita has undertaken a series of interviews with local individuals and groups to explore their communicative ecologies, and has worked up maps that represent these. Figure 8.1 shows Sita's communicative ecology map for Sabita, a community library volunteer. Figure 8.2 shows Sita's communicative ecology map for Firali, an indigenous Tharu woman. Sabita's main responsibility is to help her mother with housework. She teaches some blind students, and volunteers in the community library, spending sometimes the best part of a day there. She has access to and uses a range of ICTs, for a variety of purposes as shown in Figure 8.1. Firali, on the other hand, has limited

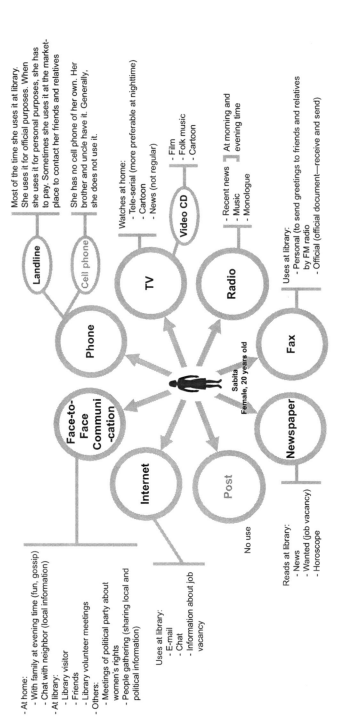

Figure 8.1. Communicative ecology map of community library volunteer, from EAR researcher Sita Adhikari, Chitwan, Nepal.

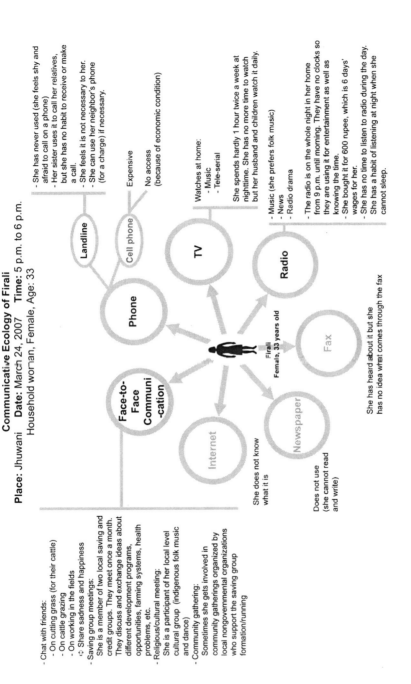

Communicative Ecology of Firali

Place: Jhuwani **Date:** March 24, 2007 **Time:** 5 p.m. to 6 p.m.

Household woman, Female, Age: 33

Phone

Landline
- She has never used (she feels shy and afraid to call on a phone)
- Her sister uses it to call her relatives, but she has no habit to receive or make a call.
- She feels it is not necessary to her.
- She can use her neighbor's phone (for a charge) if necessary.

Cell phone
Expensive
No access (because of economic condition)

TV
Watches at home:
- Music
- Tele-serial

She spends hardly 1 hour twice a week at nighttime. She has no more time to watch but her husband and children watch it daily.

Radio
- Music (she prefers folk music)
- News
- Radio drama

- The radio is on the whole night in her home from 9 p.m. until morning. They have no clocks so they are using it for entertainment as well as knowing the time.
- She bought it for 600 rupee, which is 6 days' wages for her.
- She has no time to listen to radio during the day. She has a habit of listening at night when she cannot sleep.

Face-to-Face Communication

- Chat with friends:
  - On cutting grass (for their cattle)
  - On cattle grazing
  - On working in the fields
  - Share sadness and happiness
- Saving group meetings:
  She is a member of two local saving and credit groups. They meet once a month. They discuss and exchange ideas about different development programs, opportunities, farming systems, health problems, etc.
- Religious/cultural meeting:
  She is a participant of her local level cultural group (indigenous folk music and dance)
- Community gathering:
  Sometimes she gets involved in community gatherings organized by local nongovernmental organizations who support the saving group formation/running

Internet
She does not know what it is

Newspaper
Does not use (she cannot read and write)

Fax
She has heard about it but she has no idea what comes through the fax

Firali
Female, 33 years old

Figure 8.2. Communicative ecology map of Tharu woman, from EAR researcher Sita Adhikari, Chitwan, Nepal.

access to and knowledge of newer ICTs, is illiterate, and spends her days farming her own small piece of land plus working for other land owners to earn some money, collecting grass to feed cattle or taking cattle to graze, and caring for her home and family. Firali has never used a telephone.

The comparison between these two women's communicative ecologies raised all sorts of questions and issues for the EAR researcher to reflect on and find out more about. Sita's fieldnote shows her reflecting on the challenges this comparative exercise confronted her with:

> My feelings:
> I realised the differences between those people who have access to new information and communication and those who have no access to it by undertaking two types of communicative ecology—one from library volunteers and the other from uneducated Tharu women.
> The library volunteers have access to newspapers, internet, fax, video, etc., but the Tharu women have no access to all of them. . . . Even some feel shy and afraid to use a landline phone. They know nothing about the internet and the fax. When I asked about it they started to laugh and asked me, what did I mean? . . . Firali asked me to arrange a call, she wanted to talk with me on the phone for the experience.
> I realise the importance of the women's groups and their meetings for such villager women. Those women are taking more practical information through group meetings [than through ICTs] . . . another important point that they shared with me was that they were invited by the local development organisation and NGO's [nongovernmental organisations] who are helping them to form and run those groups. So they are getting a chance to get involved in community meetings and gatherings. (Sita Adhikari fieldnote March 24, 2007, Chitwan, Nepal)

Understanding the lived experiences and communication channels and flows of people in the area is important if Sita's EAR work is to usefully inform the work of the community libraries. This research can help to ensure that their activities are appropriate and effective for as many people as they can reach. It is a real danger that ICT initiatives can widen the gap between those who have access to information and knowledge and who are able to participate in the processes that affect their lives, and those who do not. Sita's EAR work is dedicated to understanding the lives and information needs of those who have the least access to information and communication networks, and think about how the work of the community library might be made relevant to them. She is building her understanding of the people and places she works within—and as a local women, is immersed in—and sharing her research findings with her colleagues in the community libraries to ensure they listen to the voices of those less likely to enter the community libraries or speak out.

Creative Engagement

Sita is also working to involve community members in the creation of locally produced content—so far this is in the form of wall newspapers, but in the near future they hope to make short micro-documentaries or digital stories (see Ch. 9, this volume). Emphasis on local and participatory content creation in the Finding a Voice project stems directly from the research findings of the earlier ictPR project. The ictPR research (Slater & Tacchi, 2004) demonstrated the potential of developing local content and doing so in a participatory way. It demonstrated the benefits in identifying and nurturing the innovative, adventurous, and pleasurable ways in which community members might explore the possibilities of media and the mixes of traditional and new media—especially in terms of local content creation. Instead of merely seeing these technologies as tools for accessing and circulating useful information, participants engaged with them in far more complex and creative ways, combining information, entertainment, and skills development as a pleasurable activity in its own right. Content creation was found to be a powerful means of engaging people with media technologies, enabling participants to voice their concerns and share and learn locally relevant knowledge and information.

Here we consider some examples from ictPR of what we might term *creative engagement.* The short digital film, *Sonali Tantu,* was created by some women in the Nabanna project. The women decided that they wanted to make a film after a visit by one of the ictPR research coordinators, who had brought a video camera and a camera operator to make a short film about EAR. Their interest led project workers as well as participants to develop new skills and think about how to combine the limited media technologies they had access to in creative ways:

> As usual I was conducting a group discussion, more of an informal chat really, with some of the [women] on the various steps of jute process-ing. This lead to an idea of a movie. . . . As they have seen us using the digital [still] camera before, they asked me how to go about it. . . . The things that came to my mind first are how efficient this camera is to make a film. It has a very little [memory] space and is without sound. Therefore, we have to record the voiceover separately. The quality of the sound recorder is bad. However, their enthusiasm encouraged me to try to give their idea a proper shape. I [wanted them to make the

film themselves] therefore I asked them to do the whole thing. First, we discussed the various steps of the production process . . .

Day 1

[We] started at 11:30 a.m. for our first shoot. Mita selected the field, which was 5 minutes away from the ICT centre . . . it took 5 minutes by road and 15 more minutes on the field. . . . Finally we reached the right place and took the shot. . . . It was a sunny day, when we reached the centre the other girls said that they never knew that filmmaking is such a tough job. Then Geeta transferred the movie into the computer. It was very small, it got pixillated as we tried to see it on a bigger size. Well, again we have to go there. All our efforts were in vain. We decided to do it on the next day.

Day 4

To take the shots of the drying process was very easy. All the roads, houses, roofs were full of fibers. . . . On that day whole lot of people asked us how we will be able to make a film with these small shots. The girls said 'come to the centre after a month and see what we have done.' They were so confident, but I was not sure how actually . . . to edit the film. The movie editing software that I know is not available here; on the other hand I do not know how to edit an MPEG movie. Anyway, I was confident about that I could solve the problem some way.

Day 6

This was the last thing which need to be shot—the trading part. In a near by bus stand there is a place where all the farmers come and sale their jute and it is transported to various places. Girls went there to take their final shot . . . after each and every shot there was a complaint from the [women] that the memory stick is so small that they can not capture the whole thing. The shooting is almost complete. Now we have to edit the film. We have to incorporate some voice over . . . [and] make a title card. I have finally decided to make the movie in Window MovieMaker. We had already made a trial version. They suggested that jute sticks should be shown separately and their use, if possible . . . Nilima and Yashoda have already prepared a write up on jute production. We hope to finish the film after the puja holidays. (Extracts from Nabanna EAR researcher's notes on the filmmaking process quoted in full in Slater & Tacchi, 2004, pp. 13–14)

Despite the challenges facing the women, the film was made and can be viewed at http://cirac.qut.edu.au/ictpr/downloads/SonaliTantu. WMV.

In this way we can see that basic skills development can be achieved effectively through creative engagement with media technologies. Additionally, and importantly, the level of media literacy that is developed through such exercises is significant. Participants learn how to create media content, and in the process, they learn how the media content they otherwise consume is created.

In Seelampur, within the first few weeks of project operation, there was a strong demand from participants to explore technologies that they had only recently encountered. The project workers showed the women a series of informational CD-ROMs that they had made covering tailoring, candlemaking, and other activities. The intention had been to encourage the women themselves to make clothing or candles, but instead the women asked if they could make a CD-ROM:

> The community's desire emerged during the process of . . . demos [of the CD-ROMs] I have been holding in the community for past several weeks. The women kept on observing me and my demos for several days. They became very curious and inquisitive about the digital camera constantly with me and they thought filming and CD production which I outlined was not so difficult for them to handle. They asked me "Madam, can we make film also? Can we handle the camera?" At this stage, I encouraged them to make the film and start handling the camera themselves which generated tremendous excitement. (Sarita Sharma fieldnote April 1, 2003, Seelampur, India)

Through such activities, skills are developed that engage with prestige technologies and facilitate group learning. They foster project-based (rather than formal and theoretical) engagement with technologies in which skills are learned in the process of achieving a product that is interesting and relevant to the participants. It also holds the potential to explore the participant's community and issues participants feel strongly about, and such content might be used for advocacy. This potential is taken up as a specific focus of the Finding a Voice project.

In all of the ictPR projects, the desire from participants to generate local content emerged almost from the start, and project staff responded to them, sometimes reorganising much of their program to do so. Although participants' sense of the relevance of and their interest in computers and the internet was often talked about in very pragmatic ways—in order to even be considered for an office job one would need to know computing, and the internet is useful for finding information and news—it was through more creative uses of these and other ICTs that participants seemed to develop the most skills.

The ictPR findings demonstrated a need to understand and develop culturally appropriate interfaces for local content creation if there is to be a meaningful uptake of ICTs among marginalised groups and in low infrastructure areas. The Finding a Voice project aims to produce models for new articulations of technological and social networks: to promote voice; define the relationship between voice and 'local' content in a global mediascape; identify opportunities for and constraints on local content creation; and produce effective and sustainable local content creation and distribution models. By doing so, this research project seeks to demonstrate the ways in which content creation can be used for reducing poverty and creating positive social change. The research themes identified in the Finding a Voice project, including those related to identifying the poor, gender, health and welfare, literacy and sustainability, highlight the complexity of the issues that need to be considered in using ICTs for poverty alleviation.

Finding a Voice and Being Heard

The early focus of Finding a Voice, which built on the work of ictPR, was on developing multimedia formats that could use a combination of media available to the study's centres, and developing the capacity of the centres to make these work locally. We started by working with a format called digital storytelling, which is a 2-minute personal story using mostly photographs and a recorded soundtrack. These are put together using video editing software. We examine how this worked in Finding a Voice and in another Australian research project in Chapter 9. At this stage it is important to note that, rather then focusing on formats, it proved far more beneficial to focus on helping each centre to build a strong communication strategy that understands its audiences, takes advantage of as many relevant distribution channels as are available (and builds partnerships to achieve this), works to engage people locally in the creation of content—that is, develop a strong participatory approach—and use EAR to help in the content creation process and monitor how it is working.

The EAR approach places research at the heart of each local ICT initiative and each EAR researcher is connected through a research network. They are connected through an online space where local EAR researchers post their data and reports and get feedback from research supervisors in

Australia. They are all currently working to apply what they have learned about participatory content creation processes to their particular centres, and research what happens as a result of this. The wider research team are able to monitor, and compare and contrast this across the network of centres.

The ongoing cycle of the EAR process means that each EAR researcher will adapt his or her research activities relative to research findings as they emerge. At the same time, each local centre will adapt its local content creation activities in response to research findings as the EAR researcher shares research learning. This in turn provides the centres with useful and important research opportunities and findings, all of which is shared across the network. As the participatory content creation activities develop and research becomes embedded in the centres, we will start to be able to answer our research questions about the benefits of allowing people to have a voice, and the possibilities for ensuring their voices are heard. The ways in which people participate in the development of local content will vary across the network, but, at the very least, they will be involved through the research in influencing the content. The EAR researchers are well positioned to think about what kinds of content might be useful locally and what kinds of stories need to be told.

For example, Jancy Francis, the Finding a Voice EAR researcher in Kerala, identified a range of important issues to include as content:

- Employment: Lack of livelihood security and irregular employment are found to be one of the recurrent issues concerning economic poverty. The content in this regard could include the work requirements at all levels including the unorganised sector, and also the availability of the employable hands through registration so that there is an interface between these two ends, thereby addressing the problem of unemployment to a considerable extent.

- Resource management: Proper management of even the limited resources including income and credit is a skill to be developed among the resource-poor communities and people.

- Resource guidance: Low-cost quality materials for house construction; multiple technologies; raw materials.

- Educational guidance: Knowledge of different courses, their scope, offering institutions, conditions, and so on, could be of use for a better decision-making process in the area of higher education.

- Folklore: The indigenous knowledge systems, traditional heritages, and the like, that are fast disappearing could also find a place among the contents.

- Gender—women empowerment: There is a lot of gap still existing in the area of gender equity, especially in rural areas. Case histories of women empowerment and aspects of empowerment could be projected, creating greater self-confidence among women and paving way for healthy gender interaction. (Jancy Francis fieldnote extracts March 2, 2007, Kerala, India)

The list goes on to include water management, health, legal rights awareness, and so on; many of the major issues, in fact, that one would expect to uncover when researching poor communities. What EAR researchers are building are locally specific understandings of how these issues manifest in their context, and how they might be addressed through the activities at their centres.

These research projects tell us that rather than focus on macro issues and dominant forms of new media, the focus needs to be on broader capability concepts such as democratic participation, strengthening civil society and the promotion of rights, alternative configurations of old and new media, and understanding existing communicative ecologies.

Conclusion

Although the increasing proliferation of new technologies offers at least the theoretical possibility of access to and participation in a global commons, access does not automatically equate to the active or equal participation that is a precondition of voice. The notion of voice as inclusion and participation in social, political, and economic processes, meaning-making, autonomy, and expression is seen as central to development and the realisation of rights. Development theory and practice has long recognised the importance of social context, communication, and participation in facilitating poor people to realise a broad range of human rights—to development, education, health, and well-being. The voicing of needs is now considered as fundamental to most processes of human development.

The rapid emergence and new articulations of ICTs in marginalised communities, therefore, reveals a critical need to apply rigorously tested participatory methods such as EAR to the issues of use. Mayoux and Chambers (2005) called for a paradigm shift that would bring participatory approaches to the impact assessment of development projects centre stage, supported by both qualitative and quantitative approaches. Key principles of this new paradigm include prioritising the voices, views, and interests of poor people themselves, involving them in the process of impact assessment, and increasing their skills, knowledge, and networks through their inclusion in the process (Mayoux & Chambers, 2005). The successful development and testing of EAR in various south and southeast Asian countries over the past five years has been underpinned by these key principles. The case studies presented in this chapter illustrate the value of EAR as a model of embedded and ongoing participatory research and evaluation in ICTs for poverty alleviation initiatives.

Chapter 9

Creative Engagement through Local Content Creation

This chapter further explores the role of action research in creative engagement introduced in Chapter 8, with a focus on creative content creation. This is accomplished by looking at content creation in two action research projects. The first is the *Youth Internet Radio Network* (YIRN) research project, based in Australia and focusing on young people. The second is the Finding a Voice project (described in Ch. 8), which was based in south and southeast Asia and involved the community-based information and communication technology (ICT) centres.

What connects these two projects, located as they are in very different contexts, is their shared interest in harnessing the potential of 'new' media for *creative* expression. As the distinction between content creation and consumption breaks down (e.g., Gitelman, 2006), and we become readers *and* writers of content, the beneficial ways in which technologies might be harnessed is an important focus of research. It is also important, with the emergence of a culture of participation brought about by new media, to recognise the development of a participation gap and the need to examine current cultural protocols and practices surrounding content production and consumption (Jenkins, 2006). This is especially urgent in the age of YouTube (Jenkins, 2007a, 2007c). Jenkins argued that, although most people in the West have physical access at some level, we are currently living in a participatory culture where social networking has become an important social skill and cultural competence. A participation gap thus refers to the inability to participate in culture: physical access does not necessarily enable the level of activity that constitutes participation in a meaningful sense.

Both YIRN and Finding a Voice experiment with local content creation and participation, and test the creative potential of what we currently call *new media* to promote local voices. Local content and local voices were discussed in Chapter 8. Here, we continue the discussion of these issues through the two case studies, with a focus on a particular shared creative activity. This activity was one that both projects had in common—training in content creation, with a specific focus on a format called *digital storytelling*. In this chapter then, we explore what we have learned from the content creation activities in each of these action research projects with a particular emphasis on how we might think about creative engagement.[1]

This chapter introduces the YIRN project and explains how the content creation activities undertaken in YIRN influenced the content creation activities of the subsequent Finding a Voice project. We present the digital storytelling format for local content creation and describe in some detail how and why this was applied across both projects. This activity helped us to ask a common question across the two research projects: what are the local conditions and technological, cultural, social, economic, and political contexts that facilitate (or restrict) creative engagement with—rather than simply access to—digital technologies in low infrastructure areas or among marginalised groups? We conclude the chapter by discussing some of the answers we reached. YIRN asked the question of a broad range of young people in workshop situations, whereas Finding a Voice gets far more embedded into local contexts and initiatives through its use of ethnographic action research (EAR). Indeed, the YIRN project predated Finding a Voice and informed its practice, but the different contexts provided different outcomes and learnings. In particular, Finding a Voice taught us about the importance of context and the value of embedded action research in the process of encouraging participatory content creation and creative engagement.

Online Youth Network: Creating Spaces for Creativity and Innovation

Building on earlier work around the notion of *radiocracy* (radio, democracy, and development, Hartley, 2000; Hopkinson & Tacchi, 2000), the YIRN project had the following aims (Hartley et al., 2003):

---

[1]By creative *engagement* we aim to move beyond notions of physical access to technologies, to notions of meaningful engagement with those technologies. The word *creative* indicates our concern with a particular type of engagement—that is, through participatory content creation. In particular, we are talking specifically about the very local, or what Burgess (2007) called *vernacular creativity*:

> a wide range of everyday creative practices (from scrapbooking to family photography to the storytelling that forms part of casual chat). The term 'vernacular' . . . signifies the ways in which everyday creativity is practiced outside the cultural value systems of either high culture (art) or commercial creative practice (television, say). Further, and again as with language, 'vernacular' signifies the local specificity of such creative practices, and the need to pay attention to the material, cultural, and geographic contexts in which they occur. (pp. 71–72)

- to establish a network of young content providers across urban, regional, remote, and indigenous locations;

- to research how young people interact as both producers and consumers of new media content and technology;

- to identify how different communicative ecologies within the network influence and learn from each other; and

- to understanding how culture and creativity combined with new technologies can be a seedbed for innovation and enterprise development.

The project involved two main activities: the provision of content creation training for groups of young people, delivered face to face through a series of workshops; and the development of a website to host creative content and act as a communication platform for young people, both those who attended the workshops and any other young people in Queensland, Australia, who we could attract to the website. Essentially, although we did not use this term in the early stages, we were looking to explore how young people might *creatively engage* with new media content and technologies.

One of these activities—the development of a website to host creative content and act as a communication platform—proved to be a challenge that we failed to fully meet in a timely way. The design methodology for the YIRN website adopted an 'open architecture' approach. This approach was informed and influenced by the notion of the 'internet commons' or the 'innovation commons' as articulated by Lessig (2001).

Technically speaking, an open network (Lessig, 2001) refers to a network that is simple and allows innovation to come from the ends, from its users. Therefore, we aimed to build a network that began as something quite simple and open but also had a complex backend including a content management system that was ready to respond to innovations emerging from the network's users. We also wanted to build in a track-back functionality that would allow participants to hyperlink to sources on the network that influenced or were used in producing their creative content. This would be visible to the network and essentially form a 'trail' of intercreativity or related content, a feature that has since become common on blogs and other social software sites such as Flickr and YouTube.

Because we were designing a network that intended to allow users to create and innovate through their participation, all of the activity on the website was to be viewed as creative engagement that defined what the network would become. What we were aiming to achieve is similar to what is now generally referred to as the features of Web 2.0 (O'Reilly, 2005) or aspects of new technologies that prompt Jenkins (2006) to describe a participatory culture. We learned how fast moving developments in this field can be, and how easy it is to be left behind in both technological and cultural terms. As an illustration, we called the site sticky.net.au to refer to the way in which it aspired to be a 'sticky' site that people would return to often, 'sticky' being a verb commonly used to describe such web pages in 2004, and a feature of a website that was highly desirable. Since then, we have moved from 'a world of stickiness' to one of 'spreadability,' where value no longer depends on often returning to a sticky web page, but on the spreading of content across social network sites (Jenkins, 2007a). 'Indeed our new mantra is that if it doesn't spread, its dead' (Jenkins, 2007a, April 24). Spreadability is the new sticky!

Although the web development process was overtaken by Web 2.0 the content creation process is still worth examining. In terms of methodology the YIRN project aimed to employ a combination of participatory action research (PAR; see Box 1.1, Ch. 1) and ethnography.

YIRN was *action* research in the way in which all activities were intended to inform the development of the online space—the YIRN website—that it was hoped young people would use to upload and discuss their creative content. Participants in the project were intended to be actively engaged in the research process—PAR was the goal. Taking the local communicative ecologies (see Ch. 2) into account, the methodology tried to achieve a fairly deep understanding of local contexts and wanted to ensure that a participatory ethic flowed through all layers of the project, from planning and consultation to content creation and development of the website. Although in theory this was built into the project design, in practice it proved more difficult. Had the website been developed and populated, it would to a large extent have enabled the level of participation we aimed for. Nevertheless, the project did help us to understand some of the ways in which young people might engage with new media, and how it can be creatively employed to allow them to reveal something of their lives and generate discussion around the themes that concern them. This was achieved through research conducted during the content creation workshops.

We were interested in working with a diverse range of young people from different ethnic, cultural, and socioeconomic backgrounds. We conducted workshops with two predominantly Aboriginal and Torres Strait Islander communities: Cherbourg in rural southeast Queensland and Napranum in Cape York Peninsula in far north Queensland. We conducted workshops in two Brisbane (Queensland state capital city) suburbs with a higher percentage of immigrants than the state average: Carole Park and Zillmere, and in central Brisbane. We also held workshops in Townsville and Cairns, cities on the eastern coast of Queensland. In all we held workshops in 10 locations distributed across the state of Queensland including schools, youth centres, an internet centre, and a community radio station. Project partners were selected to ensure geographical, cultural, and socioeconomic diversity.

We conducted two rounds of workshops. One of them was in radio and music production, which we felt would most likely constitute the bulk of content uploaded to the site. Before that round of workshops however, we wanted to run workshops that would encourage young people to tell stories about their lives. The format we chose was digital storytelling.

Digital Storytelling as Creative Engagement?

Digital storytelling as a distinctive new media format for showcasing personal voices was first developed by Joe Lambert and the late Dana Atchley in California in the early 1990s (Lambert, 2002). Digital storytelling emerged as a new sense of personal voice and according to Lambert (2007) is a 'contemporary process for knowing ourselves.' Lambert runs the Centre for Digital Storytelling in Berkeley, California. The centre's website stresses that digital storytelling has 'its emphasis on personal voice and facilitative teaching methods' and as Dana Atchley had said, it is distinguished from other multimedia formats in that *storytelling* is the key ingredient—the technology is simply the tool (www.storycenter.org/diner/pages/da5.html). Community workshops are a key feature of digital storytelling as it has emerged from California, and are community-building activities in themselves. For Lambert, it is the process of creation through the workshops that is the most important feature of digital storytelling, and he describes the stories as emerging from a group dynamic, although they each tell very personal stories.

YIRN researchers were trained in digital storytelling by Daniel Meadows who, inspired by and trained at the Californian centre, has been teaching digital storytelling to communities in Wales for BBC Wales since 2001 (www.bbc.co.uk/wales/capturewales/). Daniel considers digital stories to be 'scrapbook television—made on the kitchen table, with feeling' (Meadows, 2007). There is a fairly clear difference between the stories produced in California and those produced in Wales. This difference is in the tone and style—with Californian stories being highly self-revelatory and fairly serious in nature, and the Welsh stories including far more humour and a little more distance. Altough this difference can be considered as partly because of the different cultural contexts, it is also likely to be influenced by who the intended audience is. In the California model the audience is the self and close social network, in the BBC Wales example it is a wider public (BBC Wales TV, and some digital BBC channels air some of the stories, all of them are placed on the Capture Wales website) plus the self, friends, and family.

Digital stories are short, 2–5 minutes personal multimedia films put together using as few as two and as many as 30 photographs. The images are used to illustrate a script that is voiced by the creator of the story, typically in the first person. Digital storytelling community workshop participants do not need to be computer experts or have any previous experience in creating content of this kind.

For the YIRN project all of this provided us with an interesting way of exploring the personal voices of young people in the process of teaching them skills in multimedia production. Although some digital stories could be considered a form of mini-documentary, what sets digital storytelling apart from mini documentaries is really the process and the purpose. The process involves community workshops that are community-building in nature, and the purpose varies slightly in different contexts, but is essentially about the expression of personal voice. Another attraction of digital storytelling is that it can be distributed in a variety of formats such as DVD, video, CD, streaming or downloadable formats on the web, television, and community screenings.

During the workshop, participants develop story ideas, create their scripts, and edit the components together using video-editing software on a computer. The YIRN digital storytelling workshops lasted five days with up to 11 participants. Through the workshops, 51 stories were created. Before the workshop, participants are asked to think about what they might like to make a story about and to bring as many possible ideas as they could think of. They were encouraged to bring any photos or objects that seem relevant to their story idea to the workshop. During the workshop their story ideas were discussed and developed and at the end of the workshop they had a completed story. We held local screenings of these stories after each workshop and participants were encouraged to invite family and friends.

YIRN Creative Content

One of the insights we gained through the creative content workshops was how the process of creating content as well as the end product itself can help us to understand how young people see themselves and the world around them. Delivering the workshops provided an opportunity to interact with and get to know young people through a process that actively encouraged, indeed required, young people to 'speak' about themselves.

During the 5-day workshop we trained young people in story writing and photography as well as in audio, video, and image editing. The workshop participants each created short personal stories about their lives and/or passions. Participants were encouraged to invite friends and families to screenings and in one case the stories were screened to a packed auditorium of peers from two schools.

We used an ethnographic approach to the analysis of this process and the creative content. Unable to conduct a fully fledged ethnography with the groups of young people, having only a limited time with them during the workshops, we essentially attempted to apply thick description to the interpretation of cultural texts in a Geertz-like approach (Titon, 2003). The finished digital stories provided us with cultural texts of course, and we attempted to unpack the meanings residing in them, using insights gained through the workshop experience and interactions. Our interpretations then were informed by dialogue with participants. We were open to an empathetic reading, especially as the stories often contained emotional elements. As Titon (2003) stated: 'empathy does not mean standing in the other person's shoes (feeling his pain) as much as it means engagement' (p. 177). We attempted, during the workshops, to 'engage' with the participants. The process of creating personal digital stories through a workshop opens itself to such a method.

The actual digital stories can be considered as texts produced through the social practice of the workshops. The workshops therefore present a process for the production of knowledge (in the form of these cultural texts). As trainers and researchers we took part in this process of knowledge production, through dialogue with the participants. We attempted to tease out the story and help the participants to construct an artifact that communicated the meanings they intended through editing together images, sound, and voice. Story ideas, scripts, and rough edits were regularly discussed as a whole group, and between individual participants. The intended audience also played a crucial role in shaping the texts. All participants knew that the stories would be screened to a group of invited friends and relatives at the end of the workshop and also, importantly, placed on a website that was intended for young people to upload and share their own content and comment on and discuss this content.

The impact of this might be seen for example in a story made by a young, White, male participant in a rural workshop. His story frames 'Australianness' as a dominantly male state of being that can be exposed through the ongoing battle between 'Ford and Holden' cars. His humourous digital story includes key stereotypical symbols of Australian maleness—beer and cars. His story is created around a narrative in which he makes a case for the superiority of Ford cars over Holden, which includes claims and counterclaims about just how Australian the cars or some of their famous drivers are. The battle between Ford and Holden is an embedded and highly symbolic part of Australian culture—many Australians would be able to express their preference, or at least would have been asked to do so at some point in their lives. This story, then, is a self-projection and a statement by the creator of his embeddedness in male Australian culture. Although tongue in cheek in style, it contains a very strong preferred reading about who the creator is and what he is like, achieved through the telling of his story. Lambert (2002) would consider this aspect of digital storytelling one of the reasons it appeals:

> it speaks to an undeniable need to constantly explain our identities to each other. Identity is changing. . . . The only real way to know about someone is through story, and not one consistent story, but a number of little stories that can adjust to countless different contexts. As we improvise our ways through our multiple identities, any tool that extends our ability to communicate information about ourselves to others becomes invaluable. (p. 17)

Taking the stories together and looking for thematic patterns, our analysis suggests that often the content creators appeared to place significance on their geographical positioning in relation to core city centres, Brisbane and Townsville. A number of recurrent themes were identified that relate to feelings of 'boredom,' 'lack of opportunities,' and 'isolation' alongside other stories that we identified as 'aspirational.' For those in non-urban areas in particular, stories told of ambitions to seek out career and other opportunities elsewhere. At the same time, we noticed a strong sense of place-based local identity. We observed the different ways that the participants constructed meaning through cultural, geographic, and social affiliations.

Other common 'themes' that emerge from the stories are 'aspirational,' 'sense of agency,' 'overcoming challenge/recovery,' 'adventure,' and 'social message.' One of the stories discusses the problem of 'sniffers' (paint sniffing) in an outer Brisbane suburb, a location with low-income and high unemployment levels. In the story she produced, a teenager addresses the negative perceptions of the place in which she lives:

> I have mixed feelings about Carole Park. . . . Other people from outside only see the bad things about this place, but if they lived here they would see the good things as well. . . . Living here has taught me to be myself, to trust myself. (Katie, 13 years old)

At the same time, Katie acknowledges the problems that she knows exist in her community and considers how they affect her:

> I find I can't walk to the shops alone because you sometimes get followed and harassed. There is also a lot of paint sniffing . . . I think they do it because they are bored, and it's easy to get. Often they get violent and some of my friends have been bashed by them. (Katie, 13 years old)

In a number of the workshops we found that by engaging young people in new media technologies, in ways that go beyond the simple transfer of technological skills to a critical engagement with ideas, concepts, experiences, and storytelling, dialogues were initiated that often surprised teachers and youth workers. This workshop experience provided them with opportunities to explore how young people felt about issues that were affecting them. In the case just described, the youth worker was able to use this story to open up discussions with local young people at the community centre about the serious issue of paint sniffing. She was able to hear their views about what they thought needed to happen to improve the situation.

Digital Storytelling and Finding a Voice

As discussed in Chapter 8, Finding a Voice is a project that aims to both embed EAR into a network of community-based media initiatives in south and southeast Asia and explore ways to generate participatory content creation activities, especially among marginalised groups. Following the experience of running digital storytelling workshops for the YIRN project in Australia, we felt that the format offered an interesting possibility for expression of local voices in the Finding a Voice project. With this in mind we set out to conduct a train the trainers digital storytelling workshop in India in early 2006 and another in Indonesia in mid-2006.

Participants in the Indian workshop were from a range of media initiatives across south Asia, some from Finding a Voice sites in India, Sri Lanka, and Nepal, plus others from Bangladesh and Bhutan. All participants were content creators, although not all of them were familiar with multimedia content creation. During the workshop, participants learned the various techniques for creating a digital story and running digital storytelling workshops. But unlike the workshops in the YIRN project, here we encouraged participants to think about linking content creation to research activities happening in their sites, and to consider using the stories as advocacy tools, highlighting social issues and so on. The work-shop produced a dozen stories on a range of topics.[2] Although all were told in the first person, they highlighted social issues or promoted their media initiative rather than reflected on some aspect of the self. That said, the creator's identity was present and made for some powerful stories that ranged from poetic and emotive accounts of annual flooding and devastation in West Bengal, to the dramatic recounting of a Maoist raid on a Nepali town and the destruction of an historic durbar.

Rajendra Negi is from Chamba, a city in the north of India, in the Himalayan ranges. He is a volunteer for a community radio initiative that operates in the mountainous region around Chamba. At the time of his story India had not legislated for community radio licences, and he and his colleagues practiced what they call *narrowcasting*—they create radio programmes on issues of interest to people in the area, place them on a cassette tape, and then take a cassette player and play the programmes to gatherings of people in towns and villages in the area. Given the hilly ter-rain and the lack of roads to many of the villages, this can involve hours of walking. Rajendra had recently been on a trip to Nepal where com-munity radio has burgeoned in recent years and was inspired on his return home to do all he could to promote community radio in India. His story tells us what community radio has meant to him, what it can do for the communities he works with, and how he has a dream that one day they will be able to broadcast community radio in his region.

Alamgir Kabir's story is located in Sitakund, an industrial area in Bangladesh. His story is about one of the main industries there—ship breaking. Titled *In Violation . . .* Almagir's story tells us about the lack of protection for labourers in this industry. Workers, he tells us, are deprived of food, drinking water and sanitation. They work long hours with no safety rules or precautions. They have no protective gloves, footwear, or goggles despite the kinds of cutting equipment that they use. Alamgir tells us that many fatal accidents occur. Accidents also leave some permanently disabled, such as his 25-year-old friend Salim, who lost his leg in a cut-ting accident. Salim, like the others, received no compensation. Children also work here. Alamgir feels that although this industry is important to the area, adequate regulatory frameworks needs to be introduced to protect the workers. The story is told by Alamgir, in his own voice, with feeling. As such it produces a powerful media artifact about an issue of critical importance to Alamgir and the labourers in ship-breaking yards

---

[2]Stories from the workshop, and some stories made subsequently, can be viewed at www.findingavoice.org

in Sitakund. Part of the power of this particular story as a media text resides in the photographs Alamgir took to illustrate this story. The well-framed photographs of the ship-breaking yard and the workers effectively emphasises his narrative.

The stories that were produced during the workshop reinforce that powerful media texts can be developed using the digital storytelling approach. In this case, mostly for advocacy rather than expressions of self, the personal voice lends itself well to this type of story. The challenge of the workshop and Finding a Voice was for those trained in the workshop to take this training back to their various media initiatives and work alongside local researchers to generate participatory content creation activities. How would they engage community members in the process of creating their own stories? What kinds of stories would be made? In what ways could the media initiatives use and distribute these stories? Who would be the audiences?

Some of the participants were able to take their training back to their media initiatives and run their own workshops. A DVD of some of these digital stories has been produced by the UNESCO (2006). Mostly, the workshops were run to train other workers in the initiative, other organisations working in their communities, or other media organisations in the vicinity. Not much was done that actively engaged with members of the community with no prior role in their initiatives. Some of those we trained, when they returned to their media initiative, were unable to generate interest among their peers to develop plans to put what they had learned into practice at the local level. Through the application of this particular approach and observation of the follow-up activities we recognised the need to re-evaluate our approach and re-examine the appropriateness of the format. In some cases, it had taken off in quite impressive ways in terms of peer training, but this was patchy, and it was proving much harder to get community participation beyond those who already participate.

In response to these observations, our digital storytelling workshop in Indonesia was designed with a clear difference. We set up a training structure that would ensure all staff and volunteers in a media initiative (not just one person) would be trained and would have a role in developing their own plans for subsequent content creation work. We trained a core team of Jakarta-based project workers and local staff in a Sulawesi telecentre, including the staff member responsible for conducting action research. We then observed as those staff conducted a workshop with a group of key volunteers at the telecentre. These two groups then created a follow-up plan for how to implement what they had learned, train others, distribute the stories that would be produced, and so on. The Jakarta-based staff went on to train staff in two other telecentres, using the same approach.

This worked well as a training model, but other issues emerged subsequently, indicating that the format itself might need to be rethought in the Finding a Voice project. The aim of developing participatory local content that allows the voices of a range of people to be heard was proving problematic. The Jakarta-based staff analysed the stories that were produced during their workshops and subsequently with community participants and found a striking similarity in both style and content. Most people made stories that promoted the telecentre where they were trained, or the organisation to which they were attached. Additionally, a 'halo effect' was identified, where the vast majority of stories started with the same kind of image, pose, and wording—'Hello, my name is X and I live in X.' The cultural, social, and political contexts in which these content creation activities were taking place were clearly having an effect on the content itself. Not necessarily bad in itself, this led us to reflect carefully on the importance of considering the various contexts in which we are working and the need to link content creation work more closely with the EAR happening in each of the Finding a Voice research sites.

At our next content creation workshop in Nepal in late 2006, and a subsequent workshop in India in early 2007, we combined research training with content creation training. We brought EAR researchers, content creators, and managers to the workshops and invited community media organisations and potential partners in training and distribution to a final day where the content and plans produced during the workshops were presented and discussed. We moved away from training in a single format to concentrate on developing *processes* of local content creation that draw on EAR researcher's work as material around which content might be produced, and on mechanisms for getting participation from the wider community. This meant a shift from one specific and fairly rigid format—a two-minute personal story using photographs and a voiceover—to considerations of audience, distribution, participation, team-based creative activities, and the use of contextually relevant media. The format would depend on the story, the purpose, the intended audience, and the distribution channel. During workshops, a range of media has been produced including wall newspapers, digital stories, micro documentaries, and radio features. Stories produced by groups rather than individuals have been explored in places where individual self-expression is culturally inappropriate. Across Finding a Voice sites in Nepal, India, and Sri Lanka, plans to develop more participatory content creation have been developed and followed by actions that demonstrate clear examples of the development of well-researched and effective creative digital engagement strategies.

One example is the ways in which two community libraries in Nepal have begun to foster greater participation in the creation of its wall newspapers. Wall newspapers are posters placed on the wall of a local community centre or village meeting room, to spread important local information. In addition to introducing ways in which more people participate in creating the content for the wall newspapers, they have started to investigate how the content of the wall newspapers might be taken up by neighbouring community radio channels, or distributed digitally to the many other community libraries in Nepal via a computer network. Additionally, these libraries have recently started using their computer facilities to create digital stories. Sita, the EAR researcher at the library, has created digital stories with local groups around issues that have emerged from her research. Following the content creation workshop that she took part in Sita went back to her libraries and conducted training for local people in script writing and digital storytelling.

The Role of Action Research in Developing Creative Engagement

Although content creation workshops and formats like digital storytelling offer highly interesting ways of encouraging creative engagement with new technologies, it is hard to know how this activity impacts on the future lives of the participants without ongoing research. In the YIRN project we found that there were some clear examples of positive follow-up, in discussions around issues raised through the stories such as glue sniffing in an outer suburb of Brisbane as discussed earlier in this chapter, but also in other ways. Some participants in the workshops found their creative skills were recognised and rewarded with follow-up work. In one case, two participants in a Brisbane workshop were given the job by the City Council of reporting on a city festival using the digital storytelling format. Another participant in a workshop in Townsville was appointed as school photographer. Her digital story had been about her passion for photography. Working toward developing more conducive environments for creative engagement would require ongoing action research. The embedded action research component of Finding a Voice provides us with just such ongoing insights, albeit in a very different context.

Conclusion

At the start of this chapter, we outlined the question asked in both YIRN and Finding a Voice: what are the local conditions, and technological, cultural, social, economic, and political contexts, that allow for (or restrict) creative engagement with—rather than simply access to—digital technologies in low infrastructure areas or among marginalised groups? YIRN tells us that producing creative content appears to allow young people to make effective statements about themselves and to subvert or challenge some of the ways they are perceived and represented by others. The restrictive information technology practices in Queensland schools do not allow this activity free reign, despite the proliferation of online spaces where this kind of content might be circulated, exchanged, consumed, and displayed. Should we be concerned that only those with access at home will become full members of the new participatory culture?

Why is this important? In a number of the digital stories produced through the YIRN workshops, young people challenge negative perceptions of themselves or their local community. They raise issues that are affecting them. This suggests that new media technologies can be used by formal and informal training organisations to allow young people to have the kind of 'speaking power' that they themselves feel they rarely have through their creative productions.

In the very different context of the Finding a Voice project we have learned that formats like digital storytelling can allow people to tell their stories, in their own voices, in powerful ways. We now need to understand more about the implications of using new technologies to promote voice. We are concerned not just with the technologies and formats, but the contexts and the part they play in the practice of participatory local content and the negotiation of meanings.

Why is this important? UNESCO advocates the concept of 'knowledge societies,' which are 'about capabilities to identify, produce, disseminate and use information to build and apply knowledge for human development' (UNESCO, 2005, p. 191). The concept of knowledge societies as promoted by UNESCO encompasses plurality, inclusion, solidarity, and participation, and is based on certain principles, including freedom of expression and the universal access to information and knowledge. But, when many of those we wish to include in knowledge societies do not have access or effective use, how do you integrate new ICTs into communities?

Chapter 10

A Community Portal for Residents in an Inner-City Development

Cities are exciting. Cities are buzzing. They are alive with movement. A rapid flow of exchange is facilitated by a meshwork of infrastructure connections: road systems, building complexes, information and communication technology (ICT), and people networks. In this environment, the internet has advanced to become the prime technology that mediates every dimension of the fabric of urban life (Graham, 2004). In the early days of the Network Society, research of online communication and community interaction led to both utopian and dystopian interpretations of escapism (DiMaggio, Hargittai, Neuman, & Robinson, 2001). However, with the internet entering into many aspects of everyday life, current viewpoints recognise that the artificially created dichotomy of cyberspace and reality no longer holds true (Wellman & Haythornthwaite, 2002). Online social relationships are being seamlessly integrated into offline activities and networks and vice versa. In a number of ways, cities represent the most connected places of any geographical location on Earth.

This chapter reports on the work in progress of a study that focuses on the interaction between online and offline communities of urban residents. Its point of departure is the stark contrast between the widespread use of mobile and ubiquitous ICTs by city dwellers on the one hand and endemic forms of urban alienation and the disappearance or nonexistence of urban neighbourhood community identity on the other. In today's networked society, e-mail, instant messaging, online chats, and other applications are instrumental in establishing and maintaining social ties, thus creating a private 'portfolio of sociability' (Castells, 2001, p. 132). Neighbours may still be part of a resident's social portfolio, but the communication devices used to maintain social ties are inherently place-independent and ephemeral. Getting to know someone in their role as a 'neighbour' is less likely than getting to know them in their role as a 'co-worker' or being the friend of a friend. Sociologists such as Wellman (2001; Wellman et al., 2003) describe how people construct their social networks with the help of new media tools. Wellman and his colleagues found patterns in their research data that led them to propose that networks are a better conceptual model to describe current social relationships in the context of new media and network ICT use. Wellman argued that although people become more accustomed with the features that new media and ICT tools offer, the nature of the social ties people establish and maintain changes from what used to be door-to-door and place-to-place relationships, to what are now person-to-person and role-to-role relationships. Wellman termed the emerging qualities of this behaviour *networked individualism*.

The vision informing the development of networked communities of place in Australia and internationally has been articulated in terms of community-building, that is, the capacity to engender a sense of community and belonging and sociability in estates and neighbourhoods. However, a large body of both theoretical and empirical work suggests that the networking and linking practices enabled by new media and ICTs are not likely to be focused on identifications based solely on collocation and *about* place but on the sociocultural meanings and usages residents derive from their interaction situated *within* place. 'Physical closeness does not mean social closeness' (Wellman, 2001, p. 234; see also Katz et al., 2004).

Previous studies that tried to make sense of contemporary new media usage rely on simple binary oppositions such as 'individual' versus 'community,' 'physical place' versus 'cyberspace,' or 'online' versus 'offline' (DiMaggio et al., 2001). This chapter departs from these compartmentalised dichotomies by trying to create a holistic theoretical framework inherent in networked individualism. For example, even as the internet grows exponentially, place-based units such as 'home,' 'work,' and 'school' remain at the core of our understanding of everyday life, and 'the economy itself increasingly takes form around real concentrations of people in real places' (Florida, 2003, p. 4). Human interaction thus takes place seamlessly in the virtual and physical 'space of flows' (Castells, 2004) that modern transportation and modern communication afford. Place and proximity continue to matter in every socioeconomic aspect. This is evident by rising car and air travel sales (Wellman, 2001), by people commuting to work instead of working from home, and by the formation of economic clusters, precincts, and hot spots where industries based along the same value chain collocate to take advantage of synergy effects. However, an empirically proven rationale has yet to be found that clarifies the conditions under which these synergy effects apply in the context of new residential urban developments. With the intensified attention to high-density residential solutions, this research project examines these conditions by grounding and testing the theoretical framework in a case study of a new master-planned residential development in inner-city Brisbane, Australia.

The chapter is divided into two parts. The first part introduces the characteristics of the residential site that has been selected for this study. The technical infrastructure of the site available to developers and future residents has been marketed by the project stakeholders with the indirect assumption that 'if you build it, they will come.' The first part discusses the sociotechnical challenges of master-planning ICT and new media systems for a community that does not exist yet, as well as additional issues that previous studies have uncovered.

Derived from this analysis, the second part of the chapter critiques conventional approaches toward community-building and proposes a way forward. This response is twofold. First, it comprises the conceptualisation of a theoretical framework around the concept of communicative ecologies that has been developed to study the place-based communication technology and new media applications used by urban residents in the context of their other ICT and media usages (see Ch. 2). Derived from the implications of this model, this chapter also presents a methodological variation combining network action research and participatory design. The aim of this chapter is not to report on final figures and results, but to highlight the utility of action research as an innovative methodology situated at the intersection of communities and technologies.

Case Study of an Inner-City Residential Development

Australia is one of the most urbanised countries in the world in terms of the high proportion of urban dwellers among its total population. Approximately two-thirds of the total population reside in major cities (Australian Bureau of Statistics, 2004). Current projections for South East Queensland (SEQ) are 3.71 million residents by 2026, an increase of around 1.05 million people, or almost 50,000 each year on average (Queensland Government, 2005). Our partners, the Department of Housing and Brisbane City Council, are aware that the continuation of the low-density urban sprawl in SEQ is not sustainable. These trends (similar in other areas elsewhere in Australia and the world) have global economic relevance and reflect the changing role of cities internationally. Compact city policies are being developed and implemented in all Australian capitals to deal with population pressures and urban expansion. Brisbane is one of the most pressured given its long history of low-density urban sprawl and now its status as the second highest growth region in the world. Randolph (2004) argued the following:

The language of community has come back with vengeance in policy areas that ignored it for many years. Cities are becoming, perhaps more than ever before, collections of distinctive communities and neighbourhoods, all the more differentiated as the cities grow in size and complexity. As the city expands, people remain focused on their small part of it. (p. 483)

Mixed-use residential developments are a small part of it. Regarded as a new way to make urban densification socially sustainable, they provide the immediate surroundings in which location-based interactions with other residents occur and informal social networks emerge. The strategies proposed in these policies open up new research questions around issues of living together creatively and population diversity, which are the focus of this research project.

Hornecker et al. (2006) examined opportunity spaces where 'there is no urgent problem to be solved, but much potential to augment and enhance practice in new ways' (p. 47). Neighbourhoods can be such opportunity spaces insofar as they provide residents with opportunities to communicate, interact, and socialise with each other. One of the primary research questions of this study is: How can the communication technology that is already well accepted by urban residents (such as e-mail, short message service [SMS] and instant messaging, and now increasingly social networking systems) play a role in realising such opportunities? Instead of providing definite answers, the chapter's aim is to discuss the theoretical and methodological underpinnings of this action research study.

The case study selected to examine this research question is the Kelvin Grove Urban Village (KGUV; www.kgurbanvillage.com.au). The KGUV (see Fig. 10.1) is a joint initiative by the Queensland State Government's Department of Housing and Queensland University of Technology (QUT) to create a mixed-use development on 16.57 hectares of land at Kelvin Grove, a suburb just 2km from Brisbane's central business district. This $800 million Australian Dollar urban renewal project is expected to be fully developed and occupied by 2010, at which stage it will comprise more than 1,000 residential units for more than 2,000 residents.

The KGUV development is guided by an integrated master plan (KGUV, 2004), which is complemented by a 4-year community development strategy to initiate and animate the neighbourhood community, the urban village, of the KGUV. We briefly summarise the main goals of the master plan here. Although the list is explicit and expansive, it helps to contextualise the underlying design principles and intentions of the development more generally and illustrate the regulatory framework and requirements

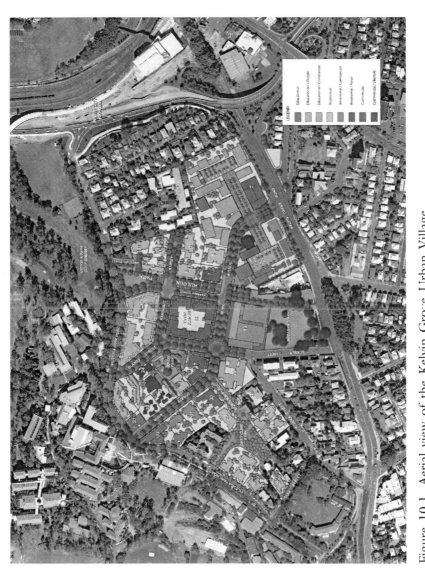

Figure 10.1. Aerial view of the Kelvin Grove Urban Village.

that the research and design of the community portal, discussed further here, is based in more specifically.

1. **Spatial framework**: Establish a clear urban outcome for the KGUV that optimises the physical, virtual, and social links with surrounding neighbourhoods, the existing QUT campus, and Brisbane's central business district. Strategies include spreading university elements within the village, creating different zones of character, and strengthening pedestrian connections.

2. **Identity and urban performance**: Position the KGUV as a dynamic, vibrant quarter of the city, with extended hours, a strong sense of place, and cultural identity. Strategies include creating attractions and events to encourage visitors and building recognisable and marketable 'signature' pieces.

3. **Built form**: Promote excellence in subtropical design, establishing the KGUV as a vibrant, interesting, richly layered, and inclusive place. Strategies include exploring innovative building methods and integrating design guidelines into the development approval process.

4. **Planning**: Establish a planning framework driven by Brisbane City Council and supported by the project partners, which encourages innovative solutions and allows the vision for the KGUV to be delivered. Strategies include using the city plan to achieve the vision for the KGUV and adopting council codes.

5. **Heritage**: Acknowledge and respond to the broad array of heritage characteristics at the village, interpreting its Indigenous culture, contribution to European history, and longstanding educational and military connections. Strategies include reusing military buildings and producing a coffee table book to record the history of the site and project.

6. **Sustainability**: Demonstrate the principles of environmentally sustainable development, delivering outcomes through design, development, and operations, and minimising the ecological 'footprint' of the KGUV. Strategies include incorporating energy efficient design and reducing demand on town water through storm/grey water reuse initiatives.

7. **Economic development**: Promote and harness innovation, stimulate enterprise, and enhance employment opportunities for everyone. Strategies include promoting mixed-use commercial outcomes and positioning the KGUV as the prime location for emerging creative businesses.

8. **Social benefit**: Create a neighbourhood that champions equality of opportunity and focuses on increasing both social capital and individual capacity. Strategies include establishing neighbourhood watch and police beat programs, integrating affordable housing sites, and linking residents to QUT facilities and activities.

9. **Community development**: Foster a sense of community by using facilities, spaces, events, and technology to deliver experiences that enrich KGUV life. Strategies include appointing a community development manager, forming a community association, and using QUT services to form a community well-being program.

10. **Transport**: Ensure that people using the KGUV are less reliant on cars than the general Brisbane population. Strategies include connecting the town centre to the new northern busway station at Brisbane Grammar School and establishing bus stops within the village.

11. **ICT**: Deliver a viable and enduring connected community, enhanced by continuing innovations in ICT. Strategies include installing a fiber optic spine throughout the KGUV, and connecting all businesses and residences to it.

12. **Research**: Deliver a dynamic research agenda using the KGUV project to improve social and urban outcomes across Queensland and beyond. Strategies include drawing together all relevant QUT faculties and promoting research and learning initiatives at the village.

13. **Delivery**: Evolve a model for the delivery of inner city, mixed-use, master-planned neighbourhoods that can be used by other Queensland Government agencies. Strategies include taking a proactive approach to tender processes, encouraging interest in the marketplace and managing all agents involved in the sale and release of land holdings.

This study is supported by the KGUV project stakeholders and part of the strategies and outcomes of Goal 12 (research) of the master plan. However, the overall theme of the research and the primary object of research, the community portal website, directly and indirectly cross other goals as well. Although the development of a community portal has been placed as a key strategy of Goal 11 (ICT) of the master plan, it is also seen as one of the tangible outcomes that are part of a range of community development initiatives being pursued in accordance with Goals 8 (social benefit) and 9 (community development). Additionally, the portal is envisioned to be a communication hub and publishing platform for community generated content to assist in the delivery of Goals 1–2, and 5–7.

The KGUV is seen as a significant showcase of Queensland's emerging information economy, designed to provide opportunities to integrate work and home through high-speed communication systems for both the local business community and the residential community. The ICT infrastructure that has been implemented at the KGUV features a 'triple-play' fiber network providing telephone, television, and data services including a 'peering link' allowing QUT students living in the KGUV to access the university's online resources from their home computers at no charge. The fiber network is complemented by wireless services allowing subscribers to access the internet in parks, restaurants, and other locations around the KGUV.

The KGUV project team acknowledges that access to this infrastructure is necessary but not sufficient per se to ensure 'effective use' (Gurstein, 2003). Therefore, the master plan calls for the design and development of a community portal that is situated on the applications layer of this infrastructure. It aims to provide an online mechanism to link the people and businesses that 'live, learn, work, and play' at the KGUV, including residents of the KGUV and nearby areas (including affordable housing residents, seniors, and students); university staff and students living and/or studying in the KGUV and nearby areas; businesses and their customers; and visitors. The portal is intended to encourage participation in the KGUV by being a key information resource of the mix of activities, programs, and facilities available. It also seeks to facilitate community uptake of ICT by hosting entertainment and information content that encourages exploration of the ICT infrastructure available at the KGUV.

Challenges for the Community Portal

Community portals are being developed and deployed to add ways for urban residents to interact with each other in an effort to revitalise and grow communities in urban neighbourhoods. However, as outlined in Chapter 6, Wellman (2001) argued that the availability of modern forms of transportation and the ubiquity of the internet and cell phones in most developed countries enable and encourage people to pursue personalised networking: to create and maintain both strong and weak ties with people who can be met easily face to face, but who do not necessarily live next door, yet are still close by.

Aurigi (2006) suggested that the term *portal* is limiting 'people's interpretations . . . to broadcasting information and providing institutional services' (p. 19). He argued for a

> need to re-address this tension and identify the emergence of the portal paradigm as something that has a lot to do with television and has

weakened the reflection on, and construction of, a civic network. . . .
But it has to be remarked how powerful and accepted the portal paradigm has become and how this type of vision can affect the shape of
things to come in the augmented city. (p. 19)

Although we continue using the term *portal*, we are challenging the
established paradigm of its expected functionality by moving away from a
pure broadcast-only medium toward a hybrid community information and
networking system.

The unique quality that sets residential community networking systems
apart from their place-independent and purely interest-based virtual coun-
terparts is proximity (see Walmsley, 2000). The KGUV project team sees a
community portal as part of a toolbox that residents can access to maintain
their private social networks, alongside and possibly interconnected with email,
phone, SMS and face-to-face interaction. Hence, the objective is to design
a community portal that learns from the issues faced by previous projects
(e.g., Cohill & Kavanaugh, 2000; Hampton & Wellman, 2003) and includes
features that allow residents to take advantage of the communication services
the internet can offer in order to conduct personalised networking (Wellman,
2002). The community portal provides access to *proximate* communication
and interaction partners—compared with other global communication tools,
this is a unique advantage (Foth, 2006b). The system would allow residents
to meet and interact online, and also to translate and continue the online
interaction into offline, real-life, collocated, and face-to-face interactions.
This offline and place-based dimension is a key challenge in the design,
development, and deployment of the portal.

In order to explain this challenge further, we build on the work by
Arnold, Gibbs, and Wright (2003) to distinguish between collective interaction for discussion *about* place and networked interaction for sociability
in place. The web development company commissioned to design and
deliver the KGUV community portal has an existing portfolio of portals
that have been installed in other place-based contexts. The features of these
systems include public discussion forums, noticeboards, events calendars,
and content management services. These functions are mostly designed
for residents in urban neighbourhoods to support collective interaction
for discussion about places that promote a one-to-many or many-to-many
broadcast mode of communication. They complement the collective community activities organised by the community development workers which
include the strategies listed under Goals 8 (social benefit) and 9 (community
development) and could extend to place-based community activism around
issues such as neighbourhood watches, traffic calming, and street rejuvenation
initiatives organised by the proposed KGUV Community Association (see
Foth & Brereton, 2004).

Activities and interactions around such place-based interests may be able to fuel social interaction for a while. Yet, a system that is solely based on a collective interaction paradigm requires a continuous effort to reach and sustain a critical mass of users. Many consider this to be a key criterion of success (Arnold et al., 2003; Patterson & Kavanaugh, 2001), and critical mass has been reported as one of the most common stumbling blocks for such systems: 'if you build it, they will not necessarily come' (Maloney-Krichmar, Abras, & Preece, 2002, p. 19).

Residents at the KGUV are going to be collocated not on the basis of a shared interest or a single demographic group. In fact, one of the guiding design principles of the KGUV is heterogeneity of housing types to encourage an inclusive collocation of 'mainstream' residents of various age and income groups together with student and seniors accommodation as well as affordable housing options for low-income earners. Although place-based initiatives and collective activities present valid motivations for neighbourhood interaction, we argue that there can be other, more inherently social reasons that do not require a critical mass of users. Analysing the interaction paradigm of social networking systems such as instant messaging shows that a network interaction paradigm may turn the problem—lack of shared place-based interest—into an advantage: social diversity.

Our previous research found that—despite not knowing many of their neighbours—urban residents believe that it is very likely that within the diversity of residents living in the same neighbourhood, there may be some who they might be socially compatible with, alas certainly not all of them. Yet, apart from serendipitous encounters, there are no convenient means to find out if they are. The aforementioned notion of the neighbourhood as an 'opportunity space' (Hornecker et al., 2006) introduces the conceptual context for such scenarios and opens up a new set of design challenges for the KGUV community portal. This view sees the portal as a way to enable, enhance, augment, or facilitate existing or emerging social networks between urban residents. This networked interaction for sociability in place describes the more private space occupied by a 'society of friendships,' that is, social networks of friends who live within relative proximity to each other. They use informal, peer-to-peer type network communication tools such as e-mail, SMS, and instant messaging to interact online, but proximity enables them to gather face to face and interact offline. They see each other primarily as 'friends who live close by' and not as 'neighbours' (Foth, 2006a).

If we regard the KGUV as an opportunity space, one of the key challenges of the portal is thus to find appropriate means to afford residents a seamless, selective, and voluntary pathway to transition from 'neighbour' to 'friend' and to link these new nodes with their existing social networks.

The other key challenge in the design of the portal is more straight-forward and easier to explain: how can we start designing a system for the future residents of the KGUV if they have not moved in yet?

Although the remainder of this chapter does not intend to provide definite answers, its contribution lies in the theoretical and methodological response to these two key challenges, which we think can be appropriated in similar cases and contexts.

Theoretical Response

The objective to deliver a community portal with interactive features that seamlessly integrate into the existing communication mix of KGUV residents requires a holistic perspective. The portal must not be seen in isolation but in the context of other communication technology employed by residents as well as other social relationships and content needs that are not necessarily related to the KGUV.

We respond to this challenge by invoking the concept of communicative ecologies. As introduced in Chapter 2, we define a communicative ecology as a milieu of agents who are connected in various ways by various media-making exchanges in various ways (Foth & Hearn, 2007). Tacchi, Slater, and Hearn (2003) suggested communicative ecologies are the 'processes that involve a mix of media, organised in specific ways, through which people connect with their social networks' (p. 17). An ecology operates as a 'web of life'; the communicative ecology framework opens up the possibility of network analyses of relationships between agents in the ecology. It refers to the context in which the communication process occurs. Such an ecology can thus be thought of as comprising a number of mediated and unmediated forms of communication.

For the purpose of this study, we conceive of a communicative ecology as having three layers: a *technological layer*, which consists of the devices and connecting media that enable communication and interaction; a *social layer*, which consists of people and social modes of organising those people—which might include, for example, everything from informal social networks to more formal community associations, as well as commercial or legal entities such as body corporates; and a *discursive layer*, which is the content, that is, the ideas, or themes that constitute the conversations and narratives of the ecology.

Furthermore, we explore three dimensions of the communicative ecology, that is, the extent to which technical, social, and discursive elements are positioned between (a) online and offline communication modi, (b) local and global contexts, and (c) collective and networked interaction paradigms (see Fig. 10.2). First, the online versus offline dichotomy is blurring. Mesch and Levanon (2003) reported that social networks that individuals generate and maintain with the help of ICT, transcend from online to offline and from offline to online seamlessly. This is supported by a number of studies that examine the use of the internet in everyday life (Wellman & Haythornthwaite, 2002). These studies find that the communication modi afforded by internet applications are becoming a well-established part of the communication mix people employ to maintain their social networks. Thus, the interactions between online and offline communities should not be separated. The design of the portal needs to allow for interoperability with major communication technology such as instant messenger and cell phone networks. If the portal is able to add value to the existing portfolio of devices and services, it has a chance of becoming an attractive addition or enhancement to the existing communicative ecology. Otherwise it risks being seen as another burden that competes with an established portfolio of communication systems.

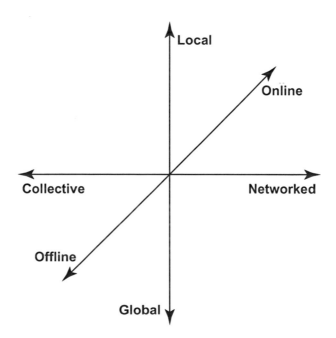

Figure 10.2. The three dimensions of a communicative ecology.

Second, the local–global axis is increasingly being occupied on the global end of the scale by a range of major and powerful Web 2.0 services such as search engines, instant messenger networks, auction sites, and social networking systems. Robertson's (1995) notion of *glocalization*, later reinterpreted by Wellman (2002), emphasises the requirement to find ways to use this global service infrastructure for meaningful usage locally. This implies that the KGUV community portal should not replicate services that compete with existing global sites or with global content. Instead, studies have highlighted a plethora of opportunities for local (and location-aware) services as well as locally produced and consumed content (Boase, Horrigan, Wellman, & Rainie 2006; Burgess et al., 2006) for which the community portal can provide a platform.

The third implication refers to the aforementioned discussion of collective and networked interaction paradigms. The KGUV community portal must be structured to allow for collective community interaction for discussion about place ('community activism') and networked community interaction for sociability in place ('social networking'). Collective interaction relates to the place in which residents are collocated and stems from the shared interest in and common purpose of the urban neighbourhood site itself. Portal features that support this aspect include body corporate affairs, community events, street rejuvenation initiatives, and lobbying activity. Features to support collective interaction are a common and necessary component of most community portals. However, they are not sufficient to ensure social sustainability.

Features that support networked interaction seek to raise awareness of who lives in the neighbourhood, provide opportunities for residents to find out about each other, and voluntarily initiate contact with selected residents of choice. For example, it is possible to publish a private white pages directory with contact details and short profiles to residents and use cell phone or e-mail contacts to begin to facilitate the development of peer-to-peer social networks. Web-based maps (e.g., Google Maps) can provide a visual and location-based overview of the community with overlaid pointers indicating network relations. If place-based issues arise, residents can migrate into the domain of a community intranet or discussion board to organise collective meetings and action. At the same time, such events can provide opportunities to meet new residents and to migrate back into the domain of the private social network. The KGUV community portal needs to be structured to allow for both collective and networked community interaction.

The communicative ecology framework provides a theoretical response to the challenge of supporting residents to transition from neighbour to friend. By taking all significant elements of the communicative ecology into account, design implications can be derived, which will guide the portal development.

Methodological Response

Community-building efforts in urban neighbourhoods require an inter-disciplinary approach in order to control for the many variables involved, such as the swarming social behaviour of urban dwellers, the systems design of the technical infrastructure, the generation of informative, useful, and creative content and assets, and so on. Therefore, a range of conceptual influences have been integrated and customised to create a suitable methodological response. A participatory action research (PAR) approach toward the development of community technology is essential to allow residents to take social ownership of the project and the resulting community portal. Embedded in the participatory and human-centred nature of action research, the PAR approach builds on aspects of several development methodologies that seek to combine community development and systems design. They include the following:

- ethnographic action research (EAR; see Ch. 5);

- asset-based community development (Kretzmann & McKnight, 1993);

- community technology and community-building (Pinkett, 2003);

- participatory design (Greenbaum & Kyng, 1991; Schuler & Namioka, 1993);

- sociocultural animation (see Chap. 5 and Foth, 2006d); and

- a networking approach to community development (Gilchrist, 2004).

The PAR approach is also informed by recent studies that examine community networks in residential environments (Day, 2002; Francisco et al., 2001; Wilcox, Greenop, & Mackie, 2002). The common ground that these methodological influences provide advocates a dual approach that integrates the technical task of designing and implementing a community network with the social task of animating and sustaining community networking among residents of the neighbourhood.

Figure 10.3 illustrates the project stages involved in this approach. After the initial phase of immersion in Stage I, the model integrates systems design (indicated on the left) with community-building efforts (on the right) in Stages II and III. Participatory design methods are utilised

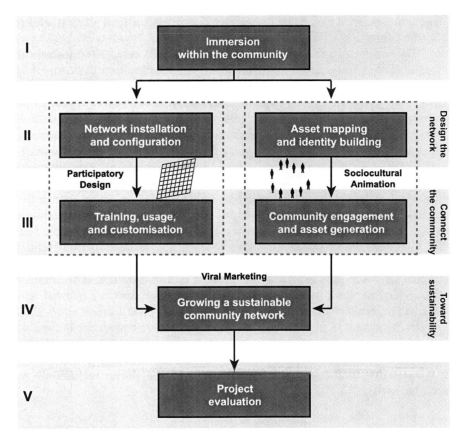

Figure 10.3. Stages of the methodological response.

to *create* the technical infrastructure, to provide *access* to information, and to ensure *usability* within the context of human–computer interaction and human-centred systems design, whereas sociocultural animation is employed to *populate* the network, to make *use* of information, and to improve *sociability* within the context of social ties and human peer-to-peer networks. Stage IV adapts principles of viral marketing to grow a socially sustainable network and to establish a culture that strengthens the community portal, so 'it becomes an institutional actor with relationships to other community institutions, as well as to individuals and their groups' (Carroll & Rosson, 2003, p. 384). Although the ongoing process of critical enquiry, reflection, and action within the action research paradigm already incorporates an ongoing commitment to evaluation within each stage, the research aspect of the model closes with a final project evaluation in Stage V.

Each stage of the methodology and individual conceptual influences are discussed in more detail in Foth (2008, forthcoming). In the context of the KGUV, research data was gathered in advance of the systems design by consulting with a group of people representative of the demographic to be expected to live in the KGUV (Meyrick & Fitzgerald, 2005). This baseline research helped us articulate the findings and considerations just discussed, which enabled more than an 'informed guess' at what type of communication features will allow the portal to add value to residents' existing communication mix. However, in order to enable an ongoing commitment to participatory design, residents have to be able to play an active role in the systems design when they move into the KGUV. The approach introduced here is thus embedded in a framework of network action research (see Ch. 6, this volume), which moves away from a pure homogenous model of community and acknowledges the fluid, dynamic, swarming, chaotic qualities of social networks that are present in communities. The primary objective of network action research is to map the existing (formal and informal) networks that operate within the KGUV and initiate small PAR projects within each of them. The task of the action researcher is then to link and harness each of these subnetworks of enquiry to form a larger networked community of practice. Cycles of reflection and informed action will then drive the continuing development of the portal technology to suit the needs of KGUV residents.

Conclusion

Interdisciplinary investigations of the communicative ecology in neighbourhoods and vertical real estate in urban capitals of the developed world are timely as they contribute to an advanced understanding of the changing facets of community in the intersection between people and place and the role technology plays to facilitate these changes. The KGUV represents a suitable case study to examine if and how urban residents connect with each other to create and maintain social networks and how new media and ICT systems can better support the interaction in those networks.

The increasingly personalised networking behaviour of urban residents together with the aspect of master planning introduces two key challenges to the design and development of community technology for the KGUV. We have discussed our theoretical response to the shifting quality of community as networks. Situating the development within a framework of a communicative ecology introduces design implications that seek to ensure the community portal is of value to KGUV residents. The methodological response combining network action research with participatory design elements is particularly suited to alleviate some of the negative side effects of a top–down approach that master planning brings with it. Both the theoretical and methodological considerations presented here on the basis of baseline research and input by KGUV project stakeholders will be backed up by further empirical data collection and user evaluations over a longer period of time.

The progressive development in the area of community and technology sees a variety of new applications and systems being introduced and disappear rapidly. We believe theory and methodology that can help researchers better understand the wider context and purpose of these developments in order to inform the design and development of community technology are valuable. This chapter hopes to make a contribution to this endeavour.

Chapter 11

Evaluating New Media
in Rural and Outback Areas

**Box 11.1 Case Study of an Australian Rural Community's Participation
in a New Media Evaluation Project**

The Tara Shire is located 330 km inland from Brisbane, the capital of Queensland, on the east coast of Australia. It has nine small townships and settlements scattered in some 11,661 km² of 'prime hard wheat country.' When our research began in 2002, the Shire's population was just over 3,800, with 1,000 people occupying the main town. It was identified as one of the top 10 most disadvantaged communities in Queensland (Tara Shire, 2001). Close to one-third of the community was classified as living in very impoverished circumstances on rural residential subdivisions with few services and facilities.

Communication problems were considerable in the Shire. As well as a lack of effective cell phone coverage, the Shire had no local newspaper or radio station and experienced extensive problems with telephone services. Furthermore, most roads were unsealed, public transport was minimal, and certain areas of the Shire had mail delivered only twice a week.

These social, economic, technological, and geographic factors played a role in what seemed to be a divided community. Many people were seen as 'apathetic and negative' and there was minimal proactive leadership apparent. As a result, the Shire lagged behind other areas in development and in the appropriation of new media.

However, in 2000, the election of a new mayor and Shire Councillors provided an encouraging fresh direction in leadership. The council's focus was on building a more cooperative, proactive community. Community leaders—in particular women—fostered this positive approach by running workshops and organising a multicultural festival. New initiatives that used new media included the following:

continued on next page

Box 11.1 *Continued*

- the Tara Shire Community website (www.tara.qld.gov.au), sponsored and managed by the Shire Council,
- public internet access at the library;
- a Learning Network Queensland Centre, which provided support to distance education students;
- computer and internet training courses;
- the 'Cyberflora' project, which used new media to collaboratively design a public mural in a botanic garden;
- a primary school website developed by its school students; and
- after-hours access to school computers and the internet for adults, who were taught by the school children.

This enthusiastic response to new media encouraged the Tara Shire Council to participate in an action research project conducted by our research team at Queensland University of Technology. They thought the action research process would improve the community's effectiveness in collaboratively reaching its goals, and generally in planning and evaluation. Additionally, council staff hoped that communication across the Shire, and training and access to new media would also be improved. The council's Community and Economic Development officer coordinated the project on a local level, assisted by the council's information technology support officer.

Eight people (seven women and one man) attended the initial community leaders' meeting and 23 people (fifteen women and eight men) took part in the first community workshop, which included presentations reporting on local new media projects and small group discussions. Participants were from diverse age groups and their occupations ranged from education and training to community and youth development, from retail and accounting to agriculture. A priest, three retirees, and an unemployed person also participated.

New media and information technologies are seen by many as vital to community and economic development in rural, regional, and outback Australia and in developing countries (Da Rin & Groves, 1999; Digital Opportunity Initiative, 2001; Dutta, Lanvin, & Paua, 2004; Groves & Da Rin, 1999). Implemented in ways that meet community and business needs and goals, and key sustainability criteria, such initiatives can help rural communities to survive and prosper, and to address key issues such as digital inequality between rural and urban areas (Geiselhart, 2004; Gurstein, 2001; L. Simpson et al., 2001; R. Simpson, 2001). However, many new media initiatives in rural Australia have failed. This has been due to factors such as the small, highly scattered populations in many rural and outback areas, limited funding and resources, lack of access to training and technical support, and reliance on enthusiastic local 'champions' (Lennie, Hearn, Simpson, & Kimber, 2005). The long-term sustainability of these initiatives is therefore a major issue. As Gurstein (2001) pointed out, new media initiatives raise several complex challenges and issues for community development and empowerment. A significant issue is the need to build community and organisational capacities in planning, developing, and evaluating new media initiatives.

This chapter considers these issues, drawing on the outcomes of two interrelated participatory action research (PAR) projects conducted at Queensland University of Technology (QUT): the LEARNERS[1] project and the EvaluateIT kit project (Lennie et al., 2004; Lennie, Hearn, & Hanrahan, 2005). Using PAR and participatory evaluation, the LEARNERS project aimed to build capacities in planning and evaluating community-based new media initiatives such as websites and information literacy programs. This type of evaluation differs from related evaluations of new media such as the user-centred approach to designing computer applications based on scenarios (Rosson & Carroll, 2002) or 'goal-directed design methodology' (Cooper & Reimann, 2003) in a number of ways. First, the evaluation is planned and conducted by the community with guidance from professionals, rather than by an outside expert. Second, the focus is on the use of new media for broad community and economic development purposes, rather than more narrow organisational or business purposes. However, we acknowledge that incorporating user-centred approaches to new media design would have broadened the scope of the project, and may have resulted in new media designs that were even more effective in meeting community needs.

We begin by introducing the project and the LEARNERS process that was trialed and evaluated in two rural communities. Following this, we discuss some of the major theoretical underpinnings of the project, including our perspectives on community empowerment and capacity-building, the role of rural women in the uptake of new media and community development, and the sustainability of new media initiatives. We then outline the multiple research, evaluation, and participation methods used in the LEARNERS project. Next we describe the development of

---

[1]LEARNERS stands for Learning, Evaluation, Action and Reflection for New technologies, Empowerment and Rural Sustainability (see Hearn et al., 2005; Lennie, 2005; Lennie et al., 2004; Lennie, Hearn, Simpson, & Kimber, 2005).

the online EvaluateIT toolkit, and present a case study of its successful use by a community group to evaluate a rural library website. The various outcomes and impacts of the LEARNERS project on participants and the rural communities involved are then discussed.

The LEARNERS Project

Building on an earlier pilot project by Lennie, Lundin, and Simpson (2000), the LEARNERS project aimed to identify and develop the existing skills, knowledge, and resources in two rural communities, and to enhance community empowerment and inclusion. An interdisciplinary research team from QUT, five public-sector partners, and participants in the Tara and Stanthorpe Shires in southern Queensland collaborated on the project from 2001 to 2004. As the case study in Box 11.1 indicated, Tara Shire has a small population scattered over a large area and was considered to be a disadvantaged community. In contrast, the Stanthorpe Shire has a smaller area with a larger population, and was more advantaged in terms of communication, education, and other services.

Figure 11.1 shows the PAR approach known as the LEARNERS process that was implemented and evaluated as part of the project. The LEARNERS process was considered innovative in that it took a 'whole of community' systems approach; used PAR and participatory evaluation methods; encouraged analysis of differences such as gender, age, ethnicity, and levels of information literacy; and sought to develop 'learning communities' (Faris, 2001). Implementation of the LEARNERS process also aimed to increase collaboration and cooperation between diverse community organisations and groups and to generate new awareness, knowledge, and ideas about the use of new media for sustainable community and economic development. The project was considered relatively unique in that few new media projects in the community development field appear to have used a combination of PAR and participatory evaluation methods.

Theoretical Underpinnings

Community Empowerment

The LEARNERS project was influenced by feminist critiques which suggest that research projects that aim to be empowering can have contradictory effects and that claims that research and evaluation projects have produced empowerment require closer examination (Anderson, 1996; Lennie, 2001).

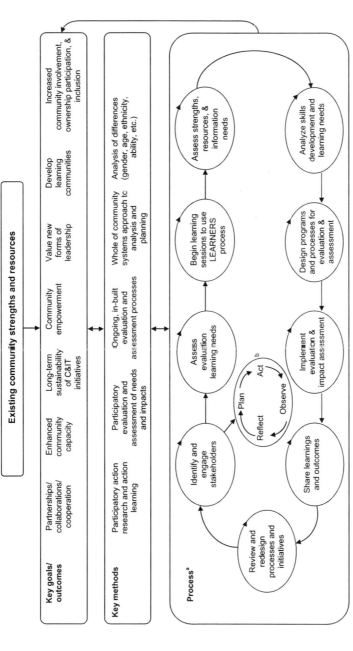

Key goals/ outcomes

| Partnerships/ collaborations/ cooperation | Enhanced community capacity | Long-term sustainability of C&IT initiatives | Community empowerment | Value new forms of leadership | Develop learning communities | Increased community involvement, ownership participation, & inclusion |

Existing community strengths and resources

Key methods

| Participatory action research and action learning | Participatory evaluation and assessment of needs and impacts | Ongoing, in-built evaluation and assessment processes | Whole of community systems approach to analysis and planning | Analysis of differences (gender, age, ethnicity, ability, etc.) |

Process[a]

Identify and engage stakeholders

Review and redesign processes and initiatives

Share learnings and outcomes

Assess evaluation learning needs

Plan — Act[b]
Reflect — Observe

Implement evaluation & impact assessment

Begin learning sessions to use LEARNERS process

Assess strengths, resources, & information needs

Design programs and processes for evaluation & assessment

Analyze skills development and learning needs

[a] All of these steps do not have to be followed and do not have to be undertaken in this sequence. They represent activities that could potentially be undertaken by stakeholders and participants.

[b] Each of the steps involves a cycle of planning, acting, observing, and reflecting

Figure 11.1. The LEARNERS process.

Empowerment was viewed as a long-term process that people undertake for themselves, rather than something that is done 'to' or 'for' another person (Lather, 1991). However, outsiders such as researchers were considered to play important roles in the process of empowerment by providing information and support, and encouraging less empowered participants to gain confidence and 'free themselves of traditional dependency' (Friedmann, 1992, p. 77). Empowerment can result in an increased sense of power, confidence and control, which is often the result of successful action (Friedmann, 1992). It can happen at the level of the individual, the group, and/or the community (Claridge, 1996).

The capacity-building methods used in the LEARNERS project were seen as underpinned by positive *power to* and *power with* models in which power is considered as social and cooperative, rather than negative and related to domination and control (Deutchman, 1991). However, the research team recognised that a community member's choice not to participate, or to only participate in a limited way, was one that is legitimate and rational (Lennie et al., 2004).

The LEARNERS research team therefore adopted a critical approach that questioned assumptions about community participation, empowerment, and the sustainability of new media initiatives. This approach recognised the often complex and contradictory nature of these processes that can affect the outcome of PAR and participatory evaluation projects. It also recognised the importance of paying attention to the communicative and relational dimensions of capacity-building and evaluation projects (McKie, 2003).

Building Community Capacities in Evaluation

A broad range of education and community development projects, including new media projects, have effectively used participatory forms of research and evaluation for more than 30 years (Brunner & Guzman, 1989; Fetterman, 2001; Hudson, 2001; Papineau & Kiely, 1996). Even so, a significant number of people in rural organisations and groups have minimal skills, knowledge, and experience in participatory forms of planning and evaluation. There is a need to build community and organisational capacities in these processes and this need has been increasingly recognised (Boyle & Lemaire, 1999; Fetterman, 2001; Khan, 1998; O'Sullivan & O'Sullivan, 1998). PAR, empowerment evaluation (Fetterman, 2001), and other forms of participatory evaluation have been found to be effective in developing these capacities (see also the strategies suggested in Bracht, 1999).

A key aim of the LEARNERS project was therefore to build community and organisational awareness, skills, confidence, and capacities in PAR and participatory planning and evaluation. Community capacity-building has been defined as 'strengthening the knowledge, skills and attitudes of people so that they can establish and sustain their area's development' (Mannion, 1996, p. 2). It is seen as the ability of communities to solve their own problems, make their own decisions, and plan their own futures. Community capacity-building programs aim to increase community participation in planning and decision making; to facilitate sustainable development by building on existing community strengths; and to create communities that are more inclusive, cooperative, and self-reliant. Local solutions to achieving sustainable community development and the effective use of new media in this process are important outcomes of a capacity-building approach.

Analysis of Gender and Other Differences

Women in Australian rural communities are making significant contributions to the social and economic development of their communities, and provide important formal and informal leadership (Alston, 1995; Grace & Lennie, 1998; Office for Women, 2003; The Rural Women and ICTs Research Team, 1999). They have also been found to be early adopters of information and communication technologies (ICTs) and new media technologies (Grace, Lundin, & Daws, 1996; Moyal, 1989; The Rural Women and ICTs Research Team, 1999). Although this suggests that gender analysis should be an important focus of the evaluation of new media projects, it is often neglected. However, as well as gender, the LEARNERS project took age, occupation, level of information literacy, and other differences, as well as issues related to social justice and power into account. This approach enabled identification of users and nonusers of new media technologies, and relevant information such as gaps in new media services and community attitudes to new technologies. Research shows that it is more often the empowered, educated members of communities who have higher levels of access to new communication technologies, rather than those who are more disadvantaged (The Rural Women and ICTs Team, 1999; Scott, Diamond, & Smith, 1997). This finding is common in innovation research in general, and in many digital-divide and knowledge-gap studies (Rice, 2002), and needs to be taken into account in any evaluation of community-based new media initiatives.

Sustainability of New Media Initiatives

Governments and rural industry organisations have positioned new media technologies such as the internet as integral to community and economic development in rural, regional, and outback Australia. Technologies such as e-mail, community websites, online discussion lists, teleconferencing, and videoconferencing are being used in these areas to access education, health and legal services and information, and for business, networking, communication, and entertainment. Rural people are expected to benefit economically from new technologies because they will provide new employment opportunities, the potential to buy and sell online, an increase in services, and access to education and training, among other impacts (Da Rin & Groves 1999; Groves & Da Rin 1999; Gurstein, 2001; Hearn et al., 2005).

However, as noted earlier, many new media initiatives in rural Australia have failed as a result of a complex range of factors. For instance, only 75% of the 600 or more telecentres established in Australia since the 1990s are still functioning today (Geiselhart, 2004). Because Australian government funding programs such as Networking the Nation have a limited life span, communities must discover methods for making new media projects economically viable and, most importantly, self-sufficient (Department of Communications, Information Technology and the Arts, 2003; Gurstein, 2001). Given this, an approach to evaluation and impact assessment that takes a wide range of social, cultural, economic, technological, and environmental factors into account is required. This type of whole of community systems approach was an important feature of the LEARNERS process.

For communities in rural, regional, and outback Australia, the long-term sustainability of new media initiatives is therefore a key imperative. Limited funding, scarce resources, and the small and widely dispersed populations in these areas all contribute to this need for new media projects that are, or can become, autonomous of outside input. Within rural communities the 'balance of contribution' is also an important factor. Successful new media initiatives in communities are often maintained by small groups of passionate 'champions' and supporters (Schuler, 1996). These volunteers, participants, and leaders may already be overcommitted or may live in the community for only a short time, thus reducing the sustainability of initiatives.

New media initiatives therefore bring to light a significant number of multifaceted challenges and concerns for rural community development and empowerment. Important issues for rural communities include the following:

- facilitating access to and adoption of new and rapidly evolving ICTs by all community groups and sectors;
- identifying the diverse ICT access and information literacy training needs of community members and groups;

- content and effective use ('If you build it, they will come');

- securing ongoing funding and resources for initiatives;

- planning, developing, and managing projects and initiatives; and

- evaluating what are often quite complex projects and initiatives that use new communication technologies (Lennie, Hearn, Simpson, & Kimber, 2005)

Designing effective strategies for access and participation that consider differences in community needs, and local social, economic, environmental, and technological factors can result in more equitable access to new media. Furthermore, research indicates that such an approach can also increase the overall sustainability and success of new media initiatives (Hearn et al., 2005; Gurstein, 2001; L. Simpson et al., 2001; The Rural Women and ICTs Research Team, 1999).

Methods Used in the LEARNERS Project

Given the approach just outlined, the local coordinators for the LEARN-ERS project were encouraged to take an inclusive approach to community participation that aimed to involve a wide cross-section of their community in workshops and other activities. In particular, they were encouraged to target people involved in or affected by specific local new media initiatives, that is, those initiatives chosen by the research participants to be evaluated. Furthermore, participants were encouraged to seek information regarding relevant differences such as those related to gender and access to new media when conducting evaluations.

In keeping with the use of PAR and participatory evaluation, the research team used a range of qualitative and quantitative methods to conduct and evaluate project activities, share information, and regularly communicate. Various forms of new media were extensively used to conduct these activities. The methods used included the following:

- meetings, workshops, teleconferences, and videoconferences involving community participants and industry partners;

- focus group discussions and individual interviews;

- workshop feedback questionnaires;

- participant observations of project activities;

- fieldwork diary entries;

- providing information via our research website (www.learners.qut. edu.au);

- sharing information and obtaining feedback through two e-mail discussion lists; and

- annual critical reflection workshops involving the research team, industry partners, and key community participants.

Use of these multiple participation, research, and evaluation methods resulted in a range of rich research data and ongoing feedback, which enabled rigorous validation of both the findings and subsequent case studies and data analysis. The coding and analysis of project impacts used the framework of rural women's empowerment developed by Lennie (2001). This framework comprises four interrelated forms of empowerment: social, technological, political, and psychological (see Lennie, 2005, for an account of the analysis of project impacts). A summary of project impacts is presented later in this chapter.

The coding process involved entering full transcripts from the interviews, focus groups, and critical reflection workshops into the NVivo program, then creating a number of tree nodes and free nodes related to the four forms of empowerment and corresponding forms of disempowerment. Each of the documents was then coded using these nodes. The data analysis process involved creating tables that list various empowering or disempowering impacts of the project. They also contained the number of women and men in each community who had reported in interviews, focus groups, or critical reflection workshops that they or others had experienced these impacts or effects. The significance of these impacts was then assessed, based on the number of participants who indicated that they or others had experienced these impacts. This data was then triangulated with data from workshop feedback questionnaires and other sources.

Development of the EvaluateIT Kit

In late 2003, in response to community feedback, the research team developed a less complex model of PAR and participatory evaluation than the LEARNERS process. Participants had stressed the need for an action research process that was easier to understand and suggested that it should include more case studies and examples. The resulting action research model was an online resource kit called EvaluateIT (see www.evaluateit.org). This kit was developed by the LEARNERS research team in collaboration with staff of the State Library of Queensland (SLQ) as part of a smaller research project conducted in 2004. The kit contained four simple steps (described later) with guiding questions and a case study of the entire evaluation process. A broad range of additional information and resources was also provided. Based on feedback from participants, a decision was made to use the term *review* rather than evaluation in the kit because the term review had fewer negative connotations.

Community groups who want to collaboratively evaluate and redesign their new media projects can easily access EvaluateIT with a basic internet connection. The resources include the following:

- a home page with links to the four EvaluateIT steps: (1) plan the review, (2) involve people in the review, (3) do the review, (4) review results and make the changes (see Fig. 11.2);

- guiding questions for each step;

- links to a 'More help with these questions' page;

- information about ways of using the kit with community groups;

- a comprehensive case study of the whole evaluation cycle, based on the fictional 'Westana' rural community (parts of this case study were adapted from actual examples);

- links to other electronic resources including toolkits, information on evaluation methods, community development and community information technology, and relevant publications;

- links from key terms to a glossary providing simple definitions of the major processes, concepts, and terms used in the kit;

- word and PDF versions of the kit that can be downloaded; and

- an online feedback form.

To obtain feedback about the prototype EvaluateIT kit, we conducted workshops and focus group discussions and distributed questionnaires in four sites representing a range of rural and regional communities in Queensland. These sites were Stanthorpe and Tara in southern Queensland, and Townsville and Charters Towers in north Queensland. Workshops conducted prior to the focus groups allowed each group to begin working through a participatory evaluation using the EvaluateIT kit.

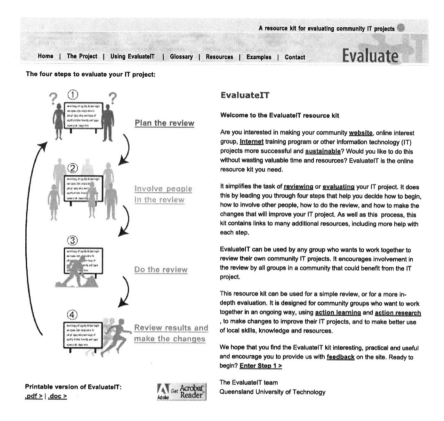

Figure 11.2. The EvaluateIT home page.

Case Study of the Use of the EvaluateIT Kit

In June 2004 a community group from Stanthorpe Shire took part in trialing and evaluating the prototype EvaluateIT kit. This Shire is located 230km southwest of Brisbane in a farming region that is popular with tourists because of its many wineries and nearby national parks. A significant outcome of the LEARNERS project in this community was the development of a group that aimed to develop the region as a learning community. The aims of learning communities are closely related to the goals of community capacity-building. They involve community members from every sector working together to enhance the social, economic, cultural, and environmental conditions of their community and to promote life-long learning (Faris, 2001).

The new library website was chosen as the focus for the evaluation workshop after discussions with local project participants, including the manager of Stanthorpe Library services. Effective local library services were a priority for this community's evaluation group, given the strong emphasis placed on life-long learning in the community.

The Stanthorpe Shire Council, which operates the library, was a key collaborator in the LEARNERS project. In total, the workshop was attended by 10 women: five local project participants, two members of the QUT research team, one representative from SLQ, one partner in the LEARNERS project, and one local school teacher. The teacher had shown interest in the project and agreed to facilitate the workshop. The local project participants were the council's web coordinator/public relations officer, a disability support group volunteer, a community development worker, a small business operator who was very active in the community, and the manager of Stanthorpe Library Services.

Participants were provided with a copy of the four EvaluateIT steps and accompanying questions. The EvaluateIT website was projected on a screen that all participants could clearly see. Notes from the workshop were displayed on butcher's paper and later typed up by a member of the research team.

Before the workshop began, the manager of Library Services outlined the library website's history. An earlier website had become outdated and was not 'user-friendly.' During the previous year, a new website for the library had been started by a skilled trainee but funding had run out before the site was completed. The manager thought there was still 'room for improvement.'

Prior to the workshop, participants were asked to review the library website and the EvaluateIT kit and to make notes and bring them to the workshop for discussion. The workshop began with a participant driven feedback forum. Participants highlighted elements of the library website that they thought worked well, or did not work so well and suggested improvements. Overall, the reaction to the new library site was positive with several ideas for improvement put forward.

The facilitator then guided participants through the process of providing comments and suggestions for the four EvaluateIT steps.

1. Plan the review.

2. Involve people in the review.

3. Do the review.

4. Review results and make the changes.

In Step 1, participants were asked to identify the purpose(s) of the review and decide who would conduct it. Some of the purposes named included:

- to get funding;

- to improve the site;

- to maximise community access and use and address community needs; and

- to assess the ongoing costs involved (time and money).

Participants also identified potential risks with doing the review. They discussed the possibility that negative feedback could be 'demotivating' and that, depending on who became involved, clashes between different opinions and needs might occur. Potential ethical issues were also discussed. For example, written consent from owners/subjects would be required for any photograph before it was used on the site.

Step 2 began with a short brainstorming session. Participants listed a variety of community groups and organisations, and types of community members who could be asked to join in the evaluation. They included Youth Council members, University of the Third Age students, 'out of towners with young families,' and students undertaking Introduction to the internet courses held by the library. Beyond this, participants proposed that non-library users, past library members, and general library clientele take part. Feedback from 'irate customers' and developers of other library websites was also considered valuable.

Next, participants discussed ways of encouraging people to become involved in the evaluation, such as:

- running evaluation sessions for different age groups;

- using captive audiences such as participants at youth group meetings;

- offering incentives such as morning tea and information about the library website;

- asking people to complete surveys while they are at the library; and

- broadcasting information about the evaluation through avenues such as community radio talk-back.

Step 3 involved participants discussing the goals of the library website. They then considered how the library was attempting to reach these goals and how the library could assess its success in reaching these goals. Some of the goals discussed included 'to provide a means of engaging people,' and 'to promote the library's services.'

The library manager explained that they currently obtained mainly verbal feedback, which was used both to check progress toward goals and to gauge the effectiveness of library services. Methods suggested for evaluating the library website included adding traffic counters to each website page, gathering feedback via a street survey, and conducting a survey as part of an Adult Learners Week forum for community groups. Participants thought this forum would be an ideal opportunity to 'showcase' the new library website.

Based on these discussions, participants considered how the website could be improved. Some participants thought the ideas generated at the initial workshop could be shaped into survey questions. Others considered small review workshops an ideal means for obtaining feedback. The library manager said she would aim to implement some of the changes suggested by the group before the Adult Learners Week forum. Participants suggested publicising these updates and the evaluation process in a press release sent to the local newspaper.

In Step 4, participants reflected on the evaluation process used in the workshop. For instance, was the group representative of the broader community? Although it was not a narrow selection, participants agreed that wider community involvement was required. They also emphasised the importance of making the evaluation results available to the Shire Council and other funding bodies or stakeholders who could be involved in improving the website. The library manager considered the feedback provided by the workshop 'thought-provoking' and 'really beneficial.' Both substantial and easy-to-make changes to the website had been identified in a short space of time.

Finally, participants brainstormed ideas for ways in which the suggested changes could actually be made. They decided that the library should be responsible for making the changes. Many of the suggested improvements could be implemented easily and quickly. Participants proposed that community organisations or arts funding bodies be approached to help cover the cost of more expensive changes. These funding campaigns could be bolstered by positive statistics gathered from the surveys that had been suggested. Most importantly, community knowledge of the website could be raised by the local media. This might also create interest in being involved in the evaluation.

Although she was 'disappointed that we couldn't get more people along,' the library manager reported that her expectations for the whole process were 'met really well.' Immediately after the workshop, a focus group was held to gather feedback on the EvaluateIT kit and the workshop process. Comments included the following:

- The workshop was easy to facilitate.

- It was good to have an experienced person to help facilitate the evaluation.

- It was easy to see what's expected of participants.

- Doing the review at the same time as planning the evaluation worked well—doing a review within a review is a natural "circles within circles process."

- Flexibility in the process is good—it's OK to jump between steps of the process.

- Everyone was able to make valuable input into the discussion.

- The discussions were stimulating.

- It was a good process for pulling together various ideas.

Participants thought the EvaluateIT kit gave structure to a process that had the potential to be chaotic and difficult. They commented that the kit helped them know what issues to consider. Furthermore, the 'precise' step-by-step process also gave 'a feeling of unity to the process.' The guiding questions for each step were described as 'useful for prompting the discussion' and the 'More help with these questions section' was considered 'very valuable.' One participant thought the opportunity for 'equal input from group members' was valuable, whereas another commented that it seemed like 'a nondiscriminatory resource.' Despite these successes, participants identified some areas for improvement. For instance, it could be a 'challenge' to get people involved in the evaluation workshop. Also, some participants found it difficult to 'visualise the experience.' Finally, it was suggested that 'what was expected from the people participating in the review' be made more explicit.

Outcomes and Impacts of the LEARNERS Project

The LEARNERS project took place in the Tara and Stanthorpe communities over three years. The development and testing of the EvaluateIT kit occurred during the final year of the project. During this time, our research team worked closely with members of the community, assisting them in the development, evaluation, and redesign of local new media systems such as community websites and internet training programs. Such new media systems aimed to allow the community to operate more effectively and to become learning communities.

The project aimed to facilitate community participation, empowerment, and capacity-building in planning and evaluation. Our meta-evaluation of the project indicated that, for those who actively participated in the project, these aims were met to varying degrees. We found that participants experienced the four forms of empowerment used in the analysis (social, technological, political, and psychological), albeit at differing levels (Lennie, 2005; Lennie et al., 2004). Overall, the outcomes and impacts were particularly positive in the Tara Shire, which was considered to be a disadvantaged community with a high level of need for improved communication systems and better community networking and cohesion.

However, because of inequalities in power and knowledge, the different values and agendas of the participants and researchers, the pre-existing relationships and networks within the communities, and other complex issues, the project also had a number of unintended and disempowering impacts. They included a perceived lack of ownership and control of some project activities, and confusion and misunderstandings about the project and the LEARNERS process. Several other barriers to community participation, empowerment, and capacity-building were identified, such as a lack of time and/or capacity to participate, the loss of key 'champions' in the community, and lack of access to or limited experience with technology. Similar barriers have been identified in other community-based projects (Boyce, 2001; Lennie, 2002; O'Meara, Chesters, & Han, 2004). Such issues and barriers indicate fundamental contextual factors that must be acknowledged when conducting capacity building and new media projects in rural and regional areas.

Because of the small number of participants who were actively involved in the project, community capacity-building was restricted. This also resulted from other barriers and issues connected with participation and empowerment. Later, however, ripple effects of the capacity-building that was achieved were experienced and reported. Skills that had been developed in the project were used in other community situations. Use of new media for communication and networking also increased. The following sections briefly provide examples of these effects.

As in the community capacity-building project reported by O'Meara et al. (2004), involving a broad range of community members and organisations became problematic. Although in the initial stages of our research a larger number of people participated in the project, over time group numbers lessened significantly. Participants were mainly women aged between 40 and 59 and tended to be White and/or with Anglo-Celtic ethnicity. Most participants worked in the areas of community development, education and training, or local government, in both paid and voluntary positions and only a few were from the business sector. Some participants held formal leadership positions in local government, community, or business groups and organisations.

The majority of core-group participants had a significant level of skills, experience, and knowledge in project-related areas and in new media usage at the beginning of the project. However, throughout the project, these participants increased their knowledge and understanding of participatory planning and evaluation. Participants also gained a deeper understanding of new media, and new knowledge, ideas and strategies for improving and making local new media initiatives more sustainable.

Several participants and community organisations made new or greater use of new media technologies (such as e-mail and teleconferencing) for communication, community development, and networking. This happened most significantly in Tara Shire. For example, the community and economic development officer in Tara Shire collaboratively developed a major funding proposal for public internet access with community members from far-reaching parts of the Shire. This was achieved using an expanded new media skill set gained during the project. In general, despite a small number of remaining problems, communication, and information-sharing initiatives—including the Tara Shire community website—were considered to have improved greatly. Moreover, Tara participants showed a significant improvement in skills and confidence related to using e-mail and other communication technologies. In Stanthorpe Shire, increased networking among the Learning Community Project group via e-mail and face-to-face meetings was considered to be a significant outcome of the project.

In both the Tara and Stanthorpe communities, many active participants, particularly women, reported that their leadership and networking activities had been enhanced and that they had obtained and shared valuable new information. In certain cases, participants and industry partners gained a different or broader perspective on the communities and new light was shed on particular community issues. In the initial stages of the project the concept of action research caused confusion, as did the purpose of the project itself. However, the workshops empowered community members by acting as a forum to voice issues of concern and an avenue to pursue interest in communication systems, life-long learning, and new media access and use.

Conclusion

The LEARNERS project employed multiple research, evaluation, and participation methods and made extensive use of new media technologies. This resulted in rich research data, ongoing feedback from participants and stakeholders, and rigorous validation of results and case studies. However, in response to community feedback about the complexity of the LEARNERS process, the online EvaluateIT toolkit was developed. Our case study of a community group's use of this kit demonstrated its value in structuring the evaluation process, facilitating community input, and suggesting key questions and issues to discuss and consider.

Our research indicates that the success of future capacity building programs in rural and regional areas may be largely dependent on facilitating rural women's empowerment. This is mainly because of rural women's significant leadership roles in community development and new media projects, and their early adoption of new media technologies such as the internet (The Rural Women and ICTs Research Team, 1999; Wells & Tanner, 1994).

Based on the outcomes of this research, we identified a number of principles and strategies that may assist researchers, government workers, and communities to plan and conduct more effective PAR and capacity-building projects and ongoing evaluations of new media initiatives (see Lennie, Hearn, Simpson, & Kimber, 2005). Our research findings indicate that, once put in place, these strategies, in conjunction with ongoing participatory evaluations, should help to increase both the sustainability of new media initiatives and rural and outback communities.

Chapter 12

Conclusion: Key Themes and Future Directions

Throughout this volume, we have shown how action research can overcome many of the problems inherent in using traditional methodologies for media and communication research by producing continuous learning, insight, and actionable knowledge. We positioned action research as a methodology, a meta-process for managing enquiry, and a research culture that can result in ongoing change and improvements to new media initiatives in ways that better meet the diverse needs and goals of organisations, community members, and others.

As an approach that engages all participants and stakeholders in a process of practical problem solving, we argued that action research is an especially appropriate methodology for developing, researching, evaluating, and managing new media projects. This approach is particularly suitable to new media initiatives because they involve constant innovation and change, have unpredictable outcomes, and require flexibility, creativity, and an open, inclusive, user-centred approach. Action research is also closely connected to the technology design or evaluation process.

New media was seen as having technology, social, and content layers. We argued that the content layer—the realm of creativity and expression—is what makes technology media. The numerous ways in which new media can be used as an integral, innovative, and effective component of action research projects for purposes such as networking and collaboration, and developing creative content, were demonstrated.

Our examples and case studies indicate the value of this approach in addressing a number of important contemporary problems and issues. For example, we showed how ethnographic action research (EAR) can enable the voices of the poor to be heard in dialogues through the use of information and communication technologies (ICTs) in community and cultural development. We indicated how anticipatory action research (AAR) can lead to more appropriate technology design and policy development

209

that takes advantage of the most desirable features of new media, while avoiding undesirable social impacts. We also discussed the value of network action research for creating more inclusive and democratic communication contexts, and how participatory action research and participatory evaluation can increase the sustainability of new media projects in rural areas.

However, we acknowledge that doing new media action research is difficult work and, as a mixed-methods approach, it 'makes heavy demands on professional social researchers' (Greenwood & Levin, 2006, p. 98). Other issues include the problems involved in working within hierarchical organisational structures and in engaging powerful stakeholders, and the highly resource and time-intensive nature of action research. Additionally, our research has also shown that, given the complex power, knowledge, and discursive issues involved, and other factors, new media action research can have contradictory effects, despite its emancipative aspirations (see Ch. 11, this volume; Lennie, 2005; Lennie et al., 2003).

In this chapter, we begin by summarising the key elements of the theoretical and conceptual framework for new media action research we have set out in this book. We then outline our broad methodological framework for new media action research. We believe that these conceptual and methodological frameworks offer a valuable means of guiding new media projects. In the final section, we consider some of the future directions for action research and new media, based on the themes and issues we have identified in this book and elsewhere, and recent debates in this field.

Theoretical and Conceptual Framework for New Media Action Research

In Chapter 2, we presented a theoretical and conceptual framework and a number of methodological principles that we argued offer a useful means of guiding new media projects. The key elements of this framework are summarised here. Our broad methodological approach, which is underpinned by the principles we outlined, is summarised in the next section.

Taking a Critical Perspective

We advocated adopting a critical perspective that questions assumptions about both action research and new media. Greenwood and Levin (2006), Reason and Bradbury (2001), and others suggest that action research is a democratic and participatory approach to practical problem solving, improvement, and change that can lead to more just, inclusive, participatory, and sustainable communities. We agree with this view, but are realistic about the many issues and challenges that must be addressed in doing action research in this field. This includes an awareness of the potentially unintended negative or undesirable effects of both action research and new media.

Considering the Communicative Ecology

We proposed that the concept *communicative ecology* is particularly valuable in new media research. This concept recognises that any 'new' connections and networks (social and technical) that develop as a result of the introduction of individual ICTs will be far more effective if they are interconnected with existing, locally appropriate systems, and structures. A communicative ecology was seen as having a technology layer (devices and connecting media), a social layer (people and ways of organising and networking them), and a discursive layer (content—the ideas and themes originating from the social layer).

We suggested that using an ecological metaphor encourages us to take the wider social and cultural context and existing local communication networks into account in our research projects. We argued that this concept enables us to analyse such things as how members of a community engage with each other, and how different features of the ecology rise and fall with time. This concept is also an important component of the holistic perspective we adopt that recognises the connectedness of everything and suggests the need to adopt multiple perspectives.

Recognising Multicausality

An implication of the connected, holistic perspective that we advocate is the recognition that any explanation of a phenomenon such as the introduction of new media technology involves multiple causes and effects. Our approach respects this multicausality and seeks to build redundancy into the systems, interventions, and enquiry processes we develop.

Adopting a Co-Evolutionary Perspective

We argued for an alternative co-evolutionary perspective on the interaction between technology and society. This was considered more useful than the bipolar positions of technological determinism and the social construction of technology. A co-evolutionary perspective assumes a reciprocal relationship between the social and the technical, and takes impacts that are not dependent on their cultural appropriation into account. We believe that new media action research is most usefully guided by this philosophical position.

A Focus on Tacit and Codified Knowledge

We pointed out that action research uses and produces both codified knowledge (theory, formal arguments, etc.) and tacit knowledge (knowledge that is embedded in the actions and everyday experiences of participants). We suggested that in new media projects, it is essential to gain access to the participant or client's tacit knowledge, given that it is an important source of the construction of knowledge about organisations and communities, and the implementation of changes in these entities. Tacit knowledge is therefore an important part of the local communicative ecology of new media projects. The interplay between tacit and codified knowledge was seen as fostered by establishing an action research culture within organisations and community initiatives.

Respecting Diversity and Difference

Diversity in such things as gender, age, ethnicity, knowledge, experience, and perspectives was seen as a valuable source of positive change and innovative ideas and solutions in new media projects. Giving value to diversity and difference was considered important because it enables a more adequate understanding of problems, and provides new insights and understanding of other perspectives (Morgan & Ramirez, 1984). It also helps us to avoid making unhelpful generalisations about particular social groups such as women, youth, the elderly, and indigenous people, and to acknowledge the multiple, sometimes conflicting roles, identities, and interests of the various groups involved in action research projects. Respecting and valuing diversity and difference also entails paying attention to gender and other equity and social justice issues that are increasingly relevant in new media projects, given the growing digital inequality experienced by people in many countries around the world.

Acknowledging Power and Knowledge Differences

We argued that instead of adopting an idealistic view that assumes that all participants in an action research project are the same and equal, it is more useful to openly acknowledge the differences between participants, and between participants and researchers, especially those related to power and knowledge. We identified the Foucauldian model of power (Humphries, 1994) as a useful one to draw on in the critical analysis and reflection phases of action research projects, given that this enables rigorous analysis of the shifting and contradictory power–knowledge relations between those involved in new media action research.

A Methodological Framework for New Media Action Research

As noted in the introduction to this chapter, action research can be seen as a *methodology*, a *meta-process* for managing new media projects, and as a *research culture* in which action research becomes embedded in new media projects and all stakeholders are engaged in constant cycles of planning, acting, observing, and reflecting. We argued that, if implemented effectively, this process can create greater levels of understanding, achievement, and improvement of new media projects. Action research was seen as an open-enquiry process in which everything is made public and challengeable. Following Wadsworth (1991), we also advocated taking an open-enquiry approach to the evaluation of new media projects that is improvement and change-oriented and takes an open, interpretative, and creative approach. The main elements of our methodological framework are summarised here.

A User-Centred Approach to Design

We highlighted the connection between existing new media and ICT design and evaluation principles and the action research process. There are three ways in which this occurs: active participation, action-based methods, and generating action. We demonstrated the value of analysing the different levels of meaning that the design and implementation process can invoke as a means of generating deeper understandings of the subjective responses and defensiveness that can often affect the technology implementation process. An EAR approach (Tacchi, Slater, & Hearn, 2003; see also Ch. 5, this volume) which emphasises user participation was seen as enabling designers and researchers to capture a maximum amount of explicit and tacit knowledge, and as providing information and insight that results in better designs. This process also ensures that new media products are more readily accepted and implemented.

Methodological Pluralism

We take a position of methodological pluralism that does not privilege one form of action research over another. We see action research as essentially multidisciplinary, and benefiting from multiple perspectives, methods, and techniques. However, we have introduced some new forms of action research that seem particularly well suited to new media projects, namely EAR, network action research, and AAR. We argued that what brings these different approaches together in a meaningful way is the guidance offered by the conceptual framework and the methodological principles outlined in Chapter 2.

In keeping with our pragmatism and methodological pluralism, we advocated using a mixed-methods approach that focuses on practical outcomes. We suggested that this approach adds rigour to action research and produces richer and better results, compared with mono-method approaches.

Multiple Skills and Competence in Research and Communication

New media action research is challenging to do well and requires multiple skills and abilities in diverse areas such as planning, organising, communication, collaboration, and small-group facilitation. Greenwood and Levin (2006) suggested that action researchers are 'obligated to be competent in all major forms of social research' (p. 6). They outlined a number of process skills that action researchers require: self-confidence, integrity, risk-taking, irony (humour and playfulness), personal security, and patience. In a similar vein, we emphasised the importance of effective communication and interpersonal skills in doing action research well, given the dialogic processes involved. These skills are required to facilitate the development of rapport and mutual understanding, and the production of actionable knowledge and insight through experiential, integrated, co-learning experiences that are enjoyable for both participants and researchers.

Future Directions

Based on the themes and issues identified in this book and elsewhere in the literature, what are the future directions for action research and new media? From his recent review of the action research literature, Dick (2006) concluded that action research is currently 'thriving' but noted that there are still gaps in the literature, particularly in relation to 'building theory from experience in action research' (p. 452). Dick's review also indicates that there appears to be limited use of action research in the new media and ICT field.

New media action research clearly faces the same issues and challenges as action research in general. We believe that there is still much to be done and many issues to address, such as developing more effective forms of collaboration and taking a more critical and rigorous approach that improves the quality of research and evaluation in this field. Designed and used appropriately, and with appropriate infrastructure and resources, we believe that new media tools can help to address some of these issues and to overcome problems related to participation and collaboration. We now consider a number of current and emerging issues and trends that we have identified as relevant to the future directions of both action research and new media.

Digital Inclusion

For more than 20 years, new ICTs have been promoted as transformative technologies, creating new 'knowledge economies' and 'networked societies' (Castells, 1996; Selwyn, 2004). In this era, the term *digital divide*, which emerged as a stark indicator of those who are part of, and those who are not part of these new developments, has increasingly been questioned. We argued in Chapter 8 that that the gap between technology and development is a more appropriate focus than the digital divide between developed and developing countries. We suggested that rather than focusing on macro issues and dominant forms of new media, it is more appropriate to focus on broader concepts such as democratic participation, strengthening civil society and the promotion of rights, alternative configurations of old and new media, and understanding existing communicative ecologies.

Therefore, we consider that the concept of the digital divide is less useful than the concepts of *digital inequality* (DiMaggio & Hargittai, 2001; Selwyn, 2004) or *digital inclusion* as ways of describing the relationships between ICTs, cultural agency, and social contexts. We suggested that although the increasing proliferation of new media technologies offers the theoretical possibility of access to and participation in a global commons, access does not automatically equate to the active or equal participation that is a precondition of voice and the empowerment of those who are disadvantaged.

This indicates that we need to consider the consequences of *engaging with* (rather than simply accessing) ICTs, the effectiveness of this engagement in terms of its short-term outcomes and longer term consequences (Selwyn, 2004), and the most appropriate ways in which this can be measured. Current Queensland University of Technology (QUT) projects such as Finding a Voice are making a significant contribution to understanding the impacts of ICTs and new media in development contexts, using a digital-inclusion perspective and EAR.

Increasing the Sustainability of New Media Projects

We acknowledge that some ICT and new media projects have failed and there is a need to address the long-term sustainability of community-based new media initiatives. This is a significant issue for disadvantaged communities and developing countries in particular. Hearn et al. (2005) suggested the following factors that can assist in achieving the sustainability of ICT initiatives undertaken in pursuit of rural and regional development:

• ensuring clarity in specifying sustainability goals;

• ensuring community involvement in deciding, planning, and evaluating ICT projects;

• adopting a learning approach through cycles of evaluation based on action research;

• leveraging micro-business enterprise development off government-funded technical and human infrastructure provision, and building on local industry strengths;

• learning from global experiences while building on local assets; and

• finding innovative business models to capitalise on new opportunities for content and applications.

Participatory Monitoring and Evaluation of New Media Projects

One of the important ways in which new media projects can become more sustainable and successful is to build in ongoing participatory monitoring and evaluation (PM&E). Combined with methodologies such as EAR, our research indicates that this method can assist in better identifying the intended and unintended impacts of new media projects. Interest in PM&E has grown as a result of:

• the trend toward performance-based accountability;

• the growing demand for greater accountability and demonstrable impact of community development initiatives;

• increased acceptance of the modification of approaches mid-project based on feedback;

• the devolution of central governments and stronger nongovernmental organisation (NGO) capacities; and

• mounting evidence that PM&E produces positive results and are particularly useful in assessing complex community-based initiatives (Hudson, 2001; Lennie, Hearn, Simpson, & Kimber, 2005; Parks, 2005).

However, despite the growing acceptance of PM&E in both developed and developing countries and recognition of its value, this methodology is still not widely used. Reasons for this include issues with defining who should be involved, PM&E seen as lacking credibility in terms of rigour and validity; and PM&E may appear to cost more than nonparticipatory approaches (Parks, 2005).

This suggests an urgent need for a practical, cost-effective, easy-to-use, yet rigorous methodology for assessing the impacts of new media initiatives in development contexts. A new research project entitled *Assessing Communication for Social Change: A New Agenda in Impact Assessment* aims to address these issues. The project, which began in 2007, is being undertaken with staff and participants in community radio projects conducted by Equal Access Nepal, an international NGO, and will run to 2010. The project is being led by Jo Tacchi (from QUT) and Andrew Skuse (from the University of Adelaide) in collaboration with June Lennie (from QUT) and Michael Wilmore (from UA). One of the aims of this project is to develop EAR into a more sophisticated yet functionally amenable project development methodology that both addresses and challenges the requirements for impact assessments of communication for development initiatives, including the blend of qualitative and quantitative assessment.

New Applications of New Media

A key argument in this book is that using new media as an integral part of action research projects can provide many benefits. Several chapters discussed how participants can use tools such as blogs, wikis, discussion boards, and community networks to improve networking and collaboration, and enable creative content development. Some of the tools described offer the capacity to engage with the fine-grained, capillary communicative structures of communities and enable information and research findings to be shared with the community. We advocated the use of simple, open-ended tools that allow informal dialogue, a degree of appropriation and user-led innovation.

Community members are demanding a greater say in planning and decision making and the global flow of information, knowledge, and ideas is accelerating, but at the same time, digital inequality is increasing. This context calls for new applications of new media and re-appropriations of existing applications in action research projects. We argued that the use of new media tools for collaboration and other purposes offers vast potential to provide more inclusive and democratic environments. Creating such environments is increasingly crucial, given the trend toward more participatory and collaborative forms of research and evaluation, and the current context in which communities are expected to take greater responsibility for the accountability and sustainability of development projects and initiatives. In this context, effective processes for community engagement and participation are becoming increasingly important.

Burgess et al. (2006) argue the following:

> The technical means for generating significantly creative and innovative ideas and concepts are becoming abundantly available. However, if Australia is to maximise its ability to capitalise—in both economic and social terms—on these digital 'lifestyle' products, it needs to understand the various dimensions of cultural citizenship and support the creative application of these tools for the purpose of participation, education and innovation. Fostering human talent and digital creativity outside formal school or workplace environments will favourably nurture societal and cultural values—promoting not only an innovation culture and economy but also an inclusive society. (pp. 12–13)

Burgess et al., Coleman (2003), and others have been calling for a more creative approach to political engagement. Some of the new media applications that support e-democracy and provide new pathways into political engagement include indymedia (Morris, 2004), the blogosphere (Bruns & Jacobs, 2006), and digital storytelling (Freidus & Hlubinka, 2002; Klaebe & Foth, 2006; Lambert, 2002).

Open Access to New Media

Open access to new media content and discussion spaces is becoming an important platform for many forms of enquiry in democratic societies. For example, Hindmarsh (2007) argued that a key challenge for the future of environmental policymaking is the creation of less formal public spaces that offer inclusive social negotiation and collective representations (e.g., deliberative forums, citizens' juries, consensus conferences; 'open science' or mode 2 science). Similarly, Fitzgerald (2007) documented the movement toward 'open access' to publicly funded research—from the Open Access Declarations of Berlin and Bethesda (2003)[1] and the Organisation for Economic Cooperation and Development (OECD) in 2004 through to the conditioning of research funding by institutions such as the U.S. National Institutes of Health (2005) and the U.K.'s Wellcome Trust (2006). The argument is that publicly funded research should be available for public

---

[1]See the Berlin Declaration on Open Access to Knowledge in the Sciences and Humanities (2003), http://www.zim.mpg.de/openaccess-berlin/berlindeclaration.html, and the Bethesda Statement on Open Access Publishing (2003), http://www.earlham.edu/~peters/fos/bethesda.htm

use (Dewatripont et al., 2006). In fact, Fitzgerald (2007) argued that this right to engage in noncommercial reproduction and communication of publicly funded research should be enshrined in the copyright law. He argued that 'the right of an individual researcher to release their outputs on the internet[2] should, subject to reasonable restrictions, trump any contractual assignment of copyright to publishers or other commercialising agents' (p. 155).[3] The Creative Commons framework provides a copyright regime suitable to these ends.

This suggests that inclusive and democratic processes are not just an ideological mandate. Rather they are necessary to solve some of the many complex problems now facing the planet.

Developing a Community of Practice of Action Researchers

The debate around case-study research in action research, the distribution of knowledge beyond the community, the transferability of findings and interventions, and the re-appropriation of prior findings to new contexts remains current (cf. Arnkil, 2004; Dick, 2003; Greenwood, 2002; Gustavsen, 2003a). Scholars who question the transferability of action research outcomes have made the argument that the individual context found in a particular community renders action research results and solutions idiographic. However, this does not deny the fact that new knowledge is generated in rigorous case-study research. Gustavsen (2003b) concluded the following:

> To learn from practices, research needs to develop social relationships, internally within the research community as well as in relation to other actors. 'The new production of knowledge' as identified by Gibbons and colleagues (Gibbons et al., 1994) is above all a *network* activity, and research cannot stay outside this process and remain as isolated individuals looking at the world from up above. (pp. 162–163; italics added)

The formation of a sustainable meta-network and the collection of ethnographic evidence in network action research can support analytical

---

[2]It is assumed that before this act of release any obligations of privacy, safety, security, or confidentiality have been satisfied.

[3]For a discussion of a proposed amendment to the German *Copyright Act* ensuring such a right see Gerd Hansen, *GRUR Int.* (2005) 378. Hansen's article, still only available in the German language version, has been self-archived at http://www.gerd-hansen.net/Hansen_GRUR_Int_2005_378ff.pdf

comparison across cases and the derivation of theory in a networked community of practice of action researchers (see Keane, 2004). If it is easy to set up mini-case studies and initiate multiple micro-action research projects within each case, the process of connecting the micro sites to a larger meta-network will contribute to exchanging valuable insights, experiences, and narratives that ultimately promote action research as a viable and effective research paradigm for the new media field.

References

Allen, R. T. (1996). Polanyi's overcoming of the dichotomy of fact and value. *Polanyiana, 5*(2), 5–20.

Alston, M. (1995). *Women on the land, the hidden heart of Australia.* Kensington: University of New South Wales Press.

Anderson, J. A. (1987). *Communication research: Issues and methods.* New York: McGraw-Hill.

Anderson, J. A. (1996). Yes, but is it empowerment? Initiation, implementation and outcomes of community action. In B. Humphries (Ed.), *Critical perspectives on empowerment* (pp. 69–83). Birmingham: Venture Press.

Argyris, C. (1982). *Reasoning, learning, and action: Individual and organizational.* San Francisco, CA: Jossey-Bass.

Argyris, C. (1987). *Personality and organization: The conflict between system and the individual.* New York: Garland.

Argyris, C. (1990). *Overcoming organizational defenses: Facilitating organisational learning.* Needham, MA: Allyn & Bacon.

Argyris, C., & Schön, D. A. (1978). *Organizational learning.* Reading, MA: Addison-Wesley.

Argyris, C., & Schön, D. A. (1996). *Organizational learning II: Theory, method and practice.* Reading, MA: Addison-Wesley.

Arnkil, R. (2004). Action research: Keeping up with the times? *Concepts and Transformation, 9*(1), 75–84.

Arnold, M. (2002). Systems design meets Habermas, Foucault and Latour. In S. Clarke (Ed.), *Socio-technical and human cognition elements of information systems* (pp. 226–248). Hershey, PA: Information Science.

Arnold, M., Gibbs, M. R., & Wright, P. (2003). Intranets and local community: "Yes, an intranet is all very well, but do we still get free beer and a barbeque?" In M. Huysman, E. Wenger, & V. Wulf (Eds.), *Proceedings of the First International Conference on Communities and Technologies* (pp. 185–204). Amsterdam, The Netherlands: Kluwer Academic.

Aurigi, A. (2006). New technologies, same dilemmas: Policy and design issues for the augmented city. *Journal of Urban Technology, 13*(3), 5–28.

Australian Bureau of Statistics. (2004). *Year book Australia: Population. How many people live in Australia's remote areas?* (No. 1301.0). Canberra, ACT: Author.

Australian Mobile Telecommunications Association (AMTA). (2004). *2004 Annual Report: AMTA.* Sydney: Author.

Avison, D., Baskerville, R., & Myers, M. (2001). Controlling action research projects. *Information Technology & People, 14*(1), 28–45.

Babbie, E. (2001). *The practice of social research.* Belmont, CA: Wadsworth Thomson.

Baily, M. (2004). Recent productivity growth: The role of information technology and other innovations. *FRBSF Economic Review 2004*, pp. 35–42.

Barabási, A.-L. (2002). *Linked: The new science of networks.* Cambridge, MA: Perseus.

Barabási, A.-L. (2003). *Linked: How everything is connected to everything else and what it means for business, science, and everyday life.* New York: Plume.

Bargh, J. A., & McKenna, K. Y. (2004). The internet and social life. *The Annual Review of Psychology 2004, 55,* 573–590.

Barr, T. (1985). *The electronic estate.* Melbourne: Penguin.

Bashaw, D., & Gifford, M. (2004, January 7). Top 10 Open Source Tools for eActivism. Posted to DoWire [Democracies Online Newswire]. Retrieved February 7, 2004, at http://www.mail-archive.com/do-wire@lists.umn.edu/msg00121.html.

Bell, D. (1982). The third technical revolution. *Business Quarterly,* Summer, 33–37.

Bloomfield, B. P. (1980). *Information technology and organisations.* Norwich, UK: Bertrams.

Boase, J., Horrigan, J. B., Wellman, B., & Rainie, L. (2006). *The strength of internet ties.* Washington, DC: Pew Internet & American Life Project.

Bonabeau, E., & Meyer, C. (2001). Swarm intelligence. *Harvard Business Review, 79*(5), 106–114.

Boyce, W. (2001). Disadvantaged persons' participation in heath promotion projects: Some structural dimensions. *Social Science and Medicine, 52,* 1551–1564.

Boyle, R., & Lemaire, D. (Eds.). (1999). *Building effective evaluation capacity: Lessons from practice.* New Brunswick, NJ: Transaction Books.

Bracht, N. (Ed.). (1999). *Health promotion at the community level: New advances* (2nd ed.). Thousand Oaks, CA: Sage.

Bracht, N. (2001). Community partnership strategies in health campaigns. In R. E. Rice & C. K. Atkin (Eds.), *Public communication campaigns* (3rd ed., pp. 323–342). Thousand Oaks, CA: Sage.

Brandt, E. (2003). Action research in user-centred product development. *AI & Society, 18*(2), 113–133.

Bruce, C. (1999). Phenomenography: Opening a new territory for library and information science research. *The New Review of Information and Library Research, 5,* 31–48.

Brunner, I. & Guzman, A. (1989). Participatory evaluation: A tool to assess projects and empower people. In R.F. Conner & M. Hendricks (Eds.), *International innovations in evaluation and methodology: New directions for program evaluation* (pp. 9–17). San Francisco: Jossey-Bass.

Bruns, A. (2006). Towards produsage: Futures for user-led content production. In F. Sudweeks, H. Hrachovec, & C. Ess (Eds.), *Proceedings: Cultural attitudes towards communication and technology* (pp. 275–284). Perth: Murdoch University.

Bruns, A., & Jacobs, J. (Eds.). (2006). *Uses of blogs.* New York: Peter Lang.

Brydon-Miller, M., Greenwood, D., & Maguire, P. (2003). Why action research? *Action Research, 1*(1), 9–28.

Burgess, J. (2006). Hearing ordinary voices: Cultural studies, vernacular creativity and digital storytelling. *Continuum: Journal of Media & Cultural Studies, 20*(2), 201–214.

Burgess, J. (2007). *Vernacular creativity and new media.* Unpublished doctoral dissertation, Queensland University of Technology, Queensland.

Burgess, J., Foth, M., & Klaebe, H. (2006, September). *Everyday creativity as civic engagement: A cultural citizenship view of new media.* Paper presented at the Communications Policy & Research Forum, Sydney, NSW.

Burrell, G., & Morgan, G. (1979). *Sociological paradigms and organisational analysis: Elements of the sociology of corporate life.* London: Heinemann.

Carroll, J. M. (Ed.). (2000). *Making use: Scenario-based design of human-computer interactions.* Cambridge, MA: MIT Press.

Carroll, J. M., & Reese, D. D. (2003, September). *Community collective efficacy: Structure and consequences of perceived capacities in the Blacksburg Electronic Village.* Paper presented at the 36th Hawaii International Conference on System Sciences (HICSS), Big Island, Hawaii.

Carroll, J. M., & Rosson, M. B. (2003). A trajectory for community networks. *The Information Society, 19*(5), 381–394.

Castells, M. (1996). *The rise of the network society.* Cambridge, MA: Blackwell.

Castells, M. (1997). *The power of identity.* Malden, MA: Blackwell.

Castells, M. (2000a). *End of millennium.* Malden, MA: Blackwell.

Castells, M. (2000b). *The rise of the network society* (2nd ed.). Oxford, UK: Blackwell.

Castells, M. (2001). Virtual communities or network society? In *The internet galaxy: Reflections on the internet, business, and society* (pp. 116–136). Oxford: Oxford University Press.

Castells, M. (2003). Global information capitalism. In D. Held & A. McGrew (Eds.), *The global transformations reader: An introduction to the globalisation debate.* Cambridge, UK: Polity Press.

Castells, M. (2004). Space of flows, space of places: Materials for a theory of urbanism in the information age. In S. Graham (Ed.), *The cybercities reader* (pp. 82–93). London: Routledge.

Castells, M., Fernandez-Ardevol, M., LinchuanQui, J., & Araba, S. (2006). *Mobile communication and society: A global perspective. A project of the Annenberg*

Research Network on International Communication. Cambridge, Mass: MIT Press.

Chambers, R. (1995). *Poverty and livelihoods: Whose reality counts?* IDS discussion paper 347. Sussex: University of Sussex.

Checkland, P., & Holwell, S. (1998). Soft systems methodology in action research. In P. Checkland & S. Howell (Eds.), *Information, systems, and information systems: Making sense of the field* (pp. 155–172). New York: Wiley.

Checkland, P., & Scholes, J. (1999). *Soft systems methodology in action: A 30-year retrospective.* New York: Wiley.

Claridge, C. (1996). *Women, development and the environment: A method to facilitate women's empowerment.* Unpublished doctoral dissertation, The University of Queensland, Brisbane.

Cockburn, A. (2002). *Agile software development.* Boston: Addison-Wesley.

Coghlan, D., & Brannick, T. (2001). *Doing action research in your own organisation.* London: Sage.

Cohen, R., Erez, K., Ben-Avraham, D., & Havlin, S. (2001). Breakdown of the internet under intentional attack. *Physical Review Letters, 86,* 3682–3685.

Cohill, A. M., & Kavanaugh, A. L. (Eds.). (2000). *Community networks: Lessons from Blacksburg, Virginia* (2nd ed.). Norwood, MA: Artech House.

Coleman, S. (2003). *A tale of two houses: The House of Commons, the Big Brother house and the people at home.* London, UK: The Hansard Society.

Cooper, A. (1999). *The inmates are running the asylum.* Indianapolis, IN: Sams.

Cooper, A., & Reimann, R. M. (2003). *About Face 2.0: The essentials of interaction design.* Indianapolis, IN: Wiley.

Cooperrider, D., Whitney, D., & Stavros, J. (2003). *Appreciative inquiry: The handbook* (1st ed.). Bedford Heights, OH: Lakeshore Communications & San Francisco, CA: Berrett-Koehler.

Cooperrider, D., & Whitney, D. (2005). *Appreciative inquiry: A positive revolution in change.* San Francisco, CA: Berrett-Koehler.

Coover, V., Deacon, E., Esser, C., & Moore, C. (1985). *Resource manual for a living revolution.* Philadelphia: New Society Publishers.

Couldry, N. (2000). *The place of media power: Pilgrims and witnesses of the media age.* Oxford, UK: Routledge.

Cracknell, B. (2000). *Evaluating development aid: Issues, problems and solutions.* New Delhi: Sage.

Crane, P., & Richardson, L. (2000). Section two: Action research processes. *Reconnect action research kit.* Canberra: Department of Family and Community Services, Australia. Available at http://www.facs.gov.au/internet/facsinternet.nsf/via/reconnect

Cross, R., & Borgatti, S. P. (2004). The ties that share: Relational characteristics that facilitate information seeking. In M. Huysman & V. Wulf (Eds.), *Social capital and information technology* (pp. 137–161). Cambridge, MA: MIT Press.

Crotty, M. (1998). *The foundation of social research, meaning and perspective in the research process.* St Leonards, NSW: Allen & Unwin.

Da Rin, J., & Groves, J. (1999). *Demand and supply of internet content for Australian farm businesses.* Canberra: Rural Industries Research and Development Corporation.

Dagron, A. (2001). *Making waves: Participatory communication for social change.* New York: Rockefeller Foundation.

Davies, R., & Dart, J. (2005). *The "Most Significant Change" (MSC) technique. A guide to its use.* Available at http://www.clearhorizon.com.au/site/index.htm

Davies, W. (2003). *You don't know me, but . . . Social capital & social software.* London: The Work Foundation.

Day, P. (2002). Designing democratic community networks: Involving communities through civil participation. In M. Tanabe, P. van den Besselaar, & T. Ishida (Eds.), *Digital cities II: Second Kyoto workshop on digital cities* (Lecture notes in computer science No. 2362, pp. 86–100). Heidelberg, Germany: Springer.

De Haan, A. (1999). *Social exclusion: Towards a holistic understanding of deprivation* (DFID social development dissemination paper Note No. 2). London: DFID.

de Koning, K., & Martin, M. (Eds.). (1996). *Participatory research in health. Issues and experience.* London & Atlantic Highlands, NJ: Zed Books.

Denzin, N., & Lincoln, Y. (Eds.). (2005). *The handbook of qualitative research* (3rd ed.). Thousand Oaks, CA: Sage.

Department of Communications, Information Technology and the Arts (DCITA). (2003). *Maintaining the viability of online access centres in regional, rural and remote Australia.* Discussion paper. Canberra: DCITA, Australia. Accessed March 12, 2005, http://www.dcita.gov.au/tel/regional,_rural_and_remote_communications/?a=7789

Deutchman, I. (1991). The politics of empowerment. *Women and Politics, 11*(2), 1–18.

Dewatripont, M, Ginsburgh, V, Legros, P., Walckiers, A., Devroey, J-P., Dujardin, M., Vandooren, F., Dubois, P., Foncel, J., Ivaldi, M., & Heusse, M.-D. (2006). *Study on the economic and technical evolution of the scientific publication markets in Europe.* Final report. Brussels: European Commission. Available at http://europa.eu.int/comm/research/science-society/pdf/scientific-publication-study_en.pdf

Diamond, J. (1999). *Guns, germs, and steel: The fates of human societies.* New York: Norton.

Dick, B. (1991). *Helping groups to be effective* (2nd ed.). Brisbane: Interchange.

Dick, B. (2002). *Action research and evaluation online (areol).* Retrieved April 17, 2003, http://www.scu.edu.au/schools/gcm/ar/areol/areolhome.html

Dick, B. (2003). Rehabilitating action research: A response to Davydd Greenwood's and Björn Gustavsen's papers on action research perspectives in *Concepts and Transformation, 7*(2), 2002 and *8*(1), 2003. *Concepts and Transformation, 8*(3), 255–263.

Dick, B. (2006). Action research literature 2004–2006. Themes and trends. *Action Research, 4*(4), 439–458.

Digital Opportunity Initiative. (2001). *Creating a development dynamic. Final report of the Digital Opportunity Initiative.* Accenture, Markle and UNDP. Available at http://www.opt-init.org/framework/DOI-Final-Report.doc

Dillman, D. A. (2007). *Mail and internet Surveys: The tailored design method* (2nd ed.). Hoboken, NJ: Wiley.

DiMaggio, P., & Hargittai, E. (2001). *From the digital divide to digital inequality* (Working Paper 15, Center for Arts and Cultural Policy Studies, Princeton University). Princeton, NJ: Princeton University.

DiMaggio, P., Hargittai, E., Neuman, W. R., & Robinson, J. P. (2001). Social implications of the internet. *Annual Review of Sociology, 27,* 307–336.

Dockery, G. (2000). Participatory research. Whose roles. Whose responsibilities? In C. Truman, D. Mertens, & B. Humphries (Eds.). *Research and inequality* (pp. 95–110). London: UCL Press.

Donath, J. (2002). A semantic approach to visualizing online conversations. *Communications of the ACM, 45*(4), 45–49.

Dutta, S., Lanvin, B., & Paua, F. (2004). *The global information technology report 2003–2004. Towards an equitable information society.* New York & Oxford: Oxford University Press.

Dutton, W. H., Carusi, A., & Peltu, M. (2006). Fostering multidisciplinary engagement: Communication challenges for social research on emerging digital technologies. *Prometheus, 24*(2), 129–149.

Ellis, D. G. (1995). Introduction to special issue. *Communication Theory, 5*(2), 93–177.

Emery, F. E. (Ed.). (1969). *Systems thinking: Selected readings.* Harmondsworth, UK: Penguin.

Emery, F. E., & Trist, E. L. (1973). *Towards a social ecology: Contextual appreciations of the future in the present.* New York: Plenum.

Erickson, T., Halverson, C., Kellogg, W. A., Laff, M., & Wolf, T. (2002). Social translucence: Designing social infrastructures that make collective activity visible. *Communications of the ACM, 45*(4), 40–44.

Fallows, D. (2004). *The internet and daily life.* Washington, DC: Pew Internet & American Life Project.

Falzone, P. (2004). Transcendent ethnography: Designing an action research approach to ethnographic film within cultures of conflict. *Action Research, 2*(3), 326–344.

Faris, R. (2001). *Learning communities: Villages, neighbourhoods, towns, cities and regions preparing for a knowledge-based society.* Retrieved February 10, 2005, http://members.shaw.ca/rfaris/docs/LCdigest.pdf

Feek, W. (2003). *The digital pulse: The current and future applications of information and communication technologies for developmental health priorities.* The Communication Initiative. Retrieved January 31, 2006, http://www.com-minit.com/strategicthinking/stdigitalpulse/sld-1569.html

Fetterman, D. (2001). *Foundations of empowerment evaluation.* Thousand Oaks, CA: Sage.

Fischer, C. S. (2005). Bowling alone: What's the score? *Social Networks, 27*(2), 155–167.

Fitzgerald, B. (2007). Copyright 2010: The need for better negotiability/usability principles. In G. Hearn & D. Rooney (Eds.), *Knowledge policy: Challenges for the 21st century*. Cheltenham, UK: Edward Elgar.

Flew, T. (2005). *New media: An introduction* (2nd ed.). Melbourne: Oxford University Press.

Florida, R. L. (2003). Cities and the creative class. *City and Community, 2*(1), 3–19.

Food and Agriculture Organization of the UN. (2003). *Revisiting the "magic box": Case studies in local appropriation of information and communication technologies (ICTs)*. Rome: Food and Agriculture Organization of the UN.

Foth, M. (2006a). Analysing the factors influencing the successful design and uptake of interactive systems to support social networks in urban neighbourhoods. *International Journal of Technology and Human Interaction, 2*(2), 65–79.

Foth, M. (2006b). Facilitating social networking in inner-city neighbourhoods. *IEEE Computer, 39*(9), 44–50.

Foth, M. (2006c). Sociocultural animation. In S. Marshall, W. Taylor, & X. Yu (Eds.), *Encyclopedia of developing regional communities with information and communication technology* (pp. 640–645). Hershey, PA: Idea Group Reference.

Foth, M. (2008, forthcoming). Participation, animation, design: The PAD approach to urban community networking. *AI & Society*.

Foth, M., & Axup, J. (2006, August). *Participatory design and action research: Identical twins or synergetic pair?* Paper presented at the Participatory Design Conference (PDC), Trento, Italy.

Foth, M., & Brereton, M. (2004). Enabling local interaction and personalised networking in residential communities through action research and participatory design. In P. Hyland & L. Vrazalic (Eds.), *Proceedings of OZCHI 2004: Supporting community interaction*. 20–24 Nov 2004. Wollongong, NSW: University of Wollongong.

Foth, M., & Hearn, G. (2007). Networked individualism of urban residents: Discovering the communicative ecology in inner-city apartment buildings. *Information, Communication & Society, 10*(5), pp. 749–772.

Foth, M., & Tacchi, J. (2004). Ethnographic action research website. In I. Pringle & S. Subramanian (Eds.), *Profiles and experiences in ICT innovation for poverty reduction* (pp. 27–32). New Delhi, India: UNESCO.

Fowler, M. (2003). *The new methodology*. Retrieved May 10, 2004, http://www.martinfowler.com/articles/newMethodology.html

Francisco, V. T., Fawcett, S. B., Schultz, J. A., Berkowitz, B., Wolff, T. J., & Nagy, G. (2001). Using internet-based resources to build community capacity: The Community Tool Box [http://ctb.ukans.edu/]. *American Journal of Community Psychology, 29*(2), 293–300.

Freidus, N., & Hlubinka, M. (2002). Digital storytelling for reflective practice in communities of learners. *ACM SIGGROUP Bulletin, 23*(2), 24–26.

Freire, P. (1970). *Pedagogy of the oppressed*. New York: Seabury Press.

Freire, P. (1982). Creating alternative research methods: Learning to do it by doing it. In B. Hall, A. Gillette, & R. Tandon (Eds.), *Creating knowledge:*

A monopoly (pp. 29–37). New Delhi: Society for Participatory Research in Asia.

Friedmann, J. (1992). *Empowerment: The politics of alternative development.* Cambridge: Blackwell.

Gardner, K., & Lewis, D. (1996). *Anthropology, development and the post modern challenge.* London: Pluto Press.

Gatenby, B., & Humphries, M. (1996). Feminist commitments in organisational communication: Participatory action research as feminist praxis. *Australian Journal of Communication, 23*(2), 73–87.

Gaved, M. B., & Foth, M. (2006). More than wires, pipes and ducts: Some lessons from grassroots initiated networked communities and master-planned neighbourhoods. In R. Meersman, Z. Tari, & P. Herrero (Eds.), *On the move to meaningful internet systems 2006: OTM 2006 workshops* (Lecture Notes in Computer Science No. 4277, pp. 171–180). Heidelberg, Germany: Springer.

Gaver, B., Dunne, T., & Pacenti, E. (1999). Cultural probes. *Interactions, 6*(1), 21–29.

Geiselhart, K. (2004). *The electronic canary: Sustainability solutions for Australian teleservice centres.* Wangaratta, Victoria: Centre for Online Regional Research. Retrieved February 10, 2005, http://www.teleservices.net.au/CTSA_Viability_Report%20Final.pdf

Gerbner, G. (1983). Ferment in the field: Communications scholars address critical issues and research tasks of the discipline. *Journal of Communication, 33*(3), 4–362.

Gergen, K. (2003). Action research and orders of democracy. *Action Research, 1*(1), 39–56.

Gibbons, M., Limoges, C., Nowotny, H., Schwartzmann, S., Scott, P., & Trow, M. (1994). *The new production of knowledge: The dynamics of science and research in contemporary societies.* London: Sage.

Gilchrist, A. (2004). *The well-connected community: A networking approach to community development.* Bristol, UK: The Policy Press.

Girard, B. (Ed.). (2003). *The one to watch: Radio, new ICTs and interactivity.* Rome: FAO.

Gitelman, L. (2006). *Always already new: Media, history and the data of culture.* Cambridge, MA: MIT Press.

Goggin, G. (2006). *Cell phone culture: Mobile technology in everyday life.* London & New York: Routledge.

Grace, M., & Lennie, J. (1998). Constructing and reconstructing rural women in Australia: The politics of change, diversity and identity. *Sociologia Ruralis, 38*(3), 351–370.

Grace, M., Lundin, R., & Daws, L. (1996). *Women and networking: Women's voices from elsewhere.* Brisbane: Centre for Policy and Leadership Studies in Education, Queensland University of Technology.

Graham, S. (Ed.). (2004). *The cybercities reader.* London: Routledge.

Granovetter, M. (1973). The strength of weak ties. *American Journal of Sociology, 78*(6), 1360–1380.

Greenbaum, J. M., & Kyng, M. (Eds.). (1991). *Design at work: Cooperative design of computer systems.* Hillsdale, NJ: Erlbaum.

Greene, J. (2002). Mixed-method evaluation: A way of democratically engaging with difference. *Evaluation Journal of Australasia, 2*(2), 23–29.

Greene, J., & Caracelli, V. (2002). Making paradigmatic sense of mixed-method practice. In A. Tashakkori & C. Teddlie (Eds.), *Handbook of mixed methods in social and behavioural research.* Thousand Oaks, CA: Sage.

Greenwood, D. (2002). Action research: Unfulfilled promises and unmet challenges. *Concepts and Transformation, 7*(2), 117–139.

Greenwood, D., & Levin, M. (2006). *Introduction to action research. Social research for social change* (2nd ed.). Thousand Oaks, CA: Sage.

Gregory, A. (2000). Problematising participation. A critical review of approaches to participation in evaluation theory. *Evaluation, 6*(2), 179–199.

Gronhaug, K., & Olson, O. (1999). Action research and knowledge creation: Merits and challenges. *Qualitative Market Research: An International Journal, 2*(1), 6–14.

Groves, J., & Da Rin, J. (1999). *Buying and selling online: The opportunities for electronic commerce for Australian farm businesses.* Canberra: Rural Industries Research and Development Corporation.

Guba, E., & Lincoln, Y. (1989). *Fourth generation evaluation.* Newbury Park, CA: Sage.

Guba, E. G., & Lincoln, Y. S. (1994). Competing paradigms in qualitative research. In N. K. Denzin & Y. S. Lincoln (Eds.), *The handbook of qualitative research* (pp. 105–117). London: Sage.

Gurstein, M. (2001). Community informatics, community networks and strategies for flexible networking. In L. Keeble & B. Loader (Eds.), *Community informatics: Shaping computer mediated social relations* (pp. 263–283). London. Routledge.

Gurstein, M. (2003a). Effective use: A community informatics strategy beyond the digital divide. *First Monday, 8*(12), http://www.firstmonday.org/issues/issue8_12/gurstein/index.html

Gustavsen, B. (2003a). Action research and the problem of the single case. *Concepts and Transformation, 8*(1), 93–99.

Gustavsen, B. (2003b). New forms of knowledge production and the role of action research. *Action Research, 1*(2), 153–164.

Habermas, J. (1979). *Communication and the evolution of society.* Boston: Beacon.

Hammersley, B. (2003). *Content syndication with RSS.* Farnham, UK: O'Reilly.

Hampton, K. N. (2001). *Living the wired life in the wired suburb: Netville, glocalization and civil society.* Unpublished doctoral dissertation, University of Toronto, Canada.

Hampton, K. N., & Wellman, B. (2003). Neighbouring in netville: How the internet supports community and social capital in a wired suburb. *City and Community, 2*(4), 277–311.

Hargie, O., & Tourish, D. (Eds.). (2000). *Handbook of communication audits for organisations.* London: Routledge.

Harrison, T. M., & Stephen, T. (1999). Researching and creating community networks. In S. G. Jones (Ed.), *Doing internet research: Critical issues and methods for examining the Net* (pp. 221–241). London: Sage.

Hartley, J. (2000). Radiocracy: Sound and citizenship. *International Journal of Cultural Studies, 3*(2), 153–159.

Hartley, J., Hearn, G., Tacchi, J., & Foth, M. (2003). The Youth Internet Radio Network: A research project to connect youth across Queensland through music, creativity and ICT. In S. Marshall & W. Taylor (Eds.), *Proceedings of the 5th International Information Technology in Regional Areas (ITiRA) Conference 2003* (pp. 335–342). Rockhampton: Central Queensland University Press.

Harvey, L. J., & Myers, M. D. (1995). Scholarship and practice: The contribution of ethnographic research methods to bridging the gap. *Information Technology and People, 8*(3), 13–27.

Hearn, G. (1999). Deconstructing modes of communication enquiry: Towards a discourse of doing. *Australian Journal of Communication, 26*(2), 47–58.

Hearn, G., & Foth, M. (2005). Action research in the design of new media and ICT systems. In K. Kwansah-Aidoo (Ed.), *Topical issues in communications and media research* (pp. 79–94). New York: Nova Science Publishers.

Hearn, G., Kimber, M., Lennie, J., & Simpson, L. (2005). A way forward: Sustainable ICTs and regional sustainability. *Journal of Community Informatics, 1*(2), 18–31.

Hearn, G., Mandeville, T. D., & Anthony, D. (1998). *The communication superhighway: Social and economic change in the digital age.* Sydney: Allen & Unwin.

Hearn, G., & Mandeville, T. (2005). How to be productive in the knowledge economy: The case of ICTs. In D. Rooney, G. Hearn, & A. Ninan (Eds.), *The knowledge economy handbook* (pp. 255–267). Cheltenham, UK: Edward Elgar.

Hearn, G., Simpson, L., Holman, L., Stevenson, T., Meara, A., Dunleavy, J., & Sikorski, G. (1993). Anticipating social and policy implications of intelligent networks: Choices for Australia. *Electronic Journal of Communication, 3*(3/4).

Hearn, G., Simpson, L., Holman, L., Stevenson, T., Meara, A., Dunleavy, J. & Sikorski, G. (1995). *Anticipating social and policy implications of intelligent networks: Complexity, choice and participation* (Research report No. 2. The Communication Centre). Brisbane: Queensland University of Technology.

Hearn, G., & Stevenson, T. (1998). Knowing through doing: Anticipating issues for the study of human communication. *Futures, 30*(2/3), 115–132.

Heron, J. (1996). Quality as primacy of the practical. *Qualitative Inquiry, 2*(1), 41–56.

Hiemstra, G. (1983). You say you want a revolution? "Information technology" in organizations. In R. N. Bostrum and B. H. Westley (Eds.), *Communication yearbook 7* (pp. 802–827). Beverly Hills: Sage.

Highsmith, J. A. (2002). *Agile software development ecosystems.* Boston: Addison-Wesley.

Hiltz, S. R., & Turoff, M. (1993). *The network nation: Human communication via computer* (Rev. ed.). Cambridge, MA: MIT Press.

Hindmarsh, R. (2007). Environment, water and energy in the 21st century: The role of deliberative governance for the knowledge society. In G. Hearn & D. Rooney (Eds.), *Knowledge policy: Challenges for the 21st century*. Cheltenham, UK: Edward Elgar.

Hine, C. (2000). *Virtual ethnography*. London: Sage.

Hine, C. (Ed.). (2005). *Virtual methods: Issues in social research on the internet*. Oxford: Berg.

Hirschheim, R. (1985). *Office automation: A social and organisational perspective*. Chichester, Sussex: Wiley.

Hopkinson, A., & Tacchi, J. (2000). Editorial. *International Journal of Cultural Studies*, *3*(2), 147–151.

Hornecker, E., Halloran, J., Fitzpatrick, G., Weal, M., Millard, D., Michaelides, D., Cruickshank, D., & De Roure, D. (2006, August). *UbiComp in opportunity spaces: Challenges for participatory design*. Paper presented at the Participatory Design Conference (PDC), Trento, Italy.

Horrigan, J. B. (2001). *Cities online: Urban development and the internet*. Washington, DC: Pew Internet & American Life Project.

Horrigan, J. B., Rainie, L., & Fox, S. (2001). *Online communities: Networks that nurture long-distance relationships and local ties*. Washington, DC: Pew Internet & American Life Project.

Horst, H., & Miller, D. (2006). *The cell phone: An anthropology of communication*. Oxford & New York: Berg.

Howard, P. N. (2002). Network ethnography and the hypermedia organisation: New media, new organisations, new methods. *New Media & Society*, *4*(4), 550–574.

Hudson, H. E. (2001). The Acacia Programme: Developing evaluation and learning systems for African telecentres. In C. Latchem & D. Walker (Eds.), *Telecentres: Case studies and key issues*. Vancouver, Canada: The Commonwealth of Learning. Retrieved February 10, 2005, http://www.col.org/telecentres/chapter%2015.pdf

Humphries, B. (1994). Empowerment and social research: Elements for an analytic framework. In B. Humphries & C. Truman (Eds.), *Re-thinking social research. Anti-discriminatory approaches in research methodology* (pp. 185–204). Aldershot: Avebury.

Humphries, B. (1996). Contradictions in the culture of empowerment. In B. Humphries (Ed.), *Critical perspectives on empowerment* (pp. 1–16). Birmingham: Venture Press.

Huysman, M., & Wulf, V. (Eds.). (2004). *Social capital and information technology*. Cambridge, MA: MIT Press.

Inayatullah, S. (1990). Deconstructing and reconstructing the future: Predictive, cultural and critical epistemologies. *Futures*, *22*(2), 115–141.

Inayatullah, S. (1999). CLA: Post-structuralism as method. *Futures*, *30*(8), 815–830.

Inayatullah, S. (Ed.). (2004). *The causal layered analysis reader*. Tamsui, Taiwan: Tamkang University Press.

Inayatullah, S. (2006). Anticipatory action learning: Theory and practice. *Futures*, *38*(6), 656–666.

Innis, H. (1950). *Empire and communication*. Oxford: Oxford University Press.

Innis, H. (1951). *The bias of communication*. Toronto: University of Toronto Press.

James, J. (2004). *Information technology and development: A new paradigm for delivering the internet to rural areas in developing countries*. Oxford: Routledge.

Jankowski, N., Jones, S., Lievrouw, L. A., & Hampton, K. (Eds.). (2004). What's changed about new media? Special issue of *New Media & Society*, *6*(1).

Jankowski, N., Jones, S., Samarajiva, R., & Silverstone, R. (Eds.). (1999). What's new about new media? Special issue of *New Media & Society*, *1*(1).

Jenkins, H. (2006). *Fans, bloggers, and gamers: Exploring participatory culture*. New York: New York University Press.

Jenkins, H. (2007a, April 24). Slash me, mash me, spread me. . . . *Confessions of an Aca-Fan: The official weblog of Henry Jenkins*. Retrieved June 1, 2007, http://www.henryjenkins.org/2007/04/slash_me_mash_me_but_please_sp.html#more

Jenkins, H. (2007b, May 28). Nine propositions towards a cultural theory of YouTube. *Confessions of an Aca-Fan: The official weblog of Henry Jenkins*. Retrieved June 1, 2007, http://www.henryjenkins.org/2007/05/9_propositions_towards_a_cultu.html

Jennings, L., & Graham, A. (1996). Exposing discourses through action research. In O. Zuber-Skerritt (Ed.), *New directions in action research* (pp. 165–181). London: The Falmer Press.

Johnson, B., & Rice, R. E. (1987). *Managing organizational innovation*. New York: Columbia University Press.

Johnson, R., & Onwuegbuzie, A. (2004). Mixed methods research: A research paradigm whose time has come. *Educational Researcher*, *33*(7), 14–26

Katz, J., & Aakhus, M. (Eds.). (2002). *Perpetual contact: Mobile communication, private talk, public performance*. Cambridge: Cambridge University Press.

Katz, J. E., & Rice, R. E. (2002). *Social consequences of internet use: Access, involvement and expression*. Cambridge, MA: MIT Press.

Katz, J. E., Rice, R. E., Acord, S., Dasgupta, K., & David, K. (2004). Personal mediated communication and the concept of community in theory and practice. In P. J. Kalbfleisch (Ed.), *Communication yearbook 28* (pp. 315–370). Mahwah, NJ: Erlbaum.

Keane, M. (2004). Network or perish? In R. Wissler, B. Haseman, S. A. Wallace, & M. Keane (Eds.), *Innovation in Australian arts, media, and design: New challenges for the tertiary sector* (pp. 135–147). Flaxton: Post Press.

Kelly, A. (1985). Action research: What is it and what can it do? In R. Burgess (Ed.), *Issues in educational research: Qualitative methods* (pp. 129–151). London & Philadelphia: The Falmer Press.

Kelvin Grove Urban Village (KGUV). (2004). *Kelvin Grove Urban Village master plan*. Retrieved November 10, 2006, http://www.kgurbanvillage.com.au/vision/masterplan.shtm

Kemmis, S., & McTaggart, R. (1988). *The action research planner* (3rd ed.). Waurn Ponds, Victoria: Deakin University.

Kemmis, S., & McTaggart, R. (2000). Participatory action research. In N. Denzin & Y. Lincoln (Eds.), *Handbook of qualitative research* (2nd ed., pp. 567–605). Beverly Hills: Sage

Kendall, K. E., & Kendall, J. E. (2005). *Systems analysis and design.* Upper Saddle River, NJ: Pearson/Prentice Hall.

Khan, M. (1998). Evaluation capacity building. *Evaluation, 4*(3), 310–328.

Khong, L. (2003). Actants and enframing: Heidegger and Latour on technology. *Studies in History and Philosophy of Science, 34,* 693–704.

Klaebe, H., & Foth, M. (2006, October). *Capturing community memory with oral history and new media: The Sharing Stories Project.* Paper presented at the third international Community Informatics Research Network (CIRN) Conference, Prato, Italy.

Klein, R. (1983). How to do what we want to do: Thoughts about feminist methodology. In G. Bowles & R. Klein (Eds.), *Theories of women's studies.* London: Routledge & Kegan Paul.

Kok, K., & van Delden, H. (2004). *Linking narrative storylines and quantitative models to combat desertification in the Guadalentin, Spain.* Wageningen, the Netherlands: Wageningen University. Available at www.iemss.org/iemss2004/pdf/scenario/koklink.pdf

Kretzmann, J. P., & McKnight, J. L. (1993). *Building communities from the inside out: A path toward finding and mobilizing a community's assets.* Chicago, IL: Institute for Policy Research.

Kristoffersen, S., Herstad, J., Ljungberg, F., Løbersli, F., Sandbakken, J. R., & Thoresen, K. (1998). Developing scenarios for mobile CSCW. In C. Johnson (Ed.), *Proceedings of the First Workshop on Human Computer Interaction for Mobile Devices.* Glasgow, Scotland: University of Glasgow.

Krug, G. (2005). *Communication, technology and cultural change.* London: Sage.

Laderchi, C. R., Saith, R., & Stewart, F. (2003). *Does it matter that we don't agree on the definition of poverty? A comparison of four approaches.* QEH Working Paper Series. Oxford: Queen Elizabeth House, University of Oxford.

Lambert, J. (2002). *Digital storytelling: Capturing lives, creating community.* Berkeley, CA: Digital Diner Press.

Lambert, J. (2007, May). *The story of digital storytelling.* Paper presented at the 57th Annual Conference of the International Communication Association, San Francisco.

Lather, P. (1991). *Getting smart. Feminist research and pedagogy with/in the postmodern.* New York: Routledge.

Latour, B. (2005). *Reassembling the social: An introduction to actor-network-theory.* Oxford: Oxford University Press.

LeCompte, M. (1995). Some notes on power, agenda, and voice: A researcher's personal evolution towards critical collaborative research. In P. McLaren & J. Giarelli (Eds.), *Critical theory and educational research* (pp. 91–112). Albany: State University of New York Press.

Lennie, J. (2001). *Troubling empowerment: An evaluation and critique of a feminist action research project involving rural women and interactive communication technologies.* Unpublished doctoral dissertation, Queensland University of Technology, Queensland.

Lennie, J. (2002). Including a diversity of rural women in a communication technology access project: Taking the macro and micro contexts into account. In G. Johanson & L. Stillman (Eds.), *Proceedings of the Electronic Networks—Building Community: 5th Community Networking Conference.* Melbourne: Monash University.

Lennie, J. (2005). An evaluation capacity-building process for sustainable community IT initiatives: Empowering and disempowering impacts. *Evaluation. The International Journal of Theory, Research and Practice, 11*(4), 390–414.

Lennie, J. (2006). Increasing the rigour and trustworthiness of participatory evaluations: Learnings from the field. *Evaluation Journal of Australasia, 6*(1), 27–35.

Lennie, J., Hatcher, C., & Morgan, W. (2003). Feminist discourses of (dis)empowerment in an action research project involving rural women and communication technologies. *Action Research, 1*(1), 57–80.

Lennie, J., & Hearn, G. (2003, September). *The potential of PAR and participatory evaluation for increasing the sustainability and success of community development initiatives using new communication technologies.* Paper presented at the Sixth Annual Conference of Action Learning, Action Research & Process Management (ALARPM) and the 10th Congress of Participatory Action Research (PAR), Pretoria, South Africa.

Lennie, J., Hearn, G., & Hanrahan, M. (2005). The EvaluateIT Kit: A method for engaging communities in evaluating IT projects. *Proceedings of the International Conference on Engaging Communities.* Brisbane: Department of Communities & Department of Main Roads, Queensland. Available at http://engagingcommunities2005.org/abstracts/Lennie-June-final.pdf

Lennie, J., Hearn, G., Simpson, L., Kennedy da Silva, E., Kimber, M., & Hanrahan, M. (2004). *Building community capacity in evaluating IT projects: Outcomes of the LEARNERS project.* Brisbane: Queensland University of Technology. Retrieved February 10, 2005. Available at http://www.eprints.qut.edu.au/archive/00004389/

Lennie, J., Hearn, G., Simpson, L., & Kimber, M. (2005). Building community capacities in evaluating rural IT projects: Success strategies from the LEARNERS project. *International Journal of Education and Development using Information and Communication Technology, 1*(1). Available at http://ijedict.dec.uwi.edu//viewarticle.php?id=14

Lennie, J., Hearn, G., Stevenson, T., Inayatullah, S., & Mandeville, T. (1996). Bringing multiple perspectives to Australia's communication futures: Beyond the superhighway. *Prometheus, 14*(1), 10–30.

Lennie, J., Lundin, R., & Simpson, L. (2000). *Development of a participatory evaluation assessment and planning framework for sustainable rural community development that uses interactive communication technologies.* Brisbane: The Communication Centre, Queensland University of Technology.

Lessig, L. (2001). *The future of ideas: The fate of the commons in a connected world.* New York: Random House.

Lessig, L. (2005). Do you floss? *London Review of Books, 27*(16).

Lewin, K. (1946). Action research and minority problems. *Journal of Social Issues, 2,* 34–46.

Ling, R. (2004). *The mobile connection: The cell phone's impact on society* (Morgan Kaufmann Series in Interactive Technologies). San Francisco, CA: Morgan Kaufmann.

Linstone, H. A., & Turoff, M. (Eds.). (1975). *The Delphi method: Techniques and applications.* Reading, MA: Addison-Wesley.

Lister, R. (2004). *Poverty.* Cambridge: Polity Press.

Livingstone, S. (2004). Media literacy and the challenge of new information and communication technologies. *The Communication Review, 7,* 3–14.

Lowe, I. (1992). Social impact analysis of information technologies. In T. Stevenson & J. Lennie (Eds.), *Australia's communication futures* (pp. 48–59). Brisbane: The Communication Centre, Queensland University of Technology.

MacColl, I., Cooper, R., Rittenbruch, M., & Viller, S. (2005). Watching ourselves watching: Ethical issues in ethnographic action research. In *Citizens Online: Considerations for Today & the Future—Proceedings of OzCHI2005.* Canberra, Australia: CHISIG.

Mackay, H., & Gillespie, G. (1992). Extending the social shaping of technology: Ideology and appropriation. *Social Studies of Science, 22,* 685–716.

MacKenzie, D., & Wajcman, J. (Eds.). (1985). *The social shaping of technology.* Milton Keynes: Open University Press.

Maguire, P. (1987). *Doing participatory research: A feminist approach.* Boston: University of Massachusetts.

Maher, D. W. (2006). *The domain name system: Reflections on the law of unintended consequences.* Available at http://www.pir.org/PDFs/LSPI177DNS-Unint-Conseq.pdf

Maloney-Krichmar, D., Abras, C., & Preece, J. (2002, June). *Revitalizing an Online Community.* Paper presented at the International Symposium on Technology and Society (ISTAS)—Social implications of information and communication technology, Raleigh, NC.

Manning, H. (2003). *The power of design personas.* Cambridge, MA: Forrester Research.

Mannion, J. (1996, October 6–10). Partnership, participation and capacity building: Rural development based on local bottom-up strategies. *Leader Magazine, 12.*

Mansell, R. (2002). From digital divides to digital entitlements in knowledge societies. *Current Sociology, 50*(3), 407–426.

Mansell, R., & Wehn, U. (Eds.). (2003). *INK—knowledge societies information technology for sustainable development.* Sussex: University of Sussex. Available at http://www.sussex.ac.uk/spru/1-4-9-1-1-2.html

Margolis, E. (2006). *Visual ethnography paradigms.* College of Education, Arizona State University. Retrieved October 18, 2006, http://courses.ed.asu.edu/margolis/va.html

Markus, L. (1984). *Systems in organizations: Bugs and features.* Cambridge, MA: Ballinger.

Martin, M. (1994). Developing a feminist participative research framework: Evaluating the process. In B. Humphries & C. Truman (Eds.), *Re-thinking social research. Anti-discriminatory approaches in research methodology* (pp. 123–143). Aldershot: Avebury.

Martin, M. (1996). Issues of power in the participatory research process. In K. de Koning & M. Martin (Eds.), *Participatory research in health. Issues and experiences* (pp. 82–93). London & Atlantic Highlands, NJ: Zed Books.

Martin, M. (1997). Critical education for participatory research. *Sociological Research Online, 2*(2), http://www.socresonline.org.uk/socres online/2/2/8.html

Martin, M. (2000). Critical education for participatory research. In C. Truman, D. Mertens, & B. Humphries (Eds.), *Research and inequality* (pp. 191–204). New York: UCL Press.

Martino, J. (2003). A review of selected recent advances in technological forecasting. *Technological Forecasting & Social Change, 70,* 719–733.

Mathie, A., & Greene, J. (1997). Stakeholder participation in evaluation: How important is diversity? *Evaluation and Program Planning, 20*(3), 279–285.

May, H., & Hearn, G. (2005). The mobile phone as media. *International Journal of Cultural Studies, 8*(2), 195–211.

Mayoux, L., & Chambers, R. (2005). Reversing the paradigm: Quantification, participatory methods and pro-poor impact assessment. *Journal of International Development, 17,* 271–298.

McGuigan, J. (2005). Towards a sociology of the mobile phone. *Human Technology: An Interdisciplinary Journal on Humans in ICT Environments, 1*(1), 45–57.

McKay, J., & Marshall, P. (2001). The dual imperatives of action research. *Information Technology & People, 14*(1), 46–59.

McKie, L. (2003). Rhetorical spaces: Participation and pragmatism in the evaluation of community health work. *Evaluation, 9*(3), 307–324.

McLuhan, M. (1967a). *The mechanical bride: Folklore of industrial man.* London: Routledge & Kegan Paul.

McLuhan, M. (1967b). *The medium is the message.* London: Penguin Press.

McTaggart, R. (1991). Principles for participatory action research. *Adult Education Quarterly, 41*(3), 168–187.

McTaggart, R. (1992). Reductionism and action research: Technology versus convivial forms of life. In C. Bruce & A. Russell (Eds.), *Proceedings of the Second World Congress on Action Learning: Reflecting the philosophy of collaborative change in government, industry, education and the community* (pp. 47–61). Brisbane: ALARPM.

Meadows, D. (2007). *What is digital storytelling?* Retrieved June 1, 2007, http://www.photobus.co.uk/dstory_pages/what_dstory.html

Mesch, G. S., & Levanon, Y. (2003). Community networking and locally-based ties in two suburban localities. *City and Community, 2*(4), 335–351.

Meyrick, K., & Fitzgerald, C. (2005). *The role of new media in the social, community and cultural development of Kelvin Grove Urban Village.* Brisbane: The Hornery Institute.

Millen, D. R., & Fontaine, M. A. (2003, November). *Improving individual and organisational performance through communities of practice.* Paper presented at the ACM GROUP conference, Sanibel Island, FL.

Millen, D. R., Fontaine, M. A., & Muller, M. J. (2002). Understanding the benefit and costs of communities of practice. *Communications of the ACM, 45*(4), 69–73.

Mitchell, W. J. (2003). *Me++: The cyborg self and the networked city.* Cambridge, MA: MIT Press.

Mitroff, I. (1983). *Stakeholders of the organisational mind.* San Francisco: Jossey-Bass.

Monk, A., & Howard, S. (1998). The rich picture: A tool for reasoning about work context. *ACM SIGCHI Interactions, 5*(2), 21–30.

Moreno, J. L. (1953). *Who shall survive: Foundations of sociometry, group psychotherapy, and sociodrama.* Beacon, NY: Beacon House.

Morgan, G., & Ramirez, R. (1984). Action learning: A holographic metaphor for guiding social change. *Human Relations, 37*(1), 1–28.

Morris, D. (2004). Globalization and media democracy: The case of indymedia. In D. Schuler & P. Day (Eds.), *Shaping the network society: The new role of civil society in cyberspace* (pp. 325–352). Cambridge, MA: MIT Press.

Moyal, A. (1989). *Women and the telephone in Australia: A study prepared for Telecom Australia.* Sydney: Telecom Australia.

Mulgan, G. (1998). *Connexity: Responsibility, freedom, business and power in the new century.* London: Vintage.

Muller, M. J., Raven, M. E., Kogan, S., Millen, D. R., & Carey, K. (2003, November). *Introducing chat into business organisations: Toward an instant messaging maturity model.* Paper presented at the ACM GROUP conference, Sanibel Island, FL.

Mumby, D. K. (1997). Modernism, postmodernism and communication studies: A re-reading of an ongoing debate. *Communication Theory, 7*(1), 1–29.

Mumford, E. (2001). Advice for an action researcher. *Information Technology & People, 14*(1), 12–27.

Nair, S., Jennaway, M., & Skuse, A. (2006). *Local information networks: Social and technological considerations.* New Delhi: UNESCO.

Naples, N. A., & Clark, E. (1996). Feminist participatory research and empowerment: Going public as survivors of childhood sexual abuse. In H. Gottfried (Ed.), *Feminism and social change: Bridging theory and practice* (pp. 160–183). Urbana: University of Illinois Press.

Narayan, D., Chambers, R., Shah, M., & Petesch, P. (Eds.). (2000). *Crying out for change.* Oxford: Oxford University Press, World Bank.

Narayan, D., & Petesch, P. (Eds.). (2002). *From many lands* (Vol. 3). Oxford: Oxford University Press, World Bank.

Narula, U. (1988). The cultural challenge of communication technology. *American Behavioral Scientist, 32*(2), 194–207.

National Institutes of Health. (2005). *Policy on enhancing public access to archived publications resulting from NIH-funded research.* Bethesda, MD: Department of Health and Human Services. Available at http://public access.nih.gov/

Neuman, W. L. (2006). *Social research methods: Qualitative and quantitative approaches.* Boston: Pearson/Allyn & Bacon.

Nissen, M., Kamel, M., & Sengupta, K. (2000). Integrated analysis and design of knowledge systems and processes. In Y. Malhotra (Ed.), *Knowledge management and virtual organisations* (pp. 214–244). Hershey, PA: Idea Group Publishing.

O'Meara, P., Chesters, J., & Han, G-S. (2004). Outside—looking in: Evaluating a community capacity building project. *Rural Society, 14*(2), 126–141.

O'Sullivan, R. G., & O'Sullivan, J. M. (1998). Evaluation voices: Promoting evaluation from within programs through collaboration. *Evaluation and Program Planning, 21*(1), 21–29.

Oakland, J. S. (2003). *Total quality management: Text with cases.* London: Butterworth-Heinemann.

Office for Women. (2003). *Women in the Smart State. Directions statement 2003–2008.* Brisbane: Queensland Government. Available at http://www.women. qld.gov.au/?id=76

Oleari, K. (2000). Making your job easier: Using whole-system approaches to involve the community in sustainable planning and development. *Public Management,* December, 4–10.

O'Reilly, T. (2005). *What is Web 2.0?* Retrieved June 1, 2007, http://www.oreillynet. com/pub/a/oreilly/tim/news/2005/07/30/what-is-web-20.html

Orlikowski, W. (1992). The duality of technology: Rethinking the concept of technology in organisations. *Organisation Science, 3*(3), 398–427.

Orlikowski, W. J. (2000). Using technology and constituting structures: A practice lens for studying technology in organisations. *Organisation Science, 11*(4), 404–428.

Papineau, D., & Kiely, M. (1996). Participatory evaluation in a community organisation: Fostering stakeholder empowerment and utilization. *Evaluation and Program Planning, 19*(1), 79–93.

Parks, W. (2005). *Who measures change: An introduction to participatory monitoring and evaluation of communication for social change.* South Orange, NJ: Communication for Social Change Consortium.

Patterson, S. J., & Kavanaugh, A. L. (2001). Building a sustainable community network: An application of critical mass theory. *The Electronic Journal of Communication, 11*(2).

Patton, M. (2002). *Qualitative research and evaluation methods* (3rd ed.). Thousand Oaks, CA: Sage.

Paulus, P., & Nijstad, B. (2003). *Group creativity: Innovation through collaboration.* New York: Oxford University Press.

Pink, S. (2006). *Doing visual ethnography: Images, media and representation in research* (2nd ed.). Thousand Oaks, CA: Sage.

Pinkett, R. D. (2003). Community technology and community building: Early results from the creating community connections project. *The Information Society, 19*(5), 365–379.

Plant, S. (2004). *On the mobile: The effects of mobile telephones on social and individual life*. Motorola. Available at http://www.motorola.com/mot/doc/0/234_MotDoc.pdf

Plato. (1956). Meno. In B. Jowett, R. M. Hare, W. H. D. Rouse, E. H. Warmington, & P. G. Rouse (Eds.), *Great dialogues of Plato*. New York: New American Library.

Polanyi, M. (1983). *The tacit dimension*. Gloucester, MA: Peter Smith.

Pool, I. (1983). *Forecasting the telephone: A retrospective technology assessment*. Norwood, NJ: Ablex.

Poole, M. S., & Desanctis, G. (1990). Understanding the use of group decision support systems: The theory of adaptive structuration. In J. Fulk & C. Steinfield (Eds.), *Organizations and communication technology* (pp. 173–193). Beverly Hills, CA: Sage.

Preece, J., Rogers, Y., & Sharp, H. (2002). *Interaction design: Beyond human–computer interaction*. New York: John Wiley & Sons.

Putnam, R. D. (2000). *Bowling alone: The collapse and revival of American community*. New York: Simon & Schuster.

Quan-Haase, A., Wellman, B., Witte, J. C., & Hampton, K. N. (2002). Capitalizing on the Net: Social contact, civic engagement, and sense of community. In B. Wellman & C. A. Haythornthwaite (Eds.), *The internet in everyday life* (pp. 291–324). Oxford: Blackwell.

Queensland Government. (2005). *South East Queensland Regional Plan 2005–2026*. Brisbane, QLD: Office of Urban Management, Department of Local Government, Planning, Sport and Recreation.

Rajbhandari, B. (2006). Sustainable livelihood and rural development in south Asia. Issues, concerns and general implications. In M.C. Behera (Ed.), *Globalising rural development: Competing paradigms and emerging realities* (pp. 211–241). New Delhi: Sage.

Rakow, L. (1988). Gendered technology, gendered practice. *Critical Studies in Mass Communication, 5*(1), 57–70.

Ramos, J. (2006). Dimensions in the confluence of futures studies and action research. *Futures, 38*(6), 642–655.

Randolph, B. (2004). The changing Australian city: New patterns, new policies and new research needs. *Urban Policy and Research, 22*(4), 481–493.

Reason, P. (1994). Three approaches to participative inquiry. In N. K. Denzin & Y. S. Lincoln (Eds.), *The handbook of qualitative research* (pp. 324–339). London: Sage.

Reason, P. (1998). Political, epistemological, ecological and spiritual dimensions of participation. *Studies in Cultures, Organisations and Societies, 4*(2), 147–167.

Reason, P., & Bradbury, H. (Eds.). (2001). *Handbook of action research: Participative inquiry and practice*. London: Sage.

Revans, R. (1998). *ABC of action learning*. London: Lomos & Crane.

Reynolds, P., Thorogood, A., & Yetton, P. (2005). A $1 billion action research IT project: Building a *"new"* bank. In *Proceedings of the 4th International Symposium on Information and Communication Technologies WISICT '05*. Dublin: Trinity College.

Rheingold, H. (2002). *Smart mobs: The next social revolution*. Cambridge, MA: Perseus.

Rice, R. E. (1984). *The new media: Communication, research and technology*. London: Sage.

Rice, R. E. (2002). Primary issues in internet use: Access, civic and community involvement, and social interaction and expression. In L. A. Lievrouw & S. M. Livingstone (Eds.), *Handbook of new media: Social shaping and consequences of ICTs* (pp. 105–129). London: Sage.

Rice, R. E., & Atkin, C. K. (Eds.). (2001). *Public communication campaigns* (3rd ed.). Thousand Oaks, CA: Sage.

Rice, R. E., & Foote, D. (2001). A systems-based evaluation planning model for health communication campaigns in developing countries. In R. E. Rice & C. Atkin (Eds.), *Public communication campaigns* (3rd ed., pp. 146–157). Thousand Oaks, CA: Sage.

Rice, R. E., & Haythornthwaite, C. (2006). Perspectives on internet use: Access, involvement and interaction. In L.A. Lievrouw & S. Livingstone (Eds.), *Handbook of new media: Social consequences of ICTs* (pp. 92–113). London: Sage.

Rice, R. E., McCreadie, M., & Chang, S. L. (2001). *Accessing and browsing information and communication*. Cambridge, MA: MIT Press.

Robertson, R. (1995). Glocalization: Time-space and homogeneity-heterogeneity. In M. Featherstone, S. Lash, & R. Robertson (Eds.), *Global modernities* (pp. 25–44). London: Sage.

Robson, C. (2000). *Small-scale evaluation*. London: Sage.

Rodriguez, C. (2001). *Fissures in the mediascape: An international study of citizens' media*. Cresskill, NJ: Hampton Press.

Rodriguez, C. (2004). The renaissance of citizens' media. *Media Development, 2*. Retrieved January 31, 2006, from http://www.wacc.org.uk/wacc/publications/media_development/2004_2/the_renaissance_of_citizens_media

Rodriguez, F., & Wilson, E. J. (1999). *Are poor countries losing the information revolution?* College Park, MD: Centre for International Development and Conflict Management, University of Maryland.

Rogers, E. (1962). *The diffusion of innovations*. New York: The Free Press.

Rogers, E. (2003). *The diffusion of innovations* (5th ed.). New York: The Free Press.

Rogers, E. M., & Kincaid, L. D. (1981). *Communication networks: Toward a new paradigm for research*. New York: The Free Press.

Rosson, M. B., & Carroll, J. M. (2002). *Usability engineering: Scenario-based development of human–computer interaction.* San Francisco, CA: Academic Press.

The Rural Women and ICTs Research Team. (1999). *The new pioneers: Women in rural Queensland collaboratively exploring the potential of communication and information technologies for personal, business and community development.* Brisbane: The Communication Centre, Queensland University of Technology.

Rust, C. (2004). Design enquiry: Tacit knowledge and invention in science. *Design Issues, 20*(4), 76–85.

Sanger, J. (1996). Managing change through action research: A postmodern perspective on appraisal. In O. Zuber-Skerritt (Ed.), *New directions in action research* (pp. 182–198). London: Falmer Press.

Santos, F., & Pacheco, J. (2005). Scale-free networks provide a unifying framework for the emergence of cooperation. *Physical Review Letters, 95.* Available at http://link.aps.org/abstract/PRL/v95/e098104

Satchell, C. (2003). The swarm: Facilitating fluidity and control in young people's use of mobile phones. In S. Viller & P. Wyeth (Eds.), *Proceedings of OZCHI 2003: New directions in interaction, information environments, media and technology.* Brisbane, QLD: Information Environments Program, University of Queensland.

Schoening, G. T., & Anderson, J. A. (1995). Social action media studies: Foundational arguments and common premises. *Communication Theory, 5*(2), 93–116.

Schön, D. A. (1995). *Reflective practitioner: How professionals think in action* (2nd ed.). Aldershot, UK: Arena.

Schuler, D. (1996). *New community networks. Wired for change.* New York: Addison-Wesley.

Schuler, D., & Namioka, A. (Eds.). (1993). *Participatory design: Principles and practices.* Hillsdale, NJ: Erlbaum.

Scott, M., Diamond, A., & Smith, B. (1997). *Opportunities for communities: Public access to networked information technology.* Canberra, ACT: Department of Social Security.

Seale, C. (Ed.). (2004). *Social research methods: A reader.* London & New York: Routledge.

Selwyn, N. (2004). Reconsidering political and popular understandings of the digital divide. *New Media and Society, 6*(3), 341–362.

Sen, A. (2000). *Development as freedom.* New York: Anchor Books.

Sen, A. (2002). *Rationality and freedom.* London: Belknap Press of Harvard University Press.

Servaes, J. (1999). *Communication for development: One world, multiple cultures.* Cresskill, NJ: Hampton Press.

Shedroff, N. (1999). Information interaction design: A unified field theory of design. In R. E. Jacobson (Ed.), *Information design.* Cambridge, MA: MIT Press.

Simpson, L., Wood, L., Daws, L., & Seinen, A. (2001). *Creating rural connections: Book 1: Project overview.* Brisbane, QLD: The Communication Centre, Queensland University of Technology.

Simpson, R. (2001). *The internet and regional Australia: How rural communities can address the impact of the internet.* Canberra, ACT: Rural Industries Research and Development Corporation.

Slater, D., & Tacchi, J. (2004). *Research: ICT innovations for poverty reduction.* New Delhi: UNESCO. Retrieved September 5, 2005, from http://cirac. qut.edu.au/ictpr/downloads/research.pdf

Slater, D., Tacchi, J., & Lewis, P. (2002). *Ethnographic monitoring and evaluation of community multimedia centres: A study of Kothmale Community Radio Internet Project, Sri Lanka.* London: DfID.

Small, S. (1995). Action-oriented research: Models and methods. *Journal of Marriage and the Family, 57,* 941–955.

Smith, M. (2002). Tools for navigating large social cyberspaces. *Communications of the ACM, 45*(4), 51–55.

Smith, S. E., Willms, D. G., & Johnson, N. A. (Eds.). (1997). *Nurtured by knowledge: Learning to do participatory action-research.* New York; Ottawa: Apex Press, International Development Research Centre.

Sobel, J. (2002). Can we trust social capital? *Journal of Economic Literature, XL,* 139–154.

Sproull, L., & Kiesler, S. (1991). *New ways of working in the networked organisation.* Cambridge, MA: MIT Press.

Stewart, C. M., Gil-Egui, G., Tian, Y., & Pileggi, M. I. (2006). Framing the digital divide: A comparison of US and EU policy approaches. *New Media and Society, 8*(5), 731–751.

Stoecker, R. (2005). *Research methods for community change: A project-based approach.* Thousand Oaks, CA: Sage.

Strauss, A. (1998). *Basics of qualitative research: Techniques and procedures for developing grounded theory.* Thousand Oaks, CA: Sage.

Streeten, P. (2002). *Empowerment, participation and the poor.* Background paper for HDR 2002. New York: Human Development Report Office, UNDP.

Stringer, E. (1999). *Action research* (2nd ed.). Thousand Oaks, CA: Sage.

Surman, M., & Diceman, J. (2004). *Choosing Open Source: A decision making guide for civil society organisations.* Retrieved February 13, 2004, http://www. commonsgroup.com/ideas/opensourceguide.html

Tacchi, J. (2004). Researching creative applications of new information and communication technologies. *International Journal of Cultural Studies, 7*(1), 91–103.

Tacchi, J. (2005). *Finding a voice: The potential of creative ICT literacy and voice in community multimedia centres in south Asia.* Working paper no. 3. Information Society Research Group. Retrieved January 31, 2006, http://www.isrg.info/ISRGWorkingPaper3.pdf

Tacchi, J., Slater, D., & Hearn, G. (2003). *Ethnographic action research: A handbook.* New Delhi: UNESCO.

Tacchi, J., Slater, D., & Lewis, P. (2003, May). *Evaluating community based media initiatives: An ethnographic action research approach.* Paper presented at the OURMedia III conference, Barranquilla, Colombia. Available at http://www. ourmedianet.org/papers/om2003/Tacchi_OM3.rtf

Tacchi, J., Fildes, J., Martin, K., Mulenahalli, K., Baulch, E., and Skuse, A. (2007). Ethnographic Action Research CD-ROM. New Delhi: UNESCO.

Tandon, R. (1996). The historical roots and contemporary tendencies in participatory research: Implications for health care. In K. de Koning & M. Martin (Eds.), *Participatory research in health. Issues and experience* (pp. 19–26). London & Atlantic Highlands, NJ: Zed Books.

Tara Shire. (2001). *Tara Shire rural subdivisions.* Report collated by Tara Shire Council, Tara Neighbourhood Centre, Tara Police Station and Tara State School, Tara, Queensland.

Thatchenkery, T., & Chowdhry, D. (2007). *Appreciative inquiry and knowledge management: A social constructionist perspective.* Cheltenham, UK: Edward Elgar.

Thompson, B., & Kinne, S. (1999). Social change theory: Applications to community health. In N. Bracht (Ed.), *Health promotion at the community level 2: New advances.* London: Sage.

Thurlow, C., Lengel, L. B., & Tomic, A. (2004). *Computer mediated communication: Social interaction and the internet.* Thousand Oaks, CA: Sage.

Titon, J. (2003). Textual analysis or thick description? In M. Clayton, T. Herbert, & R. Middleton (Eds.), *The cultural study of music: A critical introduction* (pp. 171–180) New York; London: Routledge.

Tönnies, F. (1887). *Gemeinschaft und Gesellschaft* (3rd ed.). Darmstadt, Germany: Wissenschaftliche Buchgesellschaft.

UNDP. (2001). *Human development report: Making new technologies work for human development.* New York: Oxford University Press. Available at http://hdr.undp.org/reports/global/2001/en/

UNESCO. (2005). *Draft programme and budget 2006–2007.* New Delhi: UNESCO.

UNESCO. (2006). *Narratives for the future: Digital stories about the millennium development goals.* DVD. New Delhi: UNESCO.

UNESCO. (2007). *Ethnographic action research.* CD ROM. New Delhi: UNESCO.

United Nations. (2002). *The millennium development goals and the United Nations role.* United Nations Department of Public Information. Available at http://www.un.org/millenniumgoals/MDGs-FACTSHEET1.pdf

Urquhart, C. (2007). The evolving nature of grounded theory method: The case of the information systems discipline. In K. Charmaz & T. Bryant (Eds.), *The handbook of grounded theory.* Thousand Oaks, CA: Sage.

Van Notten, P., Rotmans, J., Van Asselt, M., & Rothman, D. (2003). An updated scenario typology. *Futures, 35,* 423–443.

Van Zoonen, L. (1992). Feminist theory and information technology. *Media, Culture and Society, 14,* 9–29.

Van Zoonen, L. (2001). Feminist internet studies. *Feminist Media Studies, 1*(1), 67–72.

Volti, R. (2006). *Society and technological change.* New York: Worth Publishers.

Waddell, D., Cummings, T. G., & Worley, C. G. (2004). *Organisational development and change.* South Melbourne, VIC: Thomson.

Wadsworth, Y. (1991). *Everyday evaluation on the run* (1st ed.). Melbourne: Action Research Issues Association.

Wajcman, J. (1991). *Feminism confronts technology.* Cambridge: Polity Press.

Walmsley, D. J. (2000). Community, place and cyberspace. *Australian Geographer, 31*(1), 5–19.

Walsham, G. (1993). *Interpreting information systems in organisations.* New York: Wiley.

Warschauer, M. (2003). *Technology and social inclusion: Rethinking the digital divide.* Cambridge, MA: MIT Press.

Watters, E. (2003a). How tribes connect a city. In E. Walters, *Urban tribes: Are friends the new family?* (pp. 95–118). London: Bloomsbury.

Watters, E. (2003b). *Urban tribes: Are friends the new family?* London: Bloomsbury.

Watts, D. J. (2003). *Six degrees: The science of a connected age.* New York: Norton.

Weinberger, K. (2000). *Women's participation: An economic analysis in rural Chad and Pakistan.* New York: Peter Lang.

Wellcome Trust. (2006). *Open and unrestricted access to the outputs of published research. Policy summary.* London: Wellcome Trust. Available at http://www.wellcome.ac.uk/node3302.html

Wellman, B. (2001). Physical place and cyberplace: The rise of personalized networking. *International Journal of Urban and Regional Research, 25*(2), 227–252.

Wellman, B. (2002). Little boxes, glocalization, and networked individualism. In M. Tanabe, P. van den Besselaar, & T. Ishida (Eds.), *Digital Cities II: Second Kyoto Workshop on Digital Cities* (Vol. LNCS 2362, pp. 10–25). Heidelberg, Germany: Springer.

Wellman, B., & Haythornthwaite, C. A. (Eds.). (2002). *The internet in everyday life.* Oxford, UK: Blackwell.

Wellman, B., Quan-Haase, A., Boase, J., Chen, W., Hampton, K. N., Díaz de Isla Gómez, I., & Miyata, K. (2003). The social affordances of the internet for networked individualism. *Journal of Computer-Mediated Communication, 8*(3).

Wells, B., & Tanner, B. (1994). The Organisational Potential of Women in Agriculture to Sustain Rural Communities. *Journal of the Community Development Society, 25*(2), 246–258.

Wenger, E., McDermott, R. A., & Snyder, W. (2002). *Cultivating communities of practice: A guide to managing knowledge.* Boston: Harvard Business School Press.

West, A. R., & Selian, A. N. (J. Barker, Ed.). (2005). *Experiencing technical difficulties: The urgent need to rewire and reboot the ICT-development machine* (Thematic Reports). London: Article 19.

Wilcox, D., Greenop, D., & Mackie, D. (2002). *Making the net work for residents and their landlords: A guide to using information and communication technologies in housing associations.* York, UK: Joseph Rowntree Foundation.

Williams, R., & Edge, D. (1996). The social shaping of technology. *Research Policy, 25,* 865–899.

Winner, L. (1993). Upon opening the black box and finding it empty: Social constructivism and the philosophy of technology. *Science, Technology & Human Values, 18*(3), 362–378.

Woog, R. (1998). Using complexity and systems theory to examine the epistemological framework of self organising human activity systems, or: The knowing
of certainty and the uncertainty of knowing. In *Proceedings, Learning Communities, Regional Sustainability and the Learning Society. An International
Symposium* (pp. 344–350). Launceston, TAS: Centre for Research & Learning
in Regional Australia.

Yin, R. (2003). *Case study research: Design and methods.* Thousand Oaks, CA:
Sage.

Author Index

Subject Index

Breinigsville, PA USA
29 September 2010
246287BV00001B/22/P